Library of
Davidson College

IDIOLECTS IN DICKENS

IDIOLECTS IN DICKENS

The Major Techniques and Chronological Development

Robert Golding

St. Martin's Press   New York

© Robert Golding 1985

All rights reserved. For information write:
St. Martin's Press, Inc., 175 Fifth Avenue, New York, NY 10010
Printed in Hong Kong
Published in the United Kingdom by The Macmillan Press Ltd.
First published in the United States of America in 1985

ISBN 0-312-40481-6

Library of Congress Cataloging in Publication Data
Golding, Robert
  Idiolects in Dickens.
  Includes index.
  1. Dickens, Charles, 1812–1870 – Technique.
2. Dickens, Charles, 1812–1870 – Characters.   3. Speech
in literature.   4. Characters and characteristics in
literature.   5. English language – Variation.   6. English
language – Dialects – England – London.   I Title.
PR4591.064   1985   823'.8   84-17783
ISBN 0-312-40481-6

Contents

List of Abbreviations   vii

Introduction   1

PART I DICKENS' IDIOLECTS: THE MAJOR TECHNIQUES

1. Linguistic Identifiers   15
2. Root Dialects and Registers   25
3. Rhythmic Patterns   46
4. Representational Speech   54
5. Rhetorical Extension   60

PART II DICKENS' IDIOLECTS: THE CHRONOLOGICAL DEVELOPMENT

6. Fictional Apprenticeship   73
7. *Pickwick Papers* to *The Old Curiosity Shop*   77
8. *Barnaby Rudge* and *Martin Chuzzlewit*   102
9. *Dombey & Son* to *Bleak House*   125
10. *Hard Times* and *Little Dorrit*   157
11. *Great Expectations* to *Edwin Drood*   172
12. Dickens' Achievement   213

Notes   230
Index   245

List of Abbreviations

Unless otherwise indicated, I have used *The New Oxford Illustrated Dickens*, 21 vols (1947–59), with the following abbreviations:

AN	American Notes	MP	Miscellaneous Papers - (Geneva: Edito-Service S.A.; London: Heron Books, 1970)
BH	Bleak House		
BR	Barnaby Rudge		
CB	Christmas Books		
CS	Christmas Stories	NN	Nicholas Nickleby
DC	David Copperfield	OCS	The Old Curiosity Shop
DS	Dombey & Son	OMF	Our Mutual Friend
ED	The Mystery of Edwin Drood	OT	Oliver Twist
		PP	Pickwick Papers
GE	Great Expectations	SB	Sketches by Boz
HT	Hard Times	TTC	A Tale of Two Cities
LD	Little Dorrit	UT/RP	'The Uncommercial Traveller' and 'Reprinted Pieces'
MC	Martin Chuzzlewit		

The following are the abbreviations used for periodicals or collections of articles;

AGE	*Assessing Great Expectations*, ed. Richard Lettis and William E. Morris (San Francisco: Chandler Publishing, 1960)
AS	American Speech
CS	Critical Survey

DCr	*Dickens Critics*, ed. George H. Ford and Lauriat Lane, Jr (New York: Cornell University Press, 1961)
DTC	*Dickens and the 20th Century*, ed. John Gross and Gabriel Pearson (London: Routledge & Kegan Paul, 1962)
DtC	*Dickens the Craftsman*, ed. Robert B. Partlow, Jr (Carbondale, Ill.: Southern Illinois University Press, 1970)
ES	*English Studies*
REL	*A Review of English Literature*
TCI/BH	*Twentieth-Century Interpretations of 'Bleak House'*, ed. Jacob Korg (Englewood Cliffs, N.J.: Prentice-Hall, 1968)
TLS	*Times Literary Supplement*
VNL	*Victorian Newsletter*
WTW	*Writers and their Work*

Introduction

Part of the extreme diversity of the fictional world created by Dickens is reflected in the large number of highly individualised languages with which, to a greater or lesser degree of success, he endowed his fictional characters. In Dickens criticism, these special languages have been referred to as 'private languages',[1] or, in linguistic terminology, as *idiolects*, an idiolect being 'the totality of speech habits of a single person at a given time'.[2] An examination of some of the idiolects created by Dickens, of their origins, development, linguistic, rhetorical and rhythmic features, and their structural significance (if any) is the purpose of this book.

Of course, an idiolect shares structural features with other idiolects of the same speech community, class and religion. In other words, it has the same idiolectal roots or, to put it another way, it shares registers of the same root language, depending on the particular circumstances involved. The terms *language* and *dialect* can be differentiated thus:

> A language ... is a collection of more or less similar idiolects. A dialect is just the same thing, with this difference: when both terms are used in a single discussion, the degree of similarity of the idiolects in a single dialect is presumed to be greater than that of all the idiolects in the language.[3]

However, it is not what is shared that is decisive, but what is unique, and we must see an idiolect as the unique manner in which an individual speaks the dialectal branch of his native language.

So much is also basically true of speech in fiction, as long as one remembers to what extent such speech is only presenting a highly modified version of the language of normal intercourse, one which has been subject to considerable condensation and other alterations contingent on the needs of the kind of literature concerned as well as on the author's gifts and limitations. In Norman Page's words: 'even the most realistic fictional speech generally represents a considerable selection and simplification and conventionalization of the real language of men'.[4]

Dickens goes one step further, stylising to such a degree that the idiolects of his characters come nearer to being language collages, to being wholly synthetic, than those of any other English novelist. Hence fictional speech in Dickens, to quote Norman Page once more,

> seeks to render not the real world but a fictional world that is amazingly vivid and varied ... speech is a matter of fictional convention – the author's own code of conventions, established and fairly consistently adhered to by him – rather than accurate observation.[5]

These synthetic units sprang quite naturally from the theatrical story-telling manner of Dickens' highly stylised fictional world, one primarily rooted in the technique of mimicry, and dominated by the dynamic vigour of the author's ubiquitous urge to establish the closest contact possible with his audience.

Dickens, then, was not only a highly gifted storyteller, but possessed great dramatic genius with his mimetic ability dominating. It was this ability that accompanied the author's constant endeavours to enforce his unique vision on absolutely everything that came within the range of his highly developed aural and visual perceptions: observing, absorbing, mimicking, setting down on paper – all in this order, impressing the stamp of his own inimitable personality on everything he wrote, but above all on his fictional characters.

Dickens' natural gifts and his early environment exerted decisive influence on the development of his fictional idiolects, in my view the most important facet of his stylised world. The two most important of these gifts were his exceptionally acute powers of aural and visual observation. Only Angus Wilson, it seems, has consciously and directly brought out the relative difference between them, without detracting from the importance of either. After emphasising that 'Dickens' greatest natural gift was his ear',[6] reinforcing this a few lines later by applying the adjective 'marvellous', he goes on to point out that the author also possessed 'an only just less marvellous eye. Certainly a combination of the two that is possibly unique in the English novel.'[7]

From childhood on, these two gifts received considerable stimulus through his vividly sensitive imagination, his burning, childlike curiosity, his natural tendency to exaggeration, and his unbounded sense of the ridiculous. Within his very family, for instance, Dickens was right from the beginning surrounded by extreme forms of eccentric verbosity, for each of his parents in their different ways shone in this respect, a fact confirmed both by report and by the idiolects of their fictional representations, Mrs Nickleby, Mr and Mrs Micawber and Mr William Dorrit.

Also as a boy, the author not only absorbed with rare intensity the mythical though to him very real world of fairy tales, magic and 'Arabian Nights', but followed this by discovering and reliving with equal intensity the fictional worlds of, among others, Fielding, Smollett, Goldsmith, Scott, Defoe and Cervantes. A well-known passage from *David Copperfield* (55–6) gives a literal description of this discovery and its effect on him, an effect of considerable importance in respect to his future development of fictional speech.

However, if any specific literary influence at work in Dickens' fictional apprenticeship is to be pinpointed, it must be that exerted by the eccentric speech of some of Smollett's characters in humorous or farcical situations. A startling prefiguration of the very pronounced seafaring register of Captains Cuttle and Bunsby in *Dombey & Son* is to be found, for example, in the hilariously typified speech of that retired naval officer Hawser Trunnion in *Peregrine Pickle*.[8] And in *Humphry Clinker*, the amusing and often significant malapropisms, fusions and misspellings of Winifred Jenkins hint forcibly at similar qualities in the language distortions perpetrated by so many of Dickens' lower-class characters when attempting the genteel register.[9] As Walter Allen has pointed out:

> There is a genuinely creative gusto . . ., a recognition of ambiguities, a deliberate fusion and telescoping of words found

to be congruous. Whether Smollett intended it deliberately or not, he reveals hidden layers of character in Winifred when he makes her speak of, for instance, 'the grease of God', 'matter-money', 'a satiety' that is 'to supperate' and 'dissent terms of civility'. The misspellings themselves foreshadow Dickens's use of them in such a character as Mrs Gamp.[10]

At virtually the same time as he was making the above discoveries, Dickens came under yet another lasting influence: the theatre, then – as very often later – in the form of amateur theatricals. He became so stage-struck that he even tried his hand at composing a little tragedy. The obsession which the theatre became is of vital importance in the development of every aspect of Dickens' art, but most of all in the evolution of the dramatic aspects of his fictional speech, for, as we shall see, the idiolects were actually formed and integrated in a way that is directly related to the stage.

Various anecdotes confirm that, as he got older, Dickens' interest in the spoken language became increasingly more pronounced. It was later recorded by one of his schoolfellows, for instance – this concerns the period of school life immediately following his traumatic experience in the blacking warehouse – that the young Dickens 'invented what we termed a "lingo", produced by the addition of a few letters of the same sound to every word; and it was our ambition, walking and talking thus along the street, to be considered foreigners'.[11] He left school at fifteen and was, for several years, an office boy in a firm of attorneys, this also giving the young Dickens ample opportunity to become familiar with the legal register in a great number of its forms. During this time, his gifts of aural and visual observation were developed even further in his wide-ranging explorations of the London around him, although these were but an intensified continuation of the habit started years before when his debt-ridden father had brought the family to live here.

At about this time, too, he began to reveal the workings of that mimetic ability mentioned above. Developing hand in hand with his aural and visual powers and being, so to speak, a direct offshoot of the two, this ability played a crucial role in the emergence and later unique artistic fruition through the public readings of, above all, his fictional speech. By all accounts, even during this early part of his life, he already possessed an uncanny ability to mimic brilliantly any number of different voices, especially those of the London lower classes, for, like Sam Weller, his 'knowledge of London was extensive and peculiar' (*PP*, 269). Moreover, Mamie Dickens' oft-quoted account of how she, as a young girl, witnessed her father's strange behaviour when writing would seem to confirm that Dickens deliberately utilised in fiction his gift for mimicry.[12]

Nor can the years – almost eight in all – spent by the young Dickens as a professional recorder and transcriber of speech be safely ignored in any reference to those elements in his early life which had some influence or other on the evolution of his fictional speech technique. Without a doubt, this particular occupation must have helped to sharpen even more his already exceptional powers of aural perception. Not that he was in love with the objects of his new profession (the endlessly verbose members of the law court, and, later, of Parliament), but he was able to deepen his already extensive knowledge of the English language itself and the uses to which it was put. The as yet completely unknown teenager had, with relentless assiduity, flung himself into mastering Gurney's old-fashioned form of shorthand, one which, being unphonetic, was excessively difficult and unwieldy; nevertheless, within a remarkably short time Dickens had worked up to what was by all accounts a prodigious proficiency. Several passages in *David Copperfield* (ch. XXXVIII), obviously autobiographical, supply abundant testimony to the soul-destroying labour involved.

Finally, fed up with his job as a low-paid lawyer's clerk, he managed at the end of 1828 (he was not yet seventeen) to obtain admission as a recorder to the then still existent Doctors' Commons, where he was occasionally entrusted with the writing-down of cases.[13] Dickens' years at this institution, to which one of the 'Sketches' is devoted (*SB*, 86–91), though immensely useful as far as learning to record and transcribe speech was concerned, incited in him a lifelong aversion to the ways of the law and the dry pedantry of its speech, this being more than clear in much of his later writing.

At the age of twenty, during the exciting year (1832) which witnessed the passions set astir by the violently controversial Reform Bill, Dickens became a Parliamentary reporter, rapidly – even at this uncommonly early age – becoming well-known for the speed and accuracy of his work. Again, however, in spite of the new Parliament being, if anything, above average debating ability, the impression made upon him by such of its would-be-orators as 'Our honourable friend, the member for Verbosity' (*UT/RP*, 561) was essentially negative, and (as with the world of law) many passages in his works testify to the same.[14] Only rarely was Dickens' enthusiasm enkindled by the compelling (to our tastes, perhaps, often melodramatic or pathetic) oratory of a Russell or an O'Connell. However, the value for his subsequent career of the material collected during this time cannot be overestimated. It is more than probable that his later well-known habit of jotting down bits of dialogue and oddities of speech stems from this period of his life.

Against the above background, then, Dickens finally plunged into the writing of fiction, writing in which his unique theatrical, storytelling self was primarily able to assert itself through the speech of the characters, through the dramatic qualities of the idiolects, those complex products of his own aural and mimetic gifts. But, despite the obvious importance of the idiolects within Dickens' stylised fictional world, indeed of the author's virtually unequalled use of language in all respects, there has been no truly comprehensive, systematic criticism of the one or the other. This fact is difficult to comprehend, for in the last analysis Dickens' greatness stands and falls on his – to quote Dr Leavis – 'command of word, phrase, rhythm and image: in ease and range there is surely no greater master of English except Shakespeare'.[15]

Basically, the following examination falls into two parts. The first section concentrates on the general technical developments affecting the idiolects from their fairly simple beginnings in which the key-note is linguistic individualisation, through speech typification, whether regional, social, professional, oratorical, melodramatic, situational or personal, up to (most importantly) structural representation. Additional chapters are devoted to such pertinent aspects as the rhythmic patterns of the idiolects, free indirect speech and the important fusion later in his career of all the prose modalities, a fusion in which the rhetorical and rhythmic patterns of his fictional speech played such a decisive role.

The second section is devoted to a chronological study of Dickens' idiolects, analysing both their individual patterned complexity and their structural role, if any, in the novel in which they appear. The multifarious features and the ultimate fusion thereof in the most important idiolects of the early novels – from the period 1836–44, one of immense activity and inspired improvisation – are examined in considerably greater detail than those from the later novels. There are two reasons for adopting such a procedure: on the one hand, these early idiolects reveal an ever-growing profusion of linguistic, rhetorical and rhythmic features reaching a peak in the patterned elaboration of the speech idioms of Mrs Gamp and Pecksniff in *Martin Chuzzlewit*; on the other hand, however, they contain only haphazard indications of structural integration, although there is a slight but gradual growth in intensity in this respect. The adoption of this procedure will, it is hoped, enable the reader to gain an insight into the imaginative artistry Dickens brought in the early novels to the blending of the extremely diverse elements before him, a blending which culminated in such exceedingly complex products of what was, in effect, the transference, convincing and effective, of mimetic art to the world of the novel.

With *Dombey & Son* – a novel which marks a turning point in that the author for the first time consciously and very deliberately, though with variable success, set out to endow all the fictional elements with at least a modicum of structural significance – I have firstly selected the idiolects of more than one character, and secondly examined one of them (that of Mrs Skewton) more exhaustively in order to point out its weaknesses and advantages in contrast with those that have gone before. In the analyses of the speech of the other idiolects chosen from this novel, the accent is more on their all-round qualities, whether individualising, typifying or structural, but particularly on the last-named. I have adopted this latter procedure to an increasing extent with the novels that follow, taking four, five or more characters to show how, with varying degrees of success, they have, through their idiolect features, been integrated into the general thematic structure.

A Tale of Two Cities has been excluded from particular examination, because of all Dickens' novels this is the only one in which the fictional speech recedes into the background, the accent – an experimental one – being on the authorial prose modalities to such a degree that the speech of no individual figure can be singled out as worthy of particular note. For all that, the writing of this novel signals the oncoming of that final flowering of Dickens' command over language, 'oral style'. The stylistic unifications exhibited from the next novel, *Great Expectations*, to the end of his career (1870), in which all the stylised fictional components are so admirably balanced, makes the analytical course adopted from *David Copperfield* onwards even more imperative. From this novel on I have, correspondingly, submitted an increasing number of idiolects to an examination in which it will, I hope, become gradually clear that the emphasis during this period was much less on brilliance of utterance and far more on structural requirements.

As aids to reference throughout the following study, I have sketched out firstly a working plan facilitating speedier classification of the idiolect features, and secondly a diagram giving an approximate graphic representation of Dickens' typifying categories.

The idiolectal working plan supplies a list of headings covering the various features likely to be discovered in the speech idiom of this or that Dickens character. One will not, of course, find any single idiolect containing all of them, although a complicated language collage of such as Mrs Gamp goes a very long way in this respect. It will be observed that the speech features fall under four general headings: linguistic, typifying, rhetorical and rhythmic. At their most complete, the idiolects are artistically moulded to serve identifying, typifying (general and personal) and structural purposes. Moreover, it should continually be borne in mind that, as in everyday speech, many aspects of all fictional idiolects – and Dickens' are no exception, though the features are frequently so lush that the amount which is shared with others is reduced to a minimum – are also to be found in the speech of those rooted in the same dialect or register. It is peculiarity of usage, the unusualness of a certain characteristic – whether a word, turn of phrase, stress, intonation, or what one will – and the intensity of its application, in short the uniqueness of the sum total of language habits, which is decisive. It was this, as we shall see, that Dickens brought to a fine art.

1. Linguistic Aspects

   (a) *Individual peculiarities within standard usage*
   (b) *Colloquial deviations from the standard language*[16]
      (i) *Phonological* – indicating non-standard pronunciation and including what I shall refer to as 'eye-dialect', i.e.

the somewhat crude presentation of a word in a manner in which it is pronounced anyway, the deliberately inaccurate spelling in such cases conventionally serving rather to point out the character's lack of education, or the way such a person himself would perhaps have written the word.
(ii) *Grammatical* – under this heading is also included Dickens' version of what we can assume to have been the normal, everyday, non-standard syntax of the less-educated classes.
(iii) *Lexical* – the vocabulary and distortions thereof, e.g. malapropisms, slang and dialect words or expressions, individual coinages, etc.

2. Continually Recurring Rhetorical Devices

(a) *Set forms with varying content* – Weller comparisons; (mis-)quotations or allusions; continual use of rhetorical questions; ringing the changes on the names of people and other forms of address; the habitual piling up of adjectives, especially those of emotional character; frequent use of direct quotation when reporting the statements (supposed or otherwise) of a third (sometimes imaginary) person, e.g. Mrs Gamp's 'Mrs Harris', etc.
(b) *Speech tags* – a short phrase or even just one word or exclamation which remains unvarying or virtually so.

3. Idiosyncratic Manner of Delivery Colouring the Character's Whole Speech or a Considerable Part of It

(a) *Typifying manner* – the use of one or more speech registers.
(b) *Staccato or jerky manner* – e.g. Jingle (*PP*).
(c) *Never-ending, garrulous manner* – leading to clausal confusion and a multitude of irrelevancies, e.g. Mrs Nickleby (*NN*), Flora Finching (*LD*), Mrs Lirriper (*CS*).
(d) *'Backward' manner* – eccentric sentence construction of the type not met with in any kind of normal everday speech, e.g. Mrs Chivery and John Chivery (*LD*).

(e) *Contrast manner* – sudden changes in mid-stream from long-winded, highfalutin or pseudo-poetic style down to short, to-the-point colloquial or basic English, e.g. Dick Swiveller (*OCS*), Mr Micawber (*DC*).

4. Rhythmic Patterns

(a) *Metrical patterns* – springing from the world of poetry, even music, though presented as prose, e.g. blank verse mode of Mrs Gamp (*MC*).
(b) *Schematic patterns* – springing from the world of rhetoric and involving the regular reiteration of certain syntactic figurations, e.g. the anaphoric mode of Mrs Gamp (*MC*).

The second reference aid – the diagram below – is a very approximate graphic attempt to show how typification in Dickens can be categorised into two chief root dialects and the registers which may colour them.

The two chief root dialects in Dickens and their registers

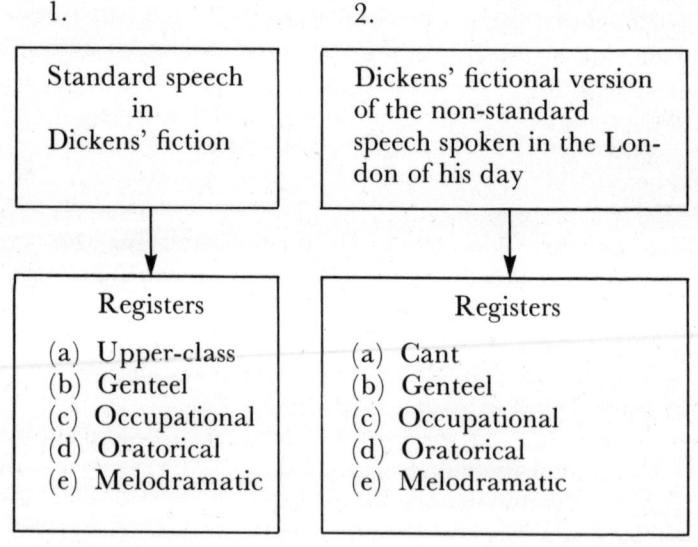

NB Further dialect roots and registers, though of secondary importance for this thesis, making up as they do but a tiny minority in the speech forms provided by the vast gallery of Dickens' characters and, except for (vi) and (vii), revealing a novelist less sure of himself, are as follows.

(i) Regional dialects: Yorkshire (e.g. Browdie, *NN*); Lancashire (e.g. Blackpool, *HT*); East Anglian (e.g. Mr Peggotty, Ham, Mrs Gummidge, *DC*);[17] American English (cf. *AN* and American scenes in *MC*);[18] odd snippets (e.g. Scottish doctor in *BH*).
(ii) The English of a Jew, e.g. Barney (*OT*) and Riah (*OMF*).
(iii) The English of foreigners, e.g. Count Smorltork (*PP*), Hortense (*BH*), Cavalletto and Rigaud (*LD*), Defarges (*TTC*), etc.
(iv) The pidgin English used by native English speakers talking to foreigners, e.g. Mrs Plornish (*LD*).
(v) So-called 'baby-talk' as practised by adults, e.g. Mrs Chick (*DS*).
(vi) The English of children, e.g. 'Schoolboy Story' (*CS*), 'Holiday Romance' (*UT/RP*).
(vii) The language differences between the sexes.

When referring to the above diagram, a number of points must be kept in mind: by 'standard speech' here, for example, is meant Dickens' fictional version of the particular English dialect generally accepted in his day and environment as the correct mode of the tongue and taught as such. The characters with this dialectal background are, in his fiction, roughly equal in numbers to those whose speech is rooted in non-standard dialect. Our impression that the latter predominate probably springs from the more striking linguistic effects produced by non-standard variations. It must also be remembered that the speech of many Dickens characters is only weakly affected, if at all, by one or more of the registers indicated; conversely, such speech may sometimes be coloured by more than one of the registers stemming from the same root dialect. Lastly, the diagram as a whole is an attempt to show not the actual linguistic divisions existing in the London of Dickens' day, but only those of the special world he created in his writings – a private world with 'private languages', so to speak.

One final word: during the following examination, it has to be assumed that despite the undeniable range of Dickens' aural, linguistic and creative gifts, his fictional idiolects perhaps never fully correspond to what he actually had in mind. It is a lack of complete correspondence between intention and achievement, the full extent of which can as little be measured in Dickens' creations as in those of any other creative artist.

Part I

Dickens' Idiolects: the Major Techniques

1 Linguistic Identifiers

THE NEED FOR AND DEVELOPMENT OF IDENTIFYING FEATURES

Very early on in Dickens' career, the general tradition of reading literary works aloud whether the listener was illiterate or not, as well as the particular needs of serial publication must, together, have forced the young writer to become aware of the substantial value of aural 'memory props'. Logically enough, then, Dickens' first attempts at fiction reveal that he individualised his characters by giving them particular linguistic constructions chiefly to make them more readily recognisable. One of the earliest, simplest, and most common of these, and certainly one of the most familiar to generations of readers and listeners, was the application of individual 'speech tags' which, as developed by Dickens, recall the character to mind in such a vivid and striking manner that the reader/listener – down to the least educated or intelligent – does not even need to be told who is actually speaking.[1]

However, although as a novelist he remained throughout his crowded, creative life acutely sensible of the desires and reactions of his public, and as a result fully realised from the very beginning that a large portion of his success was due to the popularity of those of his characters who were eccentric above all in speech, Dickens' actual wielding of his idiolects within the general structure (or what there was of this initially) was, in the primary stages, naive to say the least. In spite of – or maybe because of – this fact, the idiolects he so spontaneously created in the novels up to and including *David Copperfield* (with the partial exception of *Dombey & Son*) were often exceptionally funny and original. This simply illustrates, of course, how the highly gifted and ebulliently confident young writer at first visibly revelled in the sheer delight of spontaneous language invention.[2]

At their best, Dickens' initial methods enabled him to kill two birds with one stone: to entertain his public and to supply an important aid to quick recognition, this being absolutely essential to an uninterrupted appreciation of any single episode, the more so with a whole month (usually) elapsing between numbers. The practice of putting such identifying motifs – often eccentric ones – into the mouths of the various characters can be termed one of linguistic individualisation.

More or less parallel to and simultaneously congruent with the above procedure, Dickens also made distinct efforts to add language features which in a social (all classes), regional (primarily London), professional, oratorical or theatrical sense, helped to 'place' a whole multitude of characters in precisely that exaggerated, stylised manner so characteristic of all Dickens' fictional methods. There is, again, considerable evidence for this typification technique right from the beginning, as some of the speech in the *Sketches* demonstrates (cf. *SB*, 173), and the succeeding chapter will be devoted to a full discussion of the main typifying dialects and registers. With a few peculiar exceptions in which the linguistic background is unclear, Dickens so built up his composite idiolects that each one remained firmly rooted in one of the two major root dialects which concern us in his fiction: his own fictional versions of standard speech and non-standard London speech, these generally being coloured by one or more of the accompanying registers.

Before long, this fictional mode was taken further, at first erratically and with varying success, but finally in so perfected a form as to embrace qualities more directly personal, ones which reflected the moral, even physical, characteristics of the person concerned. This extension to the mode in question can be termed personal or individual typification. Thus, fictional speech techniques assumed a far greater and very natural significance within the stylised world of Dickens' novels and stories. Whether or not this additional development originally sprang from artistic instinct or conscious deliberation or a mixture of both is, however, impossible to determine. Suffice it to say that from *Oliver Twist* onwards, it gradually evolved until it became a firmly established weapon in Dickens' technical armoury.

CHARLES MATHEWS AND VOCAL CHARACTERISATION

A letter from Dickens to Forster[3] makes it clear that the author was, during his years as a clerk and very probably later too, a regular visitor to the one-man shows of the extremely versatile Charles Mathews, generally accepted as the greatest comedian of the day, and renowned in particular for his comic speech devices. The young, vividly impressionable Dickens was, it is clear, deeply affected by the popular comedian's extraordinarily persuasive powers in mimicry and comic variety. Even a light perusal of any of Dickens' earlier works, up to and including *David Copperfield*, supplies proof enough in this respect, for many of the abundant speech mannerisms to be found there – especially the famous 'taglines' – tally exactly in form with those of Mathews. These various language quirks are one way of individualising a character, and the young writer proceeded to incorporate them with considerable success into his own growing fictional world. One could, indeed, consider all the entries of Dickens' eccentric characters (in the earlier stages, at least) as 'one-man shows' transposed to literature.

For Dickens, however, no matter how inspired the burlesque in itself, there was, almost from the very beginning, more to such a technique than the simple transfer of variety skit to the world of fiction, and, brilliant as Mathews by all accounts was, Dickens gives his reading public more.[4] The vocal devices and idiosyncrasies of general speech manner which he borrowed from the star comedian, and which were destined to play such an important initial role in his development of fictional speech, can be divided into three groups: firstly, the speech tags; secondly, the Weller-type comparisons, sometimes called 'baroque similes';[5] and thirdly, certain features embracing the whole manner of speech delivery, such as the staccato style given to Jingle (*PP*), and the never-ending loquacity of such as Mrs Nickleby (*NN*), Flora Finching (*LD*) or Mrs Lirriper (*CS*).

The repeated use of a particular exclamation, word or expression peculiar only to the character concerned, is very much a marked feature of Dickens' early fictional speech, the technique reaching its peak in *David Copperfield*. Such a tag can also serve typifying ends, whether as drily short as the ejaculation 'hem' of Miss Knag (*NN*) – she uses it six times alone on her first appearance – or as curt and critical as the 'Trotters, you're too free' of Codlin (*ODS*), or as macabre and cynical as the ever-ready desire of Dennis, the hangman (*BR*), 'to work people off'. Mark Tapley (*MC*) is always depressingly determined to find an uncomfortable situation in order to 'be jolly'. Major Bagstock (*DS*) perpetually and brutally reminds us that he is 'tough and devilish sly'; in the same novel both the self-effacing 'It is of no consequence' of poor, good-natured Mr Toots, as well as the obsessive 'When found, make a note of' affixed to the loveable Captain Cuttle, leave an undeniable imprint on all Dickens readers.

So the speech tags, displaying linguistic eccentricity at a very simple level, serve not only as verbal memory props, but also as miniature characterisations, displaying the limitations – inarticulate or obsessive – of the characters concerned, and thus personally typifying them. For Dickens, then, even his early fictional speech was doing more than merely promoting identification, communication and the needs of the plot; it was also beginning to embody a character's view of reality (or lack of it) by presenting this in concentrated, exaggerated form. In this way, Dickens was already catching a character's essence through idiom as few authors had or have ever done, the amount of psychological insight revealed being simultaneously a measure of the artistic success.

In one of Mathews' characterisations, we find a form used of which the following is as good an example as any: 'Well, some folks have curious tastes, as my grandmother said, when I used to eat in the cinders.' All Weller fans will immediately recognise the kind of simile involved, one obviously popular at the time, for it was also put to frequent use by Splatterdash, a character in a farce called 'The Boarding House' which had a long and successful run in the 1820s.[6] This type of simile was not new – examples of it can also, for instance, be found in the German language[7] – but it would be difficult to trace its origins, lying obviously as they do in folk-humour. In a comparison embracing the comic content alone, Dickens' far-fetched, often morbidly zany, similes come off better; they are, whether read or heard, quite simply more humorous. It would be, however, as I have already pointed out, somewhat unfair to belittle in any way the achievement of Mathews, for whom the direct, personal impact possible from the stage was the most important factor. Dickens, whose novels were either read silently by people sitting alone or read aloud to others by people lacking Mathews' great histrionic gifts, was literally forced into relying on his own illimitable comic genius for creating humour in his books, above all in the fictional speech.

Taken together, the following two examples are, in manner of delivery, bafflingly similar.

> drive the Coventry stage twice a week all summer – pay for an inside place – mount the box – tip the coachy a crown – beat the mail – come in full speed – rattle down the gateway – take care of your heads – never killed but one woman and a child all my life – that's your sort!

> Heads, heads – take care of your heads! ... Terrible place – dangerous work – other day – five children – mother – tall lady, eating sandwiches – forgot the arch – crash – knock – children look round – mother's head off – sandwich in her hand – no mouth to put it in – head of family off – shocking, shocking!

The first comes from a play by Holcroft[8] and is spoken by a character called Goldfinch who, having been a jockey, automatically spoke thus when the conversation turned to horses. This was a part successfully acted later by Mathews, who so took to this jerky, staccato manner that he put it to use in many of his characterisations, and apparently it never failed to raise a laugh. The second example is, of course, the work of Dickens, being Jingle's words to an incredulous Mr Pickwick (*PP*, 11). Although it seems probable that he borrowed the essence of the anecdote – a 'sick' joke, basically trivial in concept – from Mathews' performance in the play mentioned, his humorous treatment of it is superior by far and intensely amusing. A closer examination will reveal why: Dickens reinforces the generally grotesque effect by making a seemingly trivial but realistic addition, the 'sandwich', to which, moreover, Dickens continues to draw attention, thus precipitating the reader into a comic–horrific situation that has suddenly become disquietingly alive. We are reminded, perhaps, of certain James Thurber cartoons. For obvious reasons, this manner of delivery is limited in its application. Jingle himself drops his jerky manner altogether when expressing his 'love' to Rachel, adopting the language of a cheap novelette (*PP*, 105). Further, when he reappears towards the end of the book, his speech, although he makes a brave effort, is but a shadow of its former self (*PP*, 639). Jingle stands and falls on his speech in the opening chapters.

There would seem to be a certain similarity between Jingle's manner of delivery and that of the braggartly aggressive coward Captain Dowler, introduced later in the same novel. In the speech of the latter, however, it will be noted, firstly, that the sentences, although rudely abrupt, are syntactically complete rather than jerkily half-formed, and, secondly, that the general effect is by no means so amusing. Of interest, though, is that Dowler's general style points forward to one of the author's most successful idiolects in this line, that of Major Bagstock, which appeared a decade later.

Although no exact reproduction of Jingle's speech manner reoccurs in Dickens' fiction, the author does, if circumstances demand it, allow characters in others of his novels to drop into something approaching this form of delivery: Walter Gay, for example, who becomes nervous when faced by a hostile Mr Dombey (*DS*, 131). In the succeeding novel, both Peggotty, when whispering agitatedly to young David through a keyhole (*DC*, 60–1), and Mr Micawber, beside himself with wrath (*DC*, 711), move into a form of the disjointed manner; however, without the breaks and interjections, the latter's syntax will be found to be quite normal. This is also so if one removes the 'little chords' with which Mr Skimpole intersperses his report to Esther Summerson about the tragic fate of the bailiff's children (*BH*, 206), but here there is a polished regularity about the interrupted syntactic flow that well captures this shallow parasite's heartless disinterest. The speech of that military man Matthew Bagnet (*BH*, 668) is wholly coloured by staccato rhythms, there being – logically enough – a certain resemblance to the manner of Major Bagstock (*DS*, 85). In a donkey cart driven over a bumpy road, Silas Wegg's syntax becomes 'dislocated' (*OMF*, 54), and, in the same novel, a languid Mortimer Lightwood cannot even be bothered to join his phrases on hearing of Mrs Boffin's spirited nature (*OMF*, 90). Compared with Jingle's mode, the differences, except perhaps in Lightwood's case, are obvious. They reveal, though, how Dickens could convey the form at least of everyday speech when it is moulded in unusual circumstances.

One Mathews character was called Mrs Neverend, one who once she started to talk was quite unable to stop, getting so mixed up that whatever she had in mind at the beginning was, in the ensuing verbal chaos, completely lost from view. A great many of Dickens' female characters are also loquacious in the extreme, and include – in the mouths of such as Mrs Nickleby, Mrs Gamp, Flora Finching and Mrs Lirriper – some of his most successful idiolects. They all are characterised by an erratic and continual shifting away from the goal initially intended, this being often, as with Mrs Neverend herself, utterly forgotten, each clausal shift adding more and more to the incongruity. This manner of speech delivery remains, in its illogical, garrulous wanderings, essentially the same for all of Dickens' loquacious personages, but in the later works the never-ending patterns of such idiolects become increasingly intricate and disconnected.

In the case of such a language feature, both Dickens and Mathews almost certainly drew their original inspiration from life itself, as Jane Austen probably also did regarding Miss Bates.[9] It was this character whose excitable loquacity mistakenly led Forster to believe that Dickens had modelled another such, Mrs Nickleby, on this personage. But, as his friend informed him, 'he had not at this time made the acquaintance of that fine writer', in itself a revealing remark![10] In fact, according to the novelist himself, Mrs Nickleby's speech manner was actually based on that of his own mother, albeit that she never recognised herself: 'Mrs Nickleby herself,' Dickens once wrote, 'once asked me ... if I really believed there ever was such a woman!'[11]

SPEECH IDENTIFIERS IN ACTION

A most rewarding and unusually extended illustration of the dramatic significance and polished mastery brought to what were initially relatively simple techniques is supplied by the whole of the opening chapter to the second half of *Little Dorrit*. Here, for fifteen pages, Dickens carefully avoids calling by name any of the eight characters arriving at the convent of the Great Saint Bernard who have previously, under markedly different circumstances, appeared in the novel. They are identified only by means of certain individualising and typifying language features already familiar to the reader.

The traveller who has the most to say – Rigaud, as we know him up to that point; or Blandois, as he signs himself at the end of this chapter – is only gradually led into that fictional Anglo-–French register ('Holy blue', etc.) which betrays him at once. Initially, the language merely hints (broadly enough) at its possessor by being over-elaborate, ultra-polite, and talkatively insinuating. His companion, the well-born but impoverished Henry Gowan playing the artist and on his way to Italy, can be equally quickly recognised from what we already know about him: his coldly arrogant directness alternating with the dangerous charm of his pretended indifference. As the author himself points out, there is a 'mocking inconsistency' in his manner (*LD*, 440).

Edward ('Tip') Dorrit is given but little to say; this is, however, through the drawling, affected tone ('d'ye') and free use of what he fondly imagines is the slang of young gentlemen of class ('fellows', 'immense'), enough to identify him with no difficulty. His sister Fanny says little more, but again it is the language which labels: that struggle within her public idiolect between peremptoriness and haughty gentility forces its way at once to the surface ('incommoded', 'certainly ... but not tired'). Her essentially selfish approach to life is placed in ironic contrast to the opposite quality in her younger sister Amy, in the two successive sentences wrung from them when the third young lady faints: '"Pray let me call my maid," cried the taller of the young ladies. "Pray let me put this water to her lips," said the shorter' (*LD*, 436). Without this deliberate contrast, Amy – like her counterpart Pet Gowan (née Meagles) – would be, from her speech alone, rather difficult to identify. This is in part due to her somewhat colourless, neutral register in which lexically and syntactically there is nothing unduly striking. What Amy has to say – and here is no exception – is simple, direct and to the point, and it is this that has individualised her as none of her predecessors in Dickens' standard 'hero–heroine' register.

That one of the 'two grey-haired gentlemen' (it is, of course, Frederick Dorrit, brother of William) says nothing at all is also completely in character, and no method could have placed him better. Of all the travellers, however, it is William Dorrit himself who is the easiest to identify: his entire speech idiom, in all its portentous, genteel complexity, is utterly unchanged since his prison days. He is still as painfully snobbish, as ever ready to take offence, as pompous in expression. Moreover, the nervous interjections remain, adorning his whole idiolect like scars won in the battle of Society. Compare the following two short passages, the first of which is also, in part, his first extended speech in the book, and the second from the chapter under discussion.

> I have received – hem – Testimonials in many ways, and of many degrees of value, and they have always been – ha – unfortunately acceptable; but I never was more pleased than with this – ahem – this particular Testimonial. (*LD* 84)

> Your friend, sir ... is – ha – is a little impatient; and, in his impatience, is not perhaps fully sensible of what he owes to – hum – to – but we will waive that. ... Your friend is a little impatient, sir. (*LD*, 437)

Dickens had by now so far developed this aspect of his idiolect technique that in some senses – particularly underlined by an episode such as the above – it can be likened to the *leit-motiv* technique of Wagner's mature operas.

In passing, it is worth observing that the long road travelled by Dickens (about twenty years of continuous writing) since the days when he worked out a character's speech during the actual writing of the novel concerned is not only reflected in the continuity of the above two examples, but also in the rather different language given to Mr Dorritt when he first arrives at the Marshalsea. To introduce and explain the circumstances of this character, Dickens, in Chapter 6 of the first book, moves back about 20 years in the narrative. William Dorrit's genteel speech is then not – as is to be expected – quite the same as later. Although his 'trembling lip' is mentioned several times, Dorrit's speech has not yet developed the nervous idiosyncrasies which are to spring from the appalling mental and physical pressure of over twenty years in jail. In particular, the interjections ('hem', 'ha', 'ahem', 'hum', etc.) stemming from his tremulous desire to find the right (for his situation, the least embarrassing) word, and the agitated repetitions – both of which features being very evident in the two examples given above – have not yet made their appearance. In his early works, Dickens simply had neither the time nor the experience to bear in mind such details.

For Dickens' idiolects, these individualising and typifying techniques marked the first important step towards planned structural significance. Simple in concept though these methods initially were, the results, as we have seen above, gradually began to display considerable skill and artistry over and above mere spontaneity of language production, no matter how inspired, as Dickens endeavoured to make the speech serve several functions simultaneously.

2 Root Dialects and Registers[1]

STANDARD SPEECH IN DICKENS' FICTION

Quite a few Dickens characters speak straightforward, standard, one could say written, English with next to no colouring, the resulting style giving rise to a stiff 'literary' impression rather than one of actual speech. Such a character is almost invariably a leading personage in the novel concerned, and, moreover, one normally representing moral good – the 'goodies' one might say. One thinks of Esther Summerson (*BH*), Agnes Wickfield (*DC*), Emma Haredale (*BR*) and Rose Maylie (*OT*) among others, and the expression 'goody-goody' often seems the only appropriate word when confronted with the sickly 'I-am-here-to-do-my-duty-come-what-may' attitude inherent in the artificial rhythms and lexical pretentiousness of: 'It is very bold in me ... who have lived in such seclusion, and can know so little of the world, to give you my advice so confidently, or even to have this strong opinion' (Agnes: *DC*, 367). Or even worse, Esther Summerson's answer to Allan Woodcourt's declaration of love (*BH*, 834). We are, indeed, a long way from what can be assumed was the normal colloquial idiom of even educated people, and, notwithstanding Dickens' stylised world, such a technique does not convince.

However, still more difficult to accept – at least in the eyes of those who misunderstand Dickens' intentions – is the use of this form of standard English free of any non-standard features by characters whose backgrounds preclude any such possibility. Norman Page, referring to such language as 'heroic speech',[2] goes on to define this as 'the imposing of a standard of "correct" English upon characters who enjoy a certain moral status in the novels in which they appear, being clearly intended to elicit a response of moral approbation from the reader'.[3]

For Steven Marcus, the speech idiom of Oliver Twist is 'symbolic of his alienation from the world in which he finds himself',[4] as it is, indeed, for this is what has already been referred to as one kind of personal typification. As Kathleen Tillotson has pointed out, it is part of a concept which is firmly rooted in

> the strength and indestructibility of natural, innocent virtue. [Such characters'] goodness ... may be thought implausible; but it must be seen as expressing what still survived of Dickens's own indestructible faith – expressing it almost allegorically, with the validity of fairy tale.[5]

If the presentation of such a character appears at all unconvincing, the fault will be found to lie almost completely in an uninspired application of the language mode chosen. This is the case, for instance, with Oliver Twist, in whose idiom there is a palpable lack of the vitality and originality which is otherwise so characteristic of a great deal of Dickens' fictional speech. The author was far more successful in the gradual development later in his career of the 'pure' language given to Lizzie Hexam (*OMF*).[6]

A register of the English language with which, it would appear, only England itself is cursed, is a certain manner of speaking affected by many of the English upper classes. It is non-regional, being less an individual dialect in the sense of possessing an extensive and individual range of vocabulary with its own syntactic and grammatical peculiarities, and far more a form of standard English in which the pronunciation of particular words is stressed in a non-standard manner, and to which a certain repetitive, stilted phraseology is also uniquely peculiar. It is the pronunciation more than anything else, however, which must be considered peculiarly distorted. Dickens disliked intensely people who 'yaw-yawed in their speech' (*HT*, 124) and in his early novels, especially, tended to guy them.

The upper-class register, as Dickens presents it, has six major characteristics which are particularly accentuated – or, rather, less subtly used – in the earlier novels. There is, firstly, a substitution of [w] for [r] which in certain plays, novelettes and comics was long presumed to be a typical speech impediment of the aristocratic classes. Those who have ever followed Billy Bunter's adventures at Greyfriars will be familiar with it in the mouth of the 'Honourable Arthur Augustus D'Arcy, the swell of St Jim's' ('The Wottahs! The Wuffians'). In Dickens' first novel, Lord Mutanhed, an extremely primitive attempt at satire as his name already indicates, is given extended use of this feature (*PP*, 502), though his use of '*iwon*' seems somewhat questionable, to say the least. Secondly, there is a lengthening, sometimes very pronounced, of vowels, as in Lord Verisopht's 'wa-a-x'. This particular character, indeed, provides the most sustained illustration of the upper-class register in all Dickens (*NN*, 234–9). Close behind him, though, comes the Dedlock Cousin whose sheer indolence leads him not only into the last-named distortion, but also, thirdly, into a prominent telescoped manner of speaking involving the dropping of lightly-stressed syllables as in 'fler' = fellow (*BH*, 718). Meaningless expletives, such as 'Gad', 'deuce take it' and 'you know', are a fourth feature found above all in the Verisopht–Hawk circle as well as, delightfully, in the imbecilic sentiments on 'Blood' by the 'simpering fellow with the weak legs' (*DC*, 374–5). Repetitiveness, fifthly, is common to almost all in this register, none more so than Barnacle Junior (*LD*, 108–9), and underlines their typically limited range of vocabulary. Finally, and more rarely, there is the use of special vocabulary such as 'hipped' = miserable (*BR*, 202) and that associated with hunting (*OMF*, 543).

Less linguistically pronounced, and indicating a growing subtlety with the passing of time, are the speech idioms of such as Cousin Feenix (*DS*), Steerforth (*DC*), Sir Leicester Dedlock (*BH*), James Harthouse (*HT*), Gowan (*LD*), Twemlow, Wrayburn and Lightwood (*OMF*). Their individuality arises from a smoother, more relaxed syntax plus phraseology more in keeping with the character's own personality and place in the structure of the novel concerned. In the last two cases, a general lightness of idiom is, at certain moments, particularly apparent; its roots are to be found in Steerforth, Harthouse and Gowan. The earlier speech form of Sir John Chester (*BR*), although successful within limits, is somewhat colourless. He speaks – rightly, within the context – a rather formal, old-fashioned, yet in the main elegant form of standard English, with only an occasional touch of the upper-class register. Two further characters – Mantalini (*NN*) and Mr Turveydrop (*BH*) – are not themselves products of the upper class, but resort to the by then out-dated Regency manner, aspects of which are even more affected forms of the register under discussion.

The following comment is added to the definitions of 'genteel' in the *OED*:

> A few years before the middle of the 19th century the word was much ridiculed as being characteristic of those ... possessed with a dread of being taken for 'common people', or who attached exaggerated importance to supposed marks of social superiority.

This tallies precisely with Dickens' use of the genteel register, it being in his fiction the speech form of that vast Victorian horde wandering around the snobbish wastelands not only of the central and upper-middle class, but also of its lower reaches. In this last-named case, the speech is not always – illogically enough – rooted in the author's version of the non-standard London dialect. It is clear that for Dickens, 'genteel' normally has very negative overtones, but there are odd moments when his irony is gentler, as in his authorial comment when Mlle Hortense is arrested by Inspector Bucket (*BH*, 743), or more dispassionately amused, as in his acute awareness of the subtle differences in social attitudes to the one or other profession (*GE*, 169).

The main features of Dickens' genteel register can be listed as follows: long-winded syntax forming a framework to empty, even nonsensical utterances, usually pompous, conceited or patronising, but in some cases arrogant, in others hypocritical; lexically full of highfalutin, artificial phraseology, words of Latin origin, clichés and meaningless, repetitive adjectives, combined usually with an almost pathological avoidance of what is considered vulgar (although there are some amusing lapses), all this with an exaggerated reverence for rank and title, expressed in frequent use of some respectful salutation or other.

Professor Brook refers to 'language to suit the occasion'[7] – in this case one might maintain that the so-called genteel person is permanently faced by the occasion of Society. Dickens delighted in poking fun at such types and, until the end of his career, continued with unwavering sharpness to present fictional characters whose speech, in its garrulous pomposity and sickening platitudes, is a devastating and convincing satire of the whole tawdry world under fire.[8]

The 'majestic, long-suffering' Mrs Wilfer's far-fetched, solemnly artificial speech idiom is one bitingly polished illustration of Dickens' application of this register. In her shocked prudery at the mention of underwear (*OMF*, 804–5), for example, there is a foreshadowing of Wilde's Lady Bracknell. Even better is her starchly sarcastic elucidation of the Boffins' social status:

> Mrs Boffin (of whose physiognomy I can never speak with the composure I would desire to preserve) and your mother are not on terms of intimacy. It is not for a moment to be supposed that she and her husband dare to presume to speak of this family as the Wilfers. I cannot therefore condescend to speak of them as the Boffins. No; for such a tone – call it familiarity, levity, equality, or what you will – would imply those social interchanges which do not exist. Do I render myself intelligible? (*OMF*, 312)

Just as in real life, a great many characters in Dickens whose personal manner of speaking stems from either the standard or non-standard dialect tend to add the special vocabulary – jargon, if one will – of their particular profession, a process which lends a very individual colour to the speech concerned. Dickens' interest in such occupational registers is revealed from his earliest writings onwards, there being, indeed, so many such speech idioms that one can do no more than touch on the most striking.

It is undoubtedly the legal profession which most frequently occurs in Dickens, small wonder when one remembers that after leaving school he moved as a clerk first to the law firm of Ellis and Blackmore, then to a solicitor's, when he ultimately found the profession boring, and, having learned the cumbersome shorthand of the time, then moved on to the Courts of the Doctors' Commons to take down reports of cases. All this must have given him not only an insight into the workings of the law, but also a notion of the tortuous complexities of legal language. In greatly varying forms of concentration, this register is applied with considerable contempt to the speech of a long line of solicitors, barristers and others at law, stretching from Perker, Buzfuz,

Snubbin, Phunky, Stareleigh, Dodson, Fogg, Skimpin and Pell (*PP*) through Brass (*OCS*), Kenge, Vholes and Tulkinghorn (*BH*), Bar – a form of emblematisation (*LD*), Stryver and Carton (*TTC*), Jaggers (*GE*), Wrayburn and Lightwood (*OMF*) to Grewgious (*ED*), all of whose registers are rooted (despite occasional colloquialisms) in the standard dialect.

The salient feature of Dickens' version of this register is longwindedness, probably to avoid giving anything away. A past master of this is Sampson Brass who, speaking thus even in private life, not only forces Dick Swiveller to 'set down a memorandum' concerning the 'single gentleman', but also cross-questions him as if he were in the witness-box (*OCS*, 262). Combined with this prolixity is the rhetorical tendency to build up a series of sentences all beginning with the same word or phrase. These are frequently interspersed with such meaningless qualifying locutions as 'I would say' or 'shall I say', as from the mouth of Conversation Kenge (*BH*, 20–2), plus a variety of specialised legal words and expressions,[9] inhuman legal abbreviations (*BH*, 26), often tinged with the lawyer's courtroom habit of dropping lightly stressed syllables or even whole phrases: 'Mlud, no – variety of points – feel it my duty tsubmit – ludship' (*BH*, 5). There are, of course, numerous scenes in which the legal register dominates because it must, and of which the 'Trial of Bardell against Pickwick' (*PP*, 464–88) is probably the most famous. But, like the other occupational registers, it achieves its greatest fictional effect when applied – as by Brass – in private life. Even characters who themselves have never been members of the legal profession drop into legal language, though this is normally due to continual contact, as in the case of Mr Jarndyce when talking to the lawyer's clerk, William Guppy (*BH*, 860).

Dickens' use of the educational register was satirical. He had little patience with modern teaching methods of the time that seemed to treat the child as a thing into which useless knowledge must be packed (*HT*, 5). At first sight, the actual speech register of most teachers in Dickens, which with varying success they also try to force upon their pupils, strikes the reader as somewhat colourless: grammatically and lexically pedantic rather than anything else, with a concomitant tendency to artificial rhetoric and rhythms. The individuality of the register lies far more in the actual 'over-care' with which they speak, as if they themselves have also learned off by heart what they are imparting. Bradley

Headstone, with his combination of pedantry, mistrust, halting logic and 'habit of questioning and being questioned' supplies the supreme example of such speech (*OMF*, 216–17). On occasion, Dickens goes even further, showing unadorned this register's soulless artificiality, thus becoming trenchantly satirical about what he feels is utterly wrong. This is underlined very amusingly in his authorial comments on the 'dry and sandy' Miss Blimber digging up dead languages 'like a Ghoul' (*DS*, 142-3), and, too, in Miss Twinkleton's preposterous little speech, full of pedantic irrelevancies, to the 'Ladies' of her 'Seminary' (*ED*, 83).[10]

A great many doctors plus a few medical students appear in Dickens' fiction, but in most cases the medical register is not so pronounced as the two previous registers discussed. In addition, the humour involved was, initially, more farcical than subtle and directly in the Smollett tradition, as when two medical students, Mr Benjamin Allen and Mr Bob Sawyer, deliberately 'put the horrors' into Mr Pickwick by holding 'professional' conversation at the breakfast table (*PP*, 409). Rather more to the point is the way Dickens ironically pokes fun at the doctor's habit of identifying himself with his patient, and speaking in the first person plural (*SB*, 302; *LD*, 163–4). Dickens did, in fact, gradually learn to show far greater subtlety in providing a concise but comprehensively picturesque turn of phrase in this register, a delightful illustration being Physician's zoological references to Mr Merdle's health (*LD*, 253). He also managed, in Dr Jobling's short, staccato questions to Tigg Montague to which he provides his own answers (*MC*, 434–6), to catch the breezy confidence and patronising attitude typical of the practitioner who is sure of his patient.

Outside the three registers discussed above, it would seem – in Dickens at least – that educated people are less inclined to colour their speech with professional phraseology than are those whose speech is rooted in the non-standard dialect. The example we have of the former are, therefore, all the more interesting. The armed services register, for instance, ranges from abruptly dogmatic repetitions fired at the unfortunate listener by such as the brutal Major Bagstock or the cowardly Captain Dowler, through Lieutenant Tartar's ingenuous transference of naval terms to civilian life (*ED*, 202–4), to the glorious zaniness of Mrs Bayham Badger's use of the same naval idiom (*BH*, 229). Only one member of the established church, Bishop, makes extended use of the clerical register. This is clearly the direct result of his bearing no other means of identification than his rank within his profession. Rhetorically, his observations to Merdle (*LD*, 251) are an extreme form of the Anglican sermon of the time, a form which here has sunk into pompous reflexes and unconscious hypocrisy.

From the language alone, it is sometimes difficult to decide whether a Dickens orator comes from the educated classes or whether he has acquired the rudiments of standard speech by the way. It is easier to take other, non-linguistic criteria to deduce the speaker's probable social origins. Gregsbury (*NN*) and Honeythunder (*ED*), for instance, must both stem from the educated classes; the same can, with reservations, be assumed of Chadband (*BH*). Be that as it may, they all have in common certain ever-recurring rhetorical features: the manner is almost invariably declamatory, rhetorical with an excessive use of repetition (above all in the anaphoric mode) and of archaic or pseudo-poetic words and expressions, particularly those springing from Christian sources. This last-named feature is found even in the speech of those not actually ministers of the church.[11] In addition, such orators all share a predilection for meaningless phrases, saying in effect nothing at all, and this at undue length, a fact only to be expected of characters basically being viewed as hypocrites. Allied to the above is the fraternal approach, a tendency to address the audience as the speaker's 'brother' or 'sister'. This approach can quickly change to one in which the listener is browbeaten if he or she dares to dissent, a case in point being the Rev. Crisparkle having to endure Mr Honeythunder's bullying (*ED*, 191).

As his negative representations of this type show, Dickens detested the manner and methods of speakers using this mode perhaps even more than their views. He had already had experience of such orators when taken as a child to a non-conformist chapel, and must have occasionally suffered the same later. As early as *Sketches by Boz*, two examples are to be found in his writings: the Irish orator (*SB*, 39) and the 'Parlour Orator' (*SB*, 239). The Irishman is the first of a long line in this register, through Stiggins, Howler, Chadband and Hawkyard to Honeythunder, among others. His aversion, even as a young writer, is also shown by his description of the nonconformist preacher in 'Sunday Under Three Heads' (*UT/RP*, 641) written in June 1836, just before *Pickwick* took its resounding turn for success.

When one remembers, moreover, that Dickens for many years was also subject to the equally false rhetoric of so many boring speakers in the House of Parliament, it is little wonder that he developed so deep an aversion to this register and the perpetrators of its techniques.

Even some of his greatest admirers have deplored Dickens' use of the melodramatic register, especially the crudity of some earlier forms it took. In the mouths of the straight characters, with its stiff, artificial manner, it is never, in itself, the stuff of a true Dickensian idiolect; blended with other registers and personal speech features, especially with a dash of colloquial or even non-standard English – Dick Swiveller's exotic concoction is a case in point – it can become the basis of one. The purely melodramatic manner as initially adopted by Dickens – apparently in all seriousness, especially when deeply moved by the scene he was presenting – was a direct product of the serious stage of the day, whose most famous exponent was William Macready, a firm and lifelong friend of the author. This man's acting was, by all accounts, in the grand manner: rhetorical, full of pathos and gesture, heavily and obviously emotional – in short, he must have been given to what we, by modern standards, would probably call 'overacting'.[12] And yet, paradoxically, Dickens could even make fun of the very same mode, doing so right from the *Sketches*, and even, in *Nicholas Nickleby*, putting the serious and comic forms virtually side by side, making Nicholas (one of the worst 'serious' offenders) mock the comic mode in the mouths of some of the Crummles troupe (*NN*, 379). Dickens obviously judged the value of the mode not by its own features, but by the value in his eyes of the person using it.

It is not always fully appreciated, however, that Dickens later not only learned to submit the melodramatic manner to the exigencies of the plot, but also developed it into a more strikingly effective rhetorical tool, original rather than embarrassingly hackneyed. Bradley Headstone's passionate avowal of love to Lizzie Hexam, for instance, is still undoubtedly melodrama, but now the language, through its syllabic simplicity and emphatic repetitiveness, is rhythmically tauter and well-nigh overwhelming, its vocabulary more effectively to the point, and – vital to the general structure – by revealing the ungovernable passion of the wretchedly unhappy teacher, helps raise the action of the dramatic scene to an exciting climax, as well as providing an important link in the developing chain of events forming the novel as a whole (*OMF*, 394–400). Jasper's use of the mode, when forcing his unwanted attentions upon the terrified Rosa Budd, also electrifies: the passion is irresistible, bursting through in an overwhelming rise of repetitive rhythmic intensity in which no word is superfluous or lacking in meaning, and in which there is a fundamental rhetorical simplicity. Theatrical it may be, but it is theatre that lives and whose vitality and originality cannot be ignored (*ED*, 222–3). Both Jasper and Headstone can be considered not only two of Dickens' more successful serious characterisations, but worthy of taking their place alongside the greatest villains of Victorian fiction.

DICKENS' FICTIONAL VERSION OF THE COCKNEY DIALECT

> Of all those historic dialects which still distinguish, to a greater or less degree, the speech of most Englishmen, none is of such interest as Cockney, that noble blend of East Mercian, Kentish, and East Anglian, which, written by Chaucer, printed by Caxton, spoken by Spenser and Milton, and surviving in the mouths of Sam Weller and Mrs Gamp, has, in a modified form and with an artificial pronunciation, given us the literary English of the present day.[13]

Thus Ernest Weekley. That the vast majority of Dickens' lower-class characters are depicted as Londoners is as indisputable as it is well-known; that the speech itself of these characters is not – nor is it meant to be – an exact reflection of the actual London dialect of the author's time, is far less commonly realised or accepted.[14] However, before discussing this point, there follows a general word about the fictional application of the dialect in question.

It is an unfortunate fact that Cockney – as found in Victorian literature at least – more often than not reflects the point of view that what is being presented is quite simply 'low'. This is in stark contrast to the presentation in literature of English rural dialects as, for example, in Emily Brontë, Mrs Gaskell, George Eliot and Thomas Hardy or, too, the Anglo–Scottish of Burns and Scott. It seems that this attitude has grown apace with the development and attempted fixation of a standardised form of English with its frequently artificial 'rules' of pronunciation, a process later encouraged by the necessary spread of education for all.

Two traditions can be distinguished: on the one hand there are those writers from Pierce Egon, through Dickens, to the less well known Augustus Mayhew and James Greenwood, who approach the Cockney with greater sympathy and understanding. Their application of non-standard features, although often comic in the extreme, is aimed rather at underlining eccentricity of character than otherwise. In the second tradition, on the other hand, one proceeding from Surtees, through Thackeray, down to E. J. M. Milliken and his famous figure 'Arry', there is far more a deliberate focusing on the non-standard element as something 'low'. This is a direction taken by those who, when referring to the kind of speech under discussion, would probably tend to use the prefix 'sub-' rather than 'non-'.[15] In his use of the dialect after the character's initial appearance, Dickens concentrates less on reproducing the non-standard grammatical features typical of the Cockney dialect of his day, and aims more at capturing in stylised form actual idiomatic usage, rhetorical idiosyncrasies and rhythmic patterns.

Above all it is important to realise that such characters as Sam Weller and Sairey Gamp do not speak a complete and literal phonetic transcription of Cockney dialect as it existed in the author's day; nor was an exact transcription ever considered. Far more did Dickens – who was bent on a satisfactory 'readability compromise' for his audience – begin setting up his dialect collage by deliberately selecting certain typical, easy-to-recognise non-standard features. These were primarily of a phonological nature, such as the glottal stop and the misuse of the aspirate, among others, with an admixture of non-standard grammar (particularly the weak conjugation of strong verbs), familiar colloquialisms, catch phrases or slang, the v/w transcription, prefix and suffix confusion, plus malapropisms. Only rarely does Dickens introduce an item, such as Mrs Gamp's replacement of sibilants with a [g], which is in itself unusual or out of the way. To add to the non-standard effect, Dickens also resorted (with occasional inconsistency due to the pressures of serialisation) to 'eye-dialect', the writing of a word (wrongly) in the way it is pronounced anyway, as in 'wot', 'wos', 'rekwire', etc. This is, of course, something done by many writers, probably more in order to indicate either how the character himself might have written the word, or simply to confirm in a readable way the non-standard aspect. Dickens' whole orthographical technique when presenting the Cockney dialect was, in fact, conventional rather than realistic. Finally, many of these non-standard features served a definite artistic purpose, adding to a comprehension both of the character in particular and of the novel as a whole.[16]

True idiolectal individuality was then arrived at by blending these linguistic features with a distinctive choice of such rhetorical Cockney attributes as their shrewd irony and quick wit, their habit of resorting to reported speech when citing another, and their fondness for speech tags and for the quotation – invariably inaccurate or embellished – be it from the Bible, the stage, folklore or popular ballad. In all this, Dickens showed from the very beginning an ability to re-create the rhythms of the Cockney idiom, rhythms which within the framework of his stylised fictional techniques soon developed their own highly theatrical impetus. Eventually these patterns, far from being realistic, came closer either to the metrical regularities of poetry, even music, or to the schematic syntactic structures of public rhetoric. It is this rhythmic quality which, with its exaggeration, emphatic repetition and distinctive metre, lends to the best of Dickens' fictional speech its own peculiarly personal vitality, one unrivalled in the world of the English novel, and one eminently suited to throwing each individual character into striking and significant relief.

A number of scholars have pointed to the fact that much of the non-standard detail of Dickens' Cockney dialect ('creetur', 'cowcumber', 'torter', 'furnage', etc.) was almost certainly anachronistic by the 1830s. This serves only to underline the extent to which Dickens' idiolects were language 'pasticcios'. Drawing as he did on the speech habits of young and old alike, the author inevitably and arbitrarily added certain features common to those who had learnt to speak in the previous century. Supporting this argument by quoting from, among other sources, the letters of Lady Wentworth, written early in the eighteenth century, Ernest Weekley suggests

> that, just as the dress fashions of humbler folk once followed, at a considerable interval of time, those of the wealthier class, so their speech used to reproduce the fashionable pronunciation of preceding generations. Mrs Gamp talked like an early Georgian duchess and Sam Weller like a town 'blood' of the same period.[17]

The density of non-standard detail in such hybrid mixtures varies substantially, this being the case right from the beginning. In the *Sketches*, for example, the speech idioms of Mr Sluffen (*SB*, 173) and Ikey (*SB*, 450–2) remain unequalled in Dickens in their concentrated phonetic complexity. The variable density of this phonetic complexity is evident, however, not only from book to book – reaching, with one or two later exceptions, a considerable height in the initial appearances of Mrs Gamp (*MC*) – but from character to character within the same book. Betty Higden (*OMF*), for instance, in contrast to (say) Rogue Riderhood in the same novel, speaks for no obvious reason with but a modicum of non-standard variants.[18] There may even be, particularly in the earlier works, a suggestive disparity from scene to scene for one and the same person. This could be because Dickens, overwhelmed by the pressures of serialisation, did not always have at the outset a full and exact conception of what speech features he was going to concentrate on, or even use for that matter. On the other hand, it may possibly have been dictated by rhythmic needs or, further, by the symbolic demands of the situation in particular or the novel as a whole.

The mini-idiolect of Jo (*BH*) supplies an interesting illustration of this last point, one which reveals the author making actual structural use of Jo's fictional speech. As P. J. Keating has pointed out, 'Jo is given a special speech pattern not because he is a lower-class Londoner, but because the role he plays in the novel – especially his outcast social position and pathetic death – demands it.'[19] To explain this in more detail: Jo's speech idiom presents lexically and above all phonetically an extremely complex picture, the latter feature being, as I have already pointed out, particularly unusual at this stage in the author's development. The resulting linguistic complexity, although occasionally leading to a certain artificiality, serves at its best to illustrate the undoubted care and attention Dickens devoted to this character's idiolect, an analysis of which reveals the deliberate extent to which it has been integrated into the general thematic structure: for those moving in the higher circles of the tainted Victorian society, Jo is virtually unintelligible; he in turn finds them equally unintelligible, as his encounter with Lady Dedlock (*BH*, 223–5) so devastatingly proves. He is simply a creature to be hounded through his existence, and the almost incoherent protestations and queries which form the basis of utterances which are syntactically simple but otherwise complicated, place in stark relief th[e] utter wretched hopelessness of his sorry lot. This is representati[o]nal speech in the non-standard mode of the highest quality.

To the basic Cockney dialect of the underworld characters i[n] *Oliver Twist*, Dickens added carefully sifted quantities, differin[g] strongly from character to character, of *cant*:[20] that jarg[on] common to the London criminal whose reasons for developin[g] such a register obviously lay in a desire for secrecy. Occasionall[y] one of its terms has been absorbed into general colloquial us[e]: 'yokel' (223), for example; certainly many have been taken ov[er] by the Londoner at large: 'Beak' (53), 'fence' (86), 'blab' (87[)], 'ticker' (132), 'swag' (141), and so on. However, when lookin[g] more closely at Dickens' use of this register, the modern read[er] will at once be struck by the harmlessness and relative intelligib[i]lity of what the author has selected as fit for publication. Georg[e] Gissing somewhat equivocally takes Dickens to task for n[ot] reproducing more realistically the crude language of such of h[is] underworld characters as Sikes.[21] Any examination, howeve[r,] which ignores not only Victorian moral conventions, to whic[h] Dickens was inescapably bound, but also the unusual, high[ly] personal stylisation so peculiar to his method of literary creatio[n] is bound to end up wide of the mark.

The measure of cant apportioned to the various members [of] Fagin's gang of ruffians, as well as to the two Bow Street Runne[rs] sent down to investigate the burglary at Chertsey, reveals co[n]siderable fluctuations. Characteristically, Dickens applies cant [in] large portions only when a character is being introduced to th[e] reader or on special occasions for reasons connected more with h[is] own stylised methods than with anything else. The Artful Dod[g]er's first appearance, for instance, brings a whole flood of cant [-] 'covey', 'grub', 'stump', 'on the mill', etc. (52–4) – thus addin[g] the essential touch of realism at once, doing so with words whi[ch] could hardly be considered in excessively bad taste by the ove[r] fastidious. On the other hand, his second outburst of cant (aga[in] to Oliver, who is cleaning his boots for him) is being use[d] structurally, showing the enormous gulf between their tw[o] worlds; at times, Oliver does not even understand him (130–2). [It] is revealing that, apart from the one word 'beaks' (334), th[e] Dodger uses no cant at all in his justly famous trial scene. Wi[th] the speech of the two Bow Street Runners ('prad', 'crack', 'blun[t]' etc.; 222–8), Dickens was almost certainly expressing his negati[ve] view of these forerunners of the Metropolitan police force: putting them in the same linguistic pot as Fagin's gang, so to speak.

The variability of application cuts right across all the underworld characters, some, like Fagin, exhibiting very few cant terms at all. As usual, the needs of the scene, the atmosphere, intelligibility, the sensibilities of the reader/listener, all played more important parts in the writing of *Oliver Twist*, and an impression of authenticity is retained despite the restrictions of such stylisation.

Although their social backgrounds would lead the reader to expect the opposite, the speech of many Dickens characters is completely standard. In the case, however, of those persons obviously stemming from the lower, less-educated reaches of society, but who are striving to break into the much-desired realm of gentility, Dickens has clearly made a deliberate effort to endow them with at least some non-standard language features, many of which spring from their misguided attempts to ape their social superiors. In general, there are two types comprising this nonstandard version of the genteel register: those who, having made or unexpectedly come into money (the Tuggs family (*SB*) and Mr Pumblechook (*GE*) are obvious examples), wish to insinuate themselves into a higher stratum of society; and those who, as a result of the profession they practise (such as the butlers in *Pickwick*), are forced into daily contact with people above them on the social scale.

The main rhetorical features of this register correspond in outline to those of the parallel register rooted in the standard dialect and discussed above. A major difference, one due to a lack of education, is the greatly more limited lexical content. Despite this deficiency, the speech of such characters can be equally longwinded, pompous, conceited or patronising, though far more nonsensical, Mr Bumble (*OT*) being a classic instance. There is a concomitant tendency to fall into inspired solecisms, as is supremely the case with the gloriously ridiculous Mrs Bloss, one of Dickens' first zanies, who launches the reader on a dizzy drip down the rapids of her wildly erratic English. Within a short space, she perpetrates some of the best malapropisms to be found in Dickens: 'obtrusion' = seclusion, 'unitarian' = valetudinarian, 'incited' = excited, 'pervades' = provides, 'creditable' = credible (*SB*, 292–301).

If anything, the attempts to avoid what is considered vulgar are even more extreme than in the standard branch of this register. This is hilariously brought out at the 'friendly swarry' in Bath (*PP*, 518–27), to which Sam Weller has been invited by a group of servants all bent on copying their employers both in speech and behaviour, as well as in the speech of Mr Kenwigs (*NN*, 183) and Fanny Squeers (*NN*, 175–6). Occasionally, in the early works, Dickens exhibited more the somewhat crude facetiousness of a verbosely clever young man – such as the heavily obvious play on the word 'chaise' (*SB*, 346), which he toyed with using twenty years later in *Bleak House* but then dropped – than the later artistry revealed in, for example, the fawning obsequiousness of Mr Pumblechook's syntactic pomposity and lexical aspirations (*GE*, 144–8), or the wonderous flights of Mrs Billickin so trenchantly contrasted with Miss Twinkleton's standard use of the register (*ED*, 256–8).

The combination of occupational register and non-standard detail results in considerably more complexity than in the corresponding registers rooted in the standard dialect. For this reason, Dickens' works abound with instances in which a 'translation' has to be proffered. This is done either by the one responsible or by one of the other characters present, both for the benefit of those at the receiving end and of the reader. Sometimes, the author himself interposes a gloss elucidating whatever expression it is that may be obscure. Adopting otherwise the same procedure as in his presentation of non-standard detail, Dickens frequently inserted a whole mass of occupational indicators in the initial entry of the character(s) concerned, with thereafter a mere sprinkling and that, in most cases, a repetition.

In his earliest ventures into the show world – in the *Sketches*: 'Astleys', 'Greenwich Fair' and 'Private Theatres' – Dickens sought to reduce the professional register to a minimum. In three novels (*NN*, *OCS* and *HT*) as well as in such later occasional pieces as 'Going into Society' and 'Dr Marigold', it is presented far more lavishly. The Crummles and their associates are unusual in that their use of the register, one also mixed with the melodramatic register, reveals little non-standard detail (*NN*, 278–85). It is in a later novel, however, that the reader is treated to very extensive use of the show-world register. In the first scene introducing Kidderminster ('Cupid') and Mr E. W. B. Childers, members of the lisping Mr Sleary's travelling circus, the interpolated jargon is so unintelligible that the forbidding Bounderby and Gradgrind have to be given translations: 'ochre' = money, 'missed his tip' = unsuccessful, 'ponging' = tumbling, 'Jeff' = rope, 'goosed' = drunk, 'Crackler' = speaker, etc. (*HT*, 30–2).

Waiters are continually coming and going in Dickens' works, and it is clear that Dickens had a particularly keen eye for the habits of all that vast throng who are in some way or other engaged in serving the public through the catering profession. It is also clear – as is pointedly revealed in the scene when Pip is forced to take Estella for a cup of tea, at the end of which the whole establishment has been 'bribed into a state of contempt and animosity' (*GE*, 254) – that he thought little of the general run of this kind of service. Food (and everything connected with this commodity) yields the key to this particular subdivision of the occupational register. Lexically, the usual procedure is followed, vocabulary being put, however, to satirical use when waiters start referring to customers by what they have ordered or taken.[22] Syntactically, Dickens cleverly points up the habit many waiters have of resorting to a telegraphic form of the language brought on, obviously, by the need to repeat the same phrases over and over again, these taking on the aura of an incantation. Such speech dissociation can even help to underline the parallel development taking shape within the pensive Arthur Clennam, jogged into a brown study by the dull, soul-destroying greyness of a Sunday in Victorian London, and the thoughts it arouses of his own excessively strict upbringing: '"Chaymaid! Gelen box num seven, not go sleep here, gome"' (*LD*, 30). Two further modes are those adopted by waiters when they are sure of their customer. One is impudently telegraphic, as when amiably and craftily turned on to deceive the naive boy David Copperfield; one is reminded of Jingle's manner (*DC*, 67). The other – again David, now a raw young man, is the recipient – is abruptly, imperatively familiar, with sudden and deliberate switches between the second and third persons, the whole verging on sheer insolence (*DC*, 285). It is significant that to the arrogant Steerforth, the waiter immediately becomes obsequious (*DC*, 288).

A series of articles completed at the beginning of the 1850s for his new family magazine *Household Words* clearly reflects Dickens' new-found enthusiasm for the police force, as well as the admiration he obviously felt for the detectives themselves, for their versatility, alertness and quiet efficiency. An introduction to the Liverpool police (*UT/RP*, 40–51), written about ten years later, proves equally favourable. Previous to this in his writings, it will be observed, firstly, that policemen of any kind are more conspicuous through their absence than anything else, and, secondly, that those few who do turn up are presented as either clumsily, indeed farcically inefficient with a basic non-standard dialect to match, or simply as coarse individuals sharing the same dialectal background as the criminals they hunt. The former is classically illustrated by the ignorant 'peace-officer' Grummer (*PP*, 331), the latter by the Bow Street Runners, Blathers and Duff, already referred to above. Dickens' later change of attitude is reflected in a sharp reduction of non-standard features and an increase in that lexical pedantry seemingly typical of many policemen and especially prevalent in the speech idiom of the deftly official Mr Inspector: 'clue', 'swear', 'identity', 'I presume, sir', 'consequently', 'ascertain', etc. (*OMF*, 24–7). The chief characteristic of Inspector Bucket, Dickens' one great fictional detective, is flexibility of idiom. He turns to at least eight sub-idiolects depending on what is best suited to his wily purpose. Whatever idiom he chooses, however, he remains absolutely factual; despite the apparent verbosity, not a word is wasted, nor is the end in view lost (*BH*, 729–35).[23]

The chief quality of the non-standard dialect's seafaring register is that it colours utterly the idiolects of its two most striking representatives, Captains Cuttle and Bunsby, the professional terminology being transferred completely and often grotesquely to their everyday life on shore: 'hove down', 'overhaul', 'lay your hand well to the wind', 'take an observation', etc. In the case of Cuttle, whose extensive use of an occupational register is rivalled only by that of Tony Weller, the seafaring register mirrors his whole outlook, forming his very thoughts. For all the improbability of the circumstances, a classic illustration is provided by the captain's speech in his interview with James Carker prior to Walter Gay's departure (*DS*, 233–6). It moulds, too, his attempts to philosophise as when he is trying to give Walter some encouragement (*DS*, 700). The hypocritical Rob the Grinder is so mystified by the captain's method of expressing himself that it earns him a rebuke for not knowing 'his own native alphabet' (*DS*, 454).

In the lower reaches of the world of law, many characters, from Mr Lowton (*PP*) to Chuckster (*OCS*), Uriah Heep (*DC*), Guppy and Jobling (*BH*), Wemmick (*GE*) and Young Blight

(*OMF*), hold down a position – lawyer's clerk – of which Dickens himself had direct experience. The resulting speech is more or less coloured by non-standard variants to fix the character's social level, although – as in the case of William Guppy (*BH*) – this is sometimes somewhat obscure. Two general legal modes can be determined here: one dry and to the point, as in Wemmick's official speech idiom (*GE*, 265–7), the other a splendid form of burlesque resulting from pretentious endeavours to emulate the parallel register of those that employ them. An excruciatingly funny episode in the latter mode is provided in a conversation between Guppy and his feckless, jobless friend Jobling (*BH*, 273–82).

There are so many professional registers rooted in Dickens' version of the non-standard dialect that it is impossible to go into extensive detail concerning them all. Among others, we have Tony Weller (*PP*), whose highly developed and deeply expressive use of the coaching register is to be discussed in the second part of this study. The following are also particularly distinctive: Ned Dennis, the hangman, whose euphemistic speech manner becomes horribly frightening (*BR*, 297); Mr Sweedlepipe (*MC*), barber and bird fancier; 'the Chicken', a boxer from the pre-Queensberry Rules, barefist days (*DS*, 802); the Miss Mowcher of her first appearance with her somewhat disgusting manicuring talk (*DC*, 330); the soldierly staccato of Matthew Bagnet (*BH*, 668); Mr Venus, taxidermist and articulator, with his suggestive transference of Silas Wegg's personality to the latter's amputated limb (*OMF*, 79–80); Durdles, the stonemason, with his structurally significant references in that register (*ED*, 47); and, using railway terminology, Mr Toodle, whose professional register also colours his whole speech idiom and is, indeed, essential to his thought. Here is his advice to his children: 'If you find yourselves in cuttings or in tunnels, don't you play no secret games. Keep your whistles going, and let's know where you are' (*DS*, 534).

In order to indicate that some characters using the oratorical register stem from the lower classes, Dickens is, of necessity, forced to apportion at least some non-standard features. However, it will be established that, even in the initial appearances, such features are kept down to an absolute minimum. He followed this procedure right from the beginning, concentrating primarily on drawing out the characteristic rhetoric of the oratorical register and inserting here and there a non-standard item – almost as an afterthought, it would seem; for, necessary though such were as identifying tags, too many would have spoilt the general rhetorical effect. The non-standard features of the 'Parlour Orator' from the *Sketches*, for instance, are reduced to a bare minimum ('gen'lem'n', 'says I', 'no nothing', ''em', 'ain't'). There is, instead, the usual succession of rhetorical questions or unconnected, meaningless phrases. Lexically, too, he continually overreaches himself, modelling himself both in this respect and syntactically on what he imagines – in many cases probably is – the 'Parliamentary style'. In one outburst there is, too, much of the manner of Chadband (*BH*), to appear nearly twenty years later:

> What is man? ... What is an Englishman? Is he to be trampled upon by every oppressor? Is he to be knocked down at everybody's bidding? What's freedom? Not a standing army. What's a standing army? Not freedom. What's general happiness? Not universal misery. Liberty ain't the window-tax, is it? The Lords ain't the Commons, are they? (*SB*, 239)

The 'Reverend Mr Stiggins', too, only uses 'obderrate' (=obdurate), 'buzzim' (=bosom) and 'all taps is vanities'. Otherwise, he concentrates on such a feature as the fraternal appellation: 'my friend', 'my brother', etc. (*PP*, 367–8).

We can see in the 'Parlour Orator' and before him in the Irish orator (*SB*) the genesis of all Dickens' orators, whether their speech is rooted in the standard or non-standard dialect. In his later writings, Dickens repeats again and again their fundamental speech patterns – embellishing and refining them, as well as initiating and gradually integrating them into the overall thematic structure of the works in which they appear. Many of them even preserve the red face of Mr Rogers, the 'Parlour' one, and Dickens finds it hard to conceal his contempt for them:

> A numerous race are these red-faced men; there is not a parlour, or club-room, or benefit society, or humble party of any kind, without its red-faced man. Weak-pated dolts they are, and a great deal of mischief they do to their cause, however good. (*SB*, 239)

In respect of the melodramatic register, it would seem even more difficult to use the actual language as a yardstick when deciding the social origins of the character using it. On those occasions on which characters of lower-class origin – to all intents and purposes as near uneducated as one can imagine – 'tune in' to this mode, their highly stagy language is as free of non-standard features as that of (say) Nicholas Nickleby and his sister, leaving absolutely no lines of social demarcation between groups otherwise utterly divided. Thus, it is far from easy, even in the stylised world we are dealing with, to bring conviction to the speech of those lower-class characters who slip into this mode. This is the reason, perhaps, why from *Martin Chuzzlewit* onwards, there are no more of the same, although there are a few cases – like that adopted by Jo on his deathbed (*BH*, 648–9) – which tremble on the edge of the mode in question.

Of the few examples from the mouths of lower-class characters in the works preceding *Martin Chuzzlewit*, most are found in the *Sketches* and interpolated tales of *Pickwick*. A good illustration is to be found in the young man's curse in 'The Drunkard's Death', with its complete and illogical lack of non-standard features (*SB*, 491). It will also be observed how stilted – '*stagy*' – the language is, and how Dickens deliberately (naively?) applies stage directions. He had yet to develop his own rhythmic, electrically-charged version of the register in question. Other earlier instances in this vein are: Nancy's avowal – on her knees; a favourite posture for the mode concerned! – to Rose Maylie. This from a street girl steeped in the depths of depravity (*OT*, 305). It is significant that in this chapter the author frequently – almost exclusively – refers to Nancy not by her name, but as 'the girl'. Hugh – an ostler and a man of little or no education – strikes an extreme and very out-of-character melodramatic posture at the very foot of the gallows. This episode, however, reveals that Dickens was already beginning to shake off the stiffly conventional use of the register (borrowed from the stage of his time), and was moving into a dramatic world of his own. Here, too, Dickens is making significant representational use of Hugh's speech, it corresponding to logic of situation and not realistic logic (*BR*, 596).

3 Rhythmic Patterns

> The right rhythm in prose is every bit
> as important as the right metre in a poem.[1]

The rhythmic patterns of Dickens' fictional language fall, whatever the prose modality concerned, under two headings: on the one hand, that writing which, although not presented in the conventional manner of poetry, makes use, nevertheless, of the *metrical patterns* and diction of that world, and, on the other, the *schematic patterns* springing from the regular reiteration of certain syntactic figurations.

There was nothing original in the transference of the metrical patterns of poetry to prose fiction. The usage for sentimental writing (English prose) started up in the seventeenth century, becoming firmly entrenched in the century following, above all in the works of Richardson and Sterne (sentimentally) and Smollett (ironically). By the early nineteenth century, many writers, when trying to express what was felt to be deep emotion or what were considered the more noble passions, turned to the allegedly more elevated kind of writing felt to be implicit in the application of the strict metrical forms of poetry.[2]

The metrical patterns to be found in *Oliver Twist* and *Old Curiosity Shop* simply spring, then, from one of the prose writing traditions still paramount in the 1830s.[3] However, an immediate difference began to reveal itself in the fictional speech. Whereas, initially, the other prose modalities – despite some glowing passages – remained in essence conventional, the speech idioms of many characters exhibited an extremely original and adroit development of, for example, the rhythmic patterns of blank verse. In Mrs Gamp's idiolect, Dickens actually utilises non-standard pronunciations to achieve the desired metrical symmetry, even moving within a few lines from standard to non-standard usage or from colloquial to non-colloquial to achieve this:

/I'm éasy pléased; it is but líittle ás I wánts;
/but Í must háve that líittle óf the bést,
/and tó the míinute whén the clóck strikes, élse
/we dó not párt as Í could wíish,
/but béarin' málice in our árts. (*MC*, 749)[4]

Also from the early works, the poetic snatches which so amusingly adorn the idiolect of Dick Swiveller (*OCS*) are an extremely effective satirical backlash of the conventional, usually uninspired, use of the metrical forms in question. Such aspects of Dickens' early application of poetic forms ought to be stressed, for, as John Gross has pointed out, 'critics have been frightened off far too easily by jeers at the bogus blank verse'.[5]

Indeed, the moves into metrical patterns gradually became far more adroit and less crass, infinitely more artistic on the occasions they might be used, being utilised not only for beauty of line but also for *structural significance*. A conspicuous case from a later work, for example, is the poetry – for it is nothing less – resorted to by Affery Flintwinch when Arthur Clennam questions her about the weird noises to be heard in his mother's house; the following is part of her series of answers: 'I tell you, Arthur ... noises is the secrets, rustlings and stealings about, tremblings, treads overhead and treads underneath' (*LD*, 689). The words in this case have been chosen both for their sonority in context and – such a key-word as 'secrets' is the most obvious example – for the overtones they convey in the gloom-ridden atmosphere of this uneasy, bitterly pessimistic novel with its presentation of a society enclosed in a prison of its own making. Much of the writing in *Great Expectations* – the closing lines, for instance, of the fifth chapter (*GE*, 36) – and in *Edwin Drood* – brilliantly in its opening lines – also reveals poetry of equally high quality with a similar intensity of structural import.

The scope and variety of Dickens' metrical experiments, showing how closely the rhythms of his fictional speech approach those of music, even, can be exemplified in the patterned complexity of the idiolect of Mrs Lirriper, a lady who has a yet more pronounced predilection for (seemingly) incoherent verbal rambling than Mrs Nickleby, Mrs Gamp or Flora Finching:[6]

> Mentioning my poor Lirriper brings into my head his own youngest brother the Doctor though Doctor of what I am sure it would be hard to say unless Liquor, for neither Physic nor Music nor yet Law does Joshua Lirriper know a morsel of except continually being summoned to the County Court and having orders made upon him which he runs away from, and once was taken in the passage of this very house with an umbrella up and the Major's hat on, giving his name with the door-mat round him as Sir Johnson Jones, K.C.B. in spectacles residing at the Horse Guards. On which occasion he had got into the house not a minute before, through the girl letting him on the mat when he sent in a piece of paper twisted more like one of those spills for lighting candles than a note, offering me the choice between thirty shillings in hand and his brains on the premises marked immediate and waiting for an answer. My dear it gave me such a dreadful turn to think of the brains of my poor dear Lirriper's own flesh and blood flying about the new oilcloth however unworthy to be so assisted, that I went out of my room here to ask him what he would take once for all not to do it for life when I found him in the custody of two gentlemen that I should have judged to be in the feather-bed trade if they had not announced the law, so fluffy were their personal appearance. (*CS*, 407–8)

If read aloud, it will be immediately noted that there is an almost ballad-like rhythm to the opening lines up to the word 'except', at which – if the reading is to be effective – there should be a slight pause followed by a kind of two-part 'coda' comprising the whole of the section from 'continually' down to the word 'answer', the two successive verbal torrents being marked by a slight pause after 'Guards'. It would appear that Dickens' dramatic inspiration led him quite deliberately to set the beginning of this excerpt in the fairly regular, leisurely, but dramatic rhythm of a storyteller settling down to recount an anecdote or adventure, a rhythm hinting (as I have pointed out) at that of the ballad. This then took a sudden, but for such a person as Mrs Lirriper very natural, turn as a result of which the floodgates were opened, allowing the torrent of disjointed clauses to tumble out, as it were, doing so in smoothly flowing rhythms of no consistent metre, thus creating a 'never-ending' effect. The full stop after 'answer' – and punctuation in Dickens, though sometimes unconventional, is almost invariably of paramount importance – signals not only a short, breathless pause as Mrs Lirriper comes up for air, but also the beginning in the succeeding words of a slow, gradually accelerating 'shunt-in' of a new burst of disjointed clauses. This section is rhythmically more four-square, falling into the framework of musical 6/8 time (see Figure 1 for example).[7]

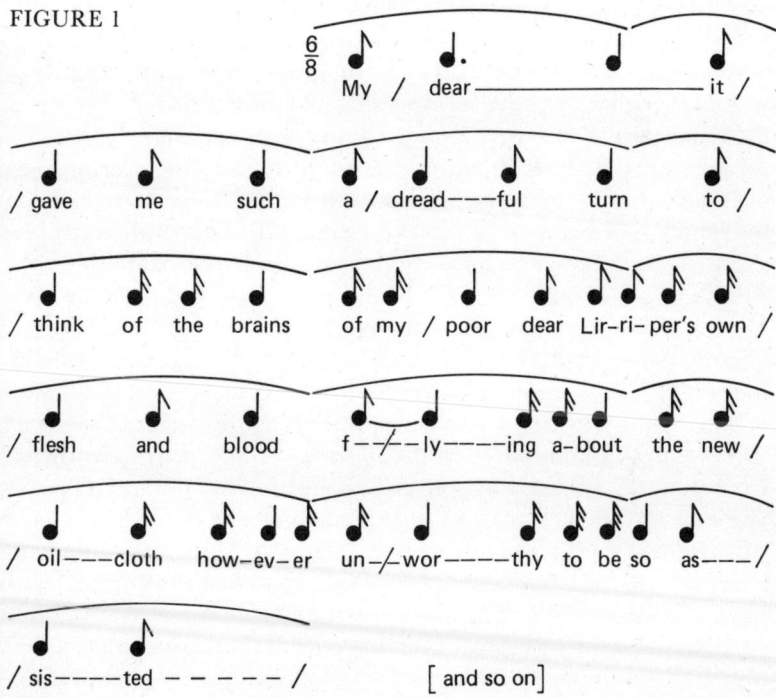

FIGURE 1

In an example such as this there is, for all practical purposes, a 'musical organisation of the prose'.[8] Assuredly, it cannot be denied that, in the quality which all such instances possess of capturing in condensed and more-explicitly patterned form rhythms otherwise spread out more thinly and haphazardly through normal everyday speech, especially that of the lower classes, they tend to resemble the rigidly stylised worlds of dramatic poetry and music rather than that of more conventional fictional prose. In all, then, just as with the linguistic and rhetorical features, the rhythmical patterns are subject to a process of selection, condensation and intensification.

We turn now to a far more obvious, if not more crucial, aspect of Dickens' prose rhythms, that coming under the general heading of *schematic patterns* referred to above, patterns which, from the works of the middle 1850s onwards, became so pervasive, indeed almost obsessive, in their effect. The decisive influence of Dickens' public readings on his general style will be discussed in more detail in a later chapter; suffice here to underline the undeniable fact that the rhetorical patterns in question received their strongest incentive from the histrionic demands made on the author during his platform appearances. The most obvious feature of these pervasive patterns is repetition, with 'doubling' and (especially) 'tripling' as the most common. It is a mode carried, on occasion, to such extreme lengths that the subsequent drumming insistency can become blatantly mannered. This is the case, for instance, in the opening of the letter written by Dr Manette in the Bastille (*TTC*, 303). Peculiar doubling patterns of an 'echoic' nature are extremely prominent in the uneasy narrative of 'George Silverman's Explanation', appearing in the late 1860s. At its best, the technique can be of superlative artistic value, as is testified by the penetrating structural effect of many passages in, to take one instance, *Our Mutual Friend*. The forms chosen range from longer, *syntagmatic progressions* embracing not merely successions of full sentences or subsidiary clauses of all kinds as in that remarkable passage in 'The Haunted Man' containing no less than thirty-two successive subsidiary clauses beginning with 'when' (*CB*, 319–21), but also repetitions of complete passages as in that of Lord Decimus Tite Barnacle's 'one indignant idea', made all the more ridiculous by the repetition being rendered in free indirect speech (*LD*, 405). The reader will find, too, innumerable examples of *anaphora*, one of the most striking of which is provided by Mrs Gamp performing 'an extemporaneous concerto' when addressing each in turn of those assembled at Merry Chuzzlewit's home, beginning each time with 'to think as I should see' (*MC*, 703–4).

There are, in addition, the following related devices: *epistrophe* which, in contrast to anaphora, resorts to repetition at the end of successive stages. Of this particular rhetorical device there are also many examples, as in the heartless reproval by Dennis, the hangman, of those Newgate prisoners pleading to be set free from the death cell. It contains no less than five successive clauses ending with 'a' purpose for you' (*BR*, 501). *Symploce* repeats the beginning at the end as in Jasper's eulogistic speech about Edwin framed by 'Look at him' (*ED*, 74). *Anadiplosis* links two sentences or sections together by beginning the new one with the same word or phrase which ended the previous one. There are a number of examples in that unusual later story 'George Silverman's Explanation' especially from the mouth of Lady Fareway, the protagonist's hard, selfishly calculating 'benefactor': 'you have no idea what she is. She is . . .' (*UT/RP*, 749). This becomes *epizeusis* if the word or phrase is repeated with no break at all, either by the same person or another. Mr Pecksniff is a master in the use of both devices (*MC*, 32–4).

In Dickens' later works especially, the schematic patterning comes right down to simple but effective paradigmatic repetition. In effect, this boils down to what can be called the incremental method, i.e. the straightforward piling up of, in particular, adjectives, verbs, nouns or short phrases. A very extended illustration of pungent effect is the description in the author's last completed novel of what the Veneerings' looking-glass reflects (*OMF*, 10–11). As a technique it is, to some degree, related to the use of key-words; it has, too, been likened to 'the telegraphic succinctness of an auctioneer's catalogue'.[9] Repetition in all its forms has long, of course, been a prominent feature of the rhetorical approach, whether written or oral. What makes it so interesting and effective in Dickens is that almost obsessive use mentioned above. The declamatory style, the relentless monomanic rhythms of the cumulative structures, make the reader – and even more the listener – feel that he is experiencing the language of some religious ritual, falling under its incantatory spell, almost, perhaps, against his will.

In respect of the narrative voice, it will be observed that writing in the repetitive mode occurs most frequently at the beginning or end of a chapter, or at those points where Dickens the storyteller is determined to buttonhole the reader/listener; this is especially true of the later works. Moreover, in the earlier works – the

Christmas Books apart – it occurs more in the fictional speech than in the other modalities. From *Bleak House* onwards, the merging process gradually sets in. At its best, it reveals through the speech of whatever character is concerned, a dramatic tension and imaginative insight the equal of which would be difficult to find. Further, the regular pulsation, the rhythmic symmetry arising from the application of the various rhetorical devices of the repetitive mode, not only gives a sometimes overwhelming impetus to the individual utterances, but also creates a firm dramatic framework capable in any one idiolect of holding together even the most disparate conglomeration of speech features. This comes out very clearly when the speech of such as Mrs Nickleby (*NN*), Mrs Gamp (*MC*) or Flora Finching (*LD*) is examined more closely. What appears at first sight complete verbal chaos – nothing but wayward streams of apparently unconnected clauses – turns out to possess distinct rhythmic patterns, as a result of which Dickens is able to impose a clear-cut system of order on the seeming formlessness of the rambling confusion, and to imbue it simultaneously with stylised dramatic qualities which made it so eminently suitable for oral presentation.

These theatrical qualities are, moreover, considerably enhanced when the symmetrical rhythmic patterns are transferred to the fictional dialogue – to the interaction of two or more idiolects – thus enabling Dickens to create set-pieces or tableaux for his highly personal fictional stage. An intriguing snippet of such rhythmic stylisation is to be found in *Dombey & Son*, the author's first serious – and only partly successful – attempt at a pre-planned, fully integrated novel. In the scene in question, the simple, good-hearted Captain Cuttle is greeting his friend Captain Bunsby, that 'great comic image of flawless stupidity',[10] and at the same time praising him for a 'helpful' opinion delivered on a previous occasion:

> 'Bunsby! ... here you are! a man as can give an opinion as is brighter than di'monds – and give me the lad with the tarry trousers as shines to me like di'monds bright, for which you'll overhaul the Stanfell's Budget, and when found make a note. Here you are, a man as gave an opinion in this here very place, that has come true, every letter on it'. .... 'For why?' growled Bunsby, looking at his friend for the first time. 'Which way? If so, why not? Therefore.' (*DS*, 551)

On paper, only a close analysis will reveal just how marked the rhythmic pattern is, and also how smoothly Bunsby's 'answer' is merged into the overall configuration. The following is an endeavour to represent this pattern graphically:

1. *Cuttle:* ... here you are!	a man as can give an opinion	as is brighter than di'monds ...	for which you'll overhaul the Stanfell's Budget, and when found make a note.
2. *Cuttle, cont.:* Here you are,	a man as gave an opinion ...	that has come true, every letter on it ...	*Bunsby:* For why? ... Which way? If so, why not? Therefore.

The diagram at once spotlights the marked syntactic symmetry of the speech form, here neatly rounded off by the other character – that he does so with nonsense is beside the point; indeed, only enhances the whole. It is a symmetry which would become even more evident if one were to hear the passage being read aloud in the way Dickens intended. This kind of dialogue was, as is known from various accounts, readily accepted – by the mass of the readers, at least – as natural within its context.[11] Indeed, it was even frequently mimicked, although no everyday speech could possibly approach such stylisation. This can be primarily put down to its being, above all in its rhythms, so completely *vocal*, so essentially *dramatic*, in conception.

No other writer of English fiction developed rhythmic patterns to quite the extent and in the manner that Dickens did. Nor, moreover, should it be forgotten how much closer this technique brought him to the world of the theatre, or rather to that world of his own theatre, his stylised storytelling world, and one within which his natural talents found far greater scope.

4 Representational Speech

From about the middle of the 1840s onwards, and with an evergrowing intensity which became particularly apparent in the later phase of his career, Dickens strove persistently to make the speech idioms of his characters serve more than simply the needs of individualisation and typification, no matter how brilliant and popular the results of these needs turned out to be, aiming at merging them in a variety of ways and for a variety of purposes into the general structure of the novels concerned. This move towards attaching structural significance to the idiolects had already become partially apparent as early as *Barnaby Rudge* (1841) and, to a fair extent, in *Martin Chuzzlewit* (1843-4), the subsequent novel. In the novels from *Dombey & Son* up to and including *Little Dorrit*, Dickens gradually learnt to weave the speech of his characters into the general structure until it became, when fully realised, a vital and artistically convincing factor, above all in those greatly more complicated though in the main unified novels of the last two decades of his life.

With the significant exception of *David Copperfield*, the step necessarily led in the novels to a general decrease in bravura, the flamboyance of the individualising and typifying qualities which had been so conspicuous in a great deal of the earlier fictional speech being toned down to a more subtle nature. Structurally, however, the gain was invaluable, for the fictional speech – especially from *Bleak House* onwards – was now so blended into the general structure (naturally, not always with equal success) that it reflected, parodied, symbolised, supported or underlined either its central themes and goals or – and this is of equal importance in Dickens – the speech of another character, cases in point being Guppy as a (subtle) parody of Inspector Bucket, and Krook (blatantly) of the Lord High Chancellor (*BH*). This metonymical mode, one infinitely more complex, artistic and effective than any of the techniques Dickens previously put to use – indeed, it incorporates all of them as well as pointing forward to the unification in the great final period of all the fictional prose elements – is one that will be referred to as *structural representation*. Any examination of the extent to which Dickens' fictional speech from *Dombey & Son* – or at the latest *Bleak House* – onwards can be considered an integrated element of the work in which it appears, should simultaneously furnish a yardstick by which we can gauge its actual structural significance.

We have just mentioned *Bleak House*, and we can turn to this novel – technically, in virtually every respect, the summit of the works of the middle period[1] – in order to illustrate what represented speech amounts to in practice. On a close reading of this novel, it will become evident that Dickens had by this stage begun a gradual move away from interpolated authorial passages – particularly of the grandiloquent, 'purple' sort – through which he indulged in personal commentary or was forced to further the narrative. Against this, the author began to rely increasingly on dialogue and action to keep the now complicated plot moving, acting out rather than informing and commenting. This method is not only more dramatically effective and economical, but also enables the author – in fact, *forces* him – to infuse the fictional speech with structural significance.

An excellent episode for demonstrating how this actually functions is that in which Mr Snagsby, the timid, hen-pecked, law-stationer, accompanies the seemingly all-powerful Inspector Bucket, whom nothing intimidates, to the appalling slum 'Tom-all-Alone's' to find Jo, the ignorant, ever-pushed-around crossing-sweeper, and bring him back to the house of Lady Dedlock's sinister, wily lawyer, Tulkinghorn, where he is to identify the lady who had given him money to show her Captain Hawdon's grave: in its entirety – although only just over four pages – a crucial passage in the novel's structural development (*BH*, 309–14).

Essentially through the fictional speech against the sparse, balanced, significantly pointed background of the narrative, descriptive and commentarial prose modalities, syntactically built up in the same urgent, simple, straightforward way, the reader is given a series of connected incidents *all* of which play a more or less important part in the general thematic structure. It can be observed to what extent the fictional speech fulfils the triple purpose of furthering the plot movement, of illuminating the character speaking, and, when the idiom of the one is contrasted with that of another, of throwing into starker relief both the idiolects concerned, hence heightening the dramatic tension. In an earlier Dickens work, much space would have been devoted to authorial explanations, much of it mannered, most of it too long, some of it clumsy. Bucket, Snagsby, Jo and the bricklayers' families (especially the wives, Jenny and Liz) are all to some extent or other key figures in the novel, and each in turn through his or her language characteristics sounds his or her ground theme and variations. Jo, the inarticulate one, understood by so few, is (significantly) given in this scene nothing to say which is actually printed. Bucket, for example, short, rapid and factual in utterance, lexically and syntactically adjusted to a simple minimum for the job in hand; his unaffected colloquial manner, full of admonitions and well-meant but superficial platitudes, with the sprinkling of non-standard features adding a touch of piquancy – all this individualises and typifies him admirably. But there is more to his idiolect than simply this: *in toto* these are the language characteristics emanating from one kind of personality inevitably thrown up by the form of society depicted in *Bleak House*, thus making him through his speech an integral part of the book. Further, what he actually says – what he conveys to those around him and thus to the reader – is, in the above passage as much as in any other in the novel, indispensable to the whole movement of the book, supplying us with important information and providing the other characters with the chance of revealing themselves through their language. Bucket's speech idiom is, therefore, working on several planes at once, both individual and general.

The same applies to Snagsby and his idiolect: even though he says still less here than is normally the case with him, we have enough of his deferential, apologetically nervous idiom with its lexical and syntactic simplicity to place him at once. We see in him, in the basic structure of his speech, each and every 'little man' tossed around by turbulent, relentless, repellent worlds of which *Bleak House* is typical.[2] In addition, he links Jo to Tulkinghorn through Bucket, but also (ironically) denying knowledge of Gridley, the ruined suitor, who is shortly to die before the very eyes of the same Bucket, and in the same place to be occupied not long after by Jo in his dying hours, with Mr Snagsby himself as witness. The thematic web is thus spun ever tighter, and even the smallest snippet of fictional speech has some significance or other.

The speech forms of the two bricklayers' wives, though, are neither strikingly individualised nor typified, for Dickens' aim here is to present as 'unsullied' a language as possible, hinting, through idiom, only here and there at their lower-class origins. This is, as we have already seen, his stylised method of presenting moral goodness, a goodness resisting (barely) the evils resulting from the squalid existence thrust upon it by an unfeeling, unthinking society. However, in the bitter comment on life – their life – by Liz, Dickens hovers dangerously close to intruding his own voice rather than continuing to mimic them as originally conceived. This comment represents, nevertheless, their chief structural role in the novel as a whole, one symbolised by the rotting misery which is Tom-all-Alone's. In addition, they are not only partly instrumental in linking Jo with Bucket (and all that this implies), but are also destined to play a small, decisive role in the closing stages of the novel, when they help Lady Dedlock foil the very man they are being lectured by in the above episode: Bucket.

In reading through the passage under discussion, we are made to realise how much more cogent, how much more pregnant, how much swifter and more alive altogether such writing can be with its shorter, more urgent sentences, its sharply alternating drama of action and dialogue, and above all the structural suggestiveness of every word spoken by the characters. Under the representational mode, as it transpired – and this is also a vital point – it was not only a *particular* case of each character through his or her fundamental speech idiosyncrasies and the variations thereof, fulfilling within the thematic structure the triple purpose discussed above, but also a *general* one. Viewed thus, the series of phrenetic – at times seemingly meaningless – variations on basically unchanging ground themes take on an additional significance, one imaging both man's growing alienation in Victorian society from those around him, and his reaction against the ugly desolation of the fixed routine forced upon him in the rigidly heterogenous system which was that baleful society.

Judging, then, by the speech manner of so many of his

characters, Dickens obviously felt that it was even less possible than it had ever been for the average person to live as a freely-developing individual within society, for he or she had now been actually *systemised* by that society – and nothing in Dickens' stylised world symbolises this more readily than the systematic, stylised jabberings which are so often the whole speech of such characters. It is a world which 'comes to us for the most part as a richly varied series of encounters between people who cannot talk with each other and who therefore can only perform their own natures in antiphonal duet with each other'.[3] An important word here is the preposition 'with', for they can and do talk *to* each other, and, moreover, they do follow the immediate functional meaning of the words poured into their ears.

A cogent illustration of the truth of the above is provided by another episode from *Bleak House*, an interview which occurs when that social parasite Harold Skimpole is 'took' by the dogged, rough-and-ready sheriff's officer, Neckett (76–7). It is clear that the characters are as much cut off from each other, make as little impression on each other's thoughts (although superficially taking in each other's words), as two people talking past each other at a cocktail party; indeed, Skimpole would have come into his own at such. Moreover, it must not be forgotten that Skimpole, regardless of the extent to which he himself is responsible, is as much (if not more) a systemised prisoner of society as Neckett is in his way, and certainly a more willing one than he himself would perhaps care to admit.

The technical development leading to controlled representational use of fictional language began little by little to make itself felt during the 1840s. Concerning its application to fictional speech, therefore, it would be logical to expect to find a *gradual* progression through to the structural triumphs of Dickens' later fiction. This is, oddly enough, not quite the case. The dialogue in *Dombey & Son* evinces, owing to the priority of structural considerations, a pointed reticence when seen against those spontaneous outpourings of improvised fictional speech in the earlier novels which reach a zenith in the unforgettable brilliance of inspiration found in the idiolects of Mrs Gamp and Seth Pecksniff (*MC*). *David Copperfield*, the novel succeeding *Dombey & Son*, displays, however, a resurgence of idiosyncratic brilliance which is the equal, at least, of much of that found in the fictional speech before *Dombey & Son*. Yet, in spite of this, *David Copperfield* is also, on the whole, a deeply satisfying work in all structural respects. How did Dickens succeed in reverting to many of the original, uninhibited speech forms while at the same time managing to fuse them so well into the general structure of the novel?

Perhaps the reason lies in the type of novel *David Copperfield* was – by casting it in the form of a *Bildungsroman*, Dickens found himself in a position which allowed him, in a sense, to let the structure look after itself, thus enabling him to concentrate with undiminished creative intensity on the perfecting of the various fictional modalities in themselves, especially the fictional speech. As his various language techniques had been moving from strength to strength anyway, we have in this novel a truly happy conjunction of factors in which both old and new stand together, ideally and significantly intertwined, thus lifting this book above its predecessors in almost every respect, and fully justifying the somewhat Janus-like position it holds in Dickens' canon. In *Bleak House*, this fusing process was taken even further and with considerable artistic success, but, generally, with a return in the fictional speech to the more subdued manner of *Dombey & Son*.

5 Rhetorical Extension

THE APPLICATION OF KEY-WORDS

In the passage introducing Littimer, Steerforth's unpleasantly enigmatic manservant, it will be observed that Dickens deliberately underlines this slimy personage's superficial respectability – his chief characteristic – by applying the words 'respectable' and 'respectability' no less than fifteen times on the two pages (*DC*, 299–300). This, as far as could be established, appears to be Dickens reader's introduction to a technique also found in patches in the subsequent novel, *Bleak House*, but not put into practice on an extensive scale until *Hard Times*, the novel after that. Its chief moment here lies in its being the first clear illustration of a move in Dickens' works towards a direct fusing of the fictional speech and the three authorial modalities. It was a move that culminated in the stylistic amalgam often called the author's 'oral style'.[1]

On the one page, for example, of that marvel of brevity the opening chapter of *Hard Times* – both structurally and artistically a very effective curtain-raiser to the plot proper – we can see the writer extending the linguistic web of identification, typification and representation from the actual speech idioms of the characters (their idiolects) to the language describing them. The whole passage, whether Gradgrind's speech itself or the description of his appearance and actions, is an elaborate play on the key-word 'Facts', and on its associations of hardness, plainness, squareness, etc. In stark contrast to the intricate, carefully built up symbolism of the openings to *Bleak House* and *Little Dorrit*, the vast panoramic novels between which *Hard Times* is sandwiched, the technique here is deliberately designed to establish through the drumming insistence of certain key-words the basic thematic idea as quickly and firmly as possible. Further, such key-words are also serving both to identify the character concerned and to evaluate him, and are continually applied throughout the novel when the thematic structure so demands:

> Dickens's remarkable metaphorical inventiveness ensures that continuity and rhetorical emphasis are not obtained at the expense of monotony. The [later] application of the key-words of the first chapter to Mr Gradgrind's house gives the same delight as the development of a metaphysical conceit.[2]

Highly contrived as its results can be, such a technique in fiction will clearly, if overdone, end up in writing which is simply extremely mannered and nothing else. In Dickens' stylised, increasingly rhetorical world, however, the obsessive emphasis falls naturally into place, helping among other things to bring the fictional speech and the authorial modalities closer together, and thus providing a further binding element in works which were becoming progressively more complex.

THE 'ORAL STYLE': STYLISTIC UNIFICATION OF THE PROSE MODALITIES

In early Dickens, especially of respect to the narrative, descriptive and commentarial voices, it would be more accurate to speak of a vast conglomeration of borrowed styles, there being only a gradual – though, for the structural integration of the idiolects decisive – move in the fictional works towards a complete takeover in these voices by the author's unique, highly stylised, storytelling manner. Here it remains to point out just how, in what forms and to what extent the influence of the fourth prose modality – the fictional speech – was exerted during the final creative period of Dickens' life.

This final flowering – often called the 'oral style' – has its roots primarily in the rhetorical approach of the storytelling manner. With the key-note technique playing a subsidiary role, it received its crucial impulse from the author's public readings.[3] The effect of these readings on the development of Dickens' later style cannot be overestimated, particularly when one bears in mind that many of those chosen from the earlier works were deliberately submitted to alteration, to the same kind of oralising process apparent in the later style, in order to bring them into rhetorical line, so to speak, as a result of which process much unnecessary material was jettisoned on the way. This procedure, continually acted upon by the public reading itself, was obviously a two-way one, working off on Dickens' writing techniques when he turned back to the writing of new fiction.

Thus, from about the middle of the 1850s onwards, the new style began so to penetrate every aspect of the narrative, descriptive and commentarial prose that the whole moved progressively nearer in tone and rhythms to that of the spoken language, albeit in stylised form. This in turn brought it much nearer in the same works to the fictional speech. Transitions, therefore, were made smoother or even eradicated altogether, the whole process being further facilitated by the judicious application of free indirect speech. So all-pervasive is the new technique, indeed, that one can at times speak of a complete merging of all the prose modalities into a multi-functional, highly expressive fictional mode that, besides having more than a little in common with free indirect speech, has become, in effect, something new, something peculiar (I would suggest) to Dickens' works alone. When it is used successfully, it is of profound dramatic expressiveness, exceeding flexibility and exquisite subtlety, conveying with greater precision and concentration biting satire, gentle irony or finer shades of feeling.

Although a number of episodes in *Hard Times* (22, 110 ff.) and *Little Dorrit* (28, 29–30 ff.), as well as in the *Christmas Stories* for 1854 and 1858 (84–5 ff.), also manifest the development, it was not until the publication of *A Tale of Two Cities* in 1859 that the new style came triumphantly into its own. One could maintain, indeed, that in this particular novel, for the first and only time in the fiction of Dickens, fictional speech plays a secondary role, almost the whole accent being on the introduction of rhetorical qualitites into the other prose modalities.[4] More balanced use of the new approach was made first in *Great Expectations* then in *Our Mutual Friend*. An excellent illustration from the latter novel is the author's sardonic attack on those who go 'into the City ... and

[have] to do with traffic in Shares' (114). It begins with a series of imperatives in which the 'cataloguing' method is used, and is followed by a series of interrogatives. Each item is answered with the insistent repetition of 'Shares', and the whole rounded off with a kind of coda – so typical, too, of many idiolect outbursts – which also uses the 'cataloguing' technique, ending with a sarcastic call in the vocative.

However, not all is sardonic comment or ironic detachment; there are also passages of moving lyricism, such as the remarkable interlude in the same novel, inserted at the point when the dead body of Gaffer Hexam lies stretched upon the shore. The passage begins by repeating his daughter's desperate call to the winds made some hours before. The words are blended into an authorial outburst of striking but bitter dramatic expressiveness, the poetry springing from the depths of the author's feeling, touching heights of eloquence which are enhanced by the rhythmic framework of the speech and movements of those who have found Gaffer. Lizzie's call is taken up, given over to be mocked by the wind, and then developed rhetorically into a series of questions rising in intensity and possessing a steady pattern of rhythmic regularity which is almost overwhelming (173–4).

The reader is, indeed, left with a total impression of being in an utterly new stylistic world, one in which the narrative modalities have been completely imbued with qualities normally peculiar to the fictional speech; qualities, moreover, of a stylised, particularly rhetorical, nature. As Norman Page puts it:

> the role of speech in this new style extends far beyond the dialogue, of course. The stylistic contrast between dialogue and non-dialogue elements ... is greatly lessened: lexical and syntactic features which might earlier have been found in the dialogue but were excluded from the more formal prose of the narrative passages are now apt to turn up in any sentence of the novel, *for the narrative style is itself permeated by the influence of speech* – not so much spontaneous, informal discourse as the more elaborate kind of rhetoric which Dickens knew from long and (in every sense) rewarding experience was capable of moving an audience.[5]

For the fictional speech and for the author's storytelling voice, then, this 'oralisation' was of reciprocal value, culminating in the ease, delicacy, compactness and that insight gained from exceptional clarity, all of which pervaded Dickens' fiction in the last decade of his life. However, perhaps the greatest reward offered to the Dickens devotee throughout these later works by the suggestive qualities of the richly plastic 'oral style', is that it enables them to be so very effectively read aloud and listened to, bringing the wonder which is Dickens' one-man theatre into every home in the way for which it is pre-eminently suitable. In this writer's hands, the English language became, finally, a medium that he was able at will to mould into those poetic-dramatic forms so ideally suited to expressing that tragi-comic outlook which dominated his whole creative vision during the period in question, these 'profoundly poetic-dramatic gifts of apprehension [being] in English literature inseparable from a profound and experimental gift of language.[6]

FREE INDIRECT SPEECH[7]

In the fictional works of Dickens, there is a fairly frequent occurrence of a mode of reporting speech which is neither completely direct nor indirect in form, but exists in a kind of blending zone between the two:

> She [Miggs] said that indeed and indeed Miss Dolly might take pattern by her blessed mother, who, she always had said, and always would say, though she were to be hanged, drawn, and quartered for it next minute, was the mildest, amiablest, forgivingest-spirited, longest-sufferingest female as ever she could have believed; the mere narration of whose excellencies had worked such a wholesome change in the mind of her own sister-in-law, that, whereas, before, she and her husband lived like cat and dog, and were in the habit of exchanging brass candlesticks, pot-lids, flat-irons, and other such strong resentments, they were now the happiest and affectionatest couple upon earth; as could be proved any day on application at Golden Lion Court, number twenty-sivin, second bell-handle on the right-hand door-post. (*BR*, 170)

It will be observed that the verbs and pronouns are regularly transposed as would be expected in normal indirect speech, but that the actual speech idiosyncrasies of the character concerned remain unaltered. The character's non-standard dialect shows itself in such deviations from the standard language as the irregular comparisons, idiosyncratic syntax, choice of phrase and the spelling of 'sivin'. In fiction, such a mode, termed 'free indirect speech', has many decided advantages, its value lying, as Randolph Quirk puts it,

> not only in the subtlety with which fast flowing narrative can be coloured by the characteristic idiom of a particular speaker, but also in the ability to convey the unspoken reflection of the speaker in the suggested language of his reflection – and even the suggested impact of one speaker upon another – without the clumsiness of explanation which would coarsen and over-sharpen the impression, and fatally simplify what the author would prefer to leave equivocal.[8]

Dickens did not extensively explore the various possibilities offered by this rhetorical device, adopting it primarily for ironic humour or caricature. One has far more the impression, indeed, of an intuitive though adroit and convincing application by a writer with a distinct flair for bending language to his own artistic purposes. It will be observed, too, that although his later use of the technique is merged far more subtly, more successfully, into the general structure, there is no real increase in the actual degree of usage, albeit he was already using it to caricature in the *Sketches*, as is shown by the reported remarks (preserving the non-standard idiom) of a 'young lady in service' about her mistress to Miss Martin, the milliner (*SB*, 250–1).

However, it was not until *Barnaby Rudge*, his fifth novel, that Dickens made extended use of the technique, doing so in the speech idiom of Miss Miggs from which the above example stems. The author's use of the mode in this character's idiolect makes it clear how irony is ever present, this being particularly apparent in the ambiguity lent to such verbs as 'suppose', 'fear', 'trust', 'have no doubt', 'dare to say', when they are involved in the transposition process. Thus, the full force of the spiteful hypocrisy ingrained in the remarks made by Miggs to Dennis, the hangman, concerning her employers, the Vardens, and the fate of their pretty, coquettish daughter, Dolly – Miggs' fellow prisoner and the object of her bitter jealousy – is delicately thrust home, so to speak. The words take on, in a subtle manner, a rather different meaning from that intended by the speaker (*BR*, 541).

With irony of varying degrees of sharpness supplying a firm basis, the application of free indirect speech from Miggs onwards embraces a wide variety of subtly expressed meanings which in time took on an ever-increasing effectivity of structural significance. In *Martin Chuzzlewit*, for instance, these range from the delicate understatement of feeling conveyed through John Westlock's transposed answers when he insists on accompanying Tom and Ruth Pinch home (696) to the dramatic shock-effect on the reader of the questions which shoot through Jonas Chuzzlewit's guilt-ridden mind when, alone, shortly after he had murdered Tigg Montague, he looks out of the window and sees a group obviously discussing the heinous deed (778), or, but a few lines before this, to the heightened sense of emergency aroused when the same character – as full of suspicion as he is of guilt – questions a maidservant regarding the whereabouts of his wife (775). By judiciously mixing the mode in question with normal direct speech, Dickens considerably sharpens the general dramatic effect. Also penetratingly presented is the mocking sarcasm aimed by the author at Pecksniff's two daughters (and, indirectly, at Pecksniff himself, by their echoing in chorus both his hypocrisy and certain of his speech habits) through the transposition of their simulated shock when hearing of young Martin's alleged treachery towards his grandfather (160–1).

Although *Dombey & Son* marks a turning point in that, among other things, it is Dickens' first concentrated, overall attempt to make the fictional speech also serve definite structural ends, its use of free indirect speech reveals no radical change from the clever though rather haphazard, more instinctive, approach previously apparent. Delightful, though, is the mocking burlesque (with its liberal use of professional language) which comes through the transposition of the two opposing explanations, one private, one official, given for the disfiguring injuries sustained by Mr Toots' companion, the 'Chicken', in a prizefight contest (662). Amusing, too, is the vivid and economic presentation of schoolboy speech reported of Briggs as he lies in bed at Dr Blimber's educational establishment (191).

Of its very nature, a first person narrative seems to offer but little necessity for the merging qualities of free indirect speech. Be that as it may, there are indeed only a few scattered passages –

almost without exception short – in the few works falling within this category. One of these snippets in *David Copperfield*, for instance, the representation of Mrs Micawber's account of the reaction in court of one of her husband's creditors (170), serves admirably, however, to illustrate how imperceptible the merging of narrative and fictional speech can be, that merging so typical of the mode under discussion. Another – her husband's airy, impossible plans about where he wishes to live on 'something satisfactory turning up' (421–2) – through its choice of such linking phrases as 'he explained' and 'he expressly said' helps to underline the narrator's commonsensical, somewhat sarcastic attitude to the preposterous plans. A decade later, in *Great Expectations*, an equally small excerpt also shows how neatly and elegantly the mode enabled Dickens to slip even the words of a blacksmith's song into Pip's narrative without detriment to the one or other; nor is the excerpt as out of place as might appear, for there is a certain grotesque significance in Miss Havisham's evident relish of the rhythms and text (*GE*, 89). In the first-person narrative of *George Silverman's Explanation*, there is one unexpected example blended into the text which – brief though it is – adds a certain grimly sarcastic touch to the uneasy story as a whole (*UT/RP*, 745).

Returning to the early 1850s: it is true that in *Bleak House*, Dickens does not resort over much to this technique – about half the novel, be it remembered, is taken up by Esther Summerson's first person narrative, anyway – yet what we do find is of considerable value as demonstrating not only the novelist's growing command over the technique in itself, but also the structural use to which it was now being put. Let us take, for instance, the oft-quoted and justly famous example provided by the transposition of Jo's spoken evidence at the inquest held on Captain Hawdon's death.[9] To an unusually high degree, this episode, when set against the now generally accepted original as it appeared in the *Household Narrative*, reveals the exceptionally rich transmuting qualities innate in Dickens' power over language. Even to the most casual eye, Dickens' version will be seen to be more dramatic, more vivid, more imaginative – quite simply telling us a great deal more. In addition – and of no little structural significance – the pregnant brevity of the condensed passage also succeeds in reproducing the shocked reaction of the coroner: 'Don't know that everybody has two names'; the mur-

mured remarks of the clerk of court: 'No father, no mother, no friends'; as well as suggesting with incisive subtlety the unwritten questions (148).

It will be established that the use of free indirect speech in *Little Dorrit* reveals that the technique not only stands as part of the transition between the author's 'old' and 'new' styles, with indications, no matter how slight, of the gradually developing innovations to come, but that it also reaches a high point in excellence as far as the 'older' style is concerned, taking even further the possibilities offered by this mode of tightening and speeding up the narrative. There is a yet greater economy of means than in *Bleak House*, as well as a more dramatically and ironically effective transposition of the fictional speech, a transposition which strikingly points up the thematic needs of this massively sombre comment on Society. In the presentation, for example, of Lord Decimus Barnacle's preposterously verbose parliamentary manner – one Dickens had learned to hate in his days as a reporter – the mode involved actually reinforces the parody, the general effect of the caricature being strengthened by an exact repetition of the lines within the same paragraph (405). Also, Mr Dorrit's almost pathological sense of the dignity of his family is ironically underlined by the transposition of the pompous little lecture to which he submits his daughter Amy (463). In a further interesting excerpt, Dickens comprehensively but in the minimum amount of space shows how the 'Merdle-fever' has seeped through even to the lower reaches of society: we have the non-standard speech characteristics of Mrs Plornish's female customers, but it is the economy and speed of the technique which is telling (571–2). Surpassing, however, all these examples in the dramatic effectivity of the underlying irony is the homily delivered by Mr Dorrit after the bizarre scene in which he gives his brother advice. Put into free indirect speech, Mr Dorrit's words reduce him himself to a naked mockery of the very moral he is trying to draw (224–5).

Bearing in mind that it was during the years immediately following the completion of *Little Dorrit* that Dickens' new 'oral style' began to come into its own, it is surely no coincidence that the free indirect speech of the later novels should also turn out to be somewhat less conventional in character, displaying the features peculiar to the altered style. In *A Tale of Two Cities*, the cross-questioning of the spy, Barsad (Solomon Pross), by Darney's defence counsel, Stryver – whose questions obviously arise from Carton's inspiration (63) – demonstrates this in an exemplary manner. The new, concentrated, strongly rhythmical effect shines through so decidedly that one almost has the impression of direct speech, and yet this is not the case; it is, in fact, transposed into the mode under discussion. The brief questions – unremitting, to the point, and devastatingly penetrating on the part of the lawyer, and the equally brief answers of the witness, shifty, ineffectively truculent and petulantly indignant – entirely stripped of any kind of superfluous description, thrown back and forth with the relentlessness of a table-tennis match between an offensive, self-confident player, and a defensive, wavering opponent, lend a taut vitality and a hint, too, of true Dickensian humour (otherwise lacking in the novel as a whole) to the irony underlying the exposure of Barsad's true character, which is not only in itself of high dramatic effectualness, but also underscores verbal qualities running right through Dickens' tale. It should be barely necessary to mention either the structural significance of the whole passage, with the foreboding insistency of its references to prison, or the inspired manipulation of language which leads, among other instances, to such a telling apposition as: 'Gentleman. Ever been kicked?'; sufficient to say that the short excerpt admirably reflects more than one aspect of the forceful action writing dominating a great many pages in the book.[10]

In that masterpiece of fictional writing techniques, *Our Mutual Friend*, the differences between the fictional speech and the other prose modalities are, as we have seen, constantly reduced to a minimum. This blurring of the boundaries means that the free indirect speech either does not stand out in such sharp relief or becomes virtually superfluous, for in a sense one can actually regard the 'new' style permeating this book as a branch of the mode in question – 'Dickensian free indirect speech', if one will. This unique integration of the various fictional modes gives a new impulse to the dramatic flow of Dickens' theatrical storytelling methods. When coloured by the penetrating rhetoric of repetitive clause patterns – as in the excerpt in which Mrs Veneering, bent on helping her husband to get a seat in Parliament, calls on Lady Tippins – the free indirect speech lends itself ideally both to the novel's devastating satire on Society and to the need, at this point, to be brief (249–50).

In the fascinating stylistic developments of the half-finished

Edwin Drood, Dickens builds on yet newer techniques. A case in point is a conversation between Neville Landless and his sister Helena. It is a dialogue which within a few lines manages to fuse direct, indirect and free indirect speech (158). A further illustration is the telling but ironically amusing satire implied in the author's dig (mirrored in the transposed speech of Miss Twinkleton) at snobbish private schools and the affected genteel register of their teachers. An excellent passage in this mode is provided when Miss Twinkleton, in a typical combination of moral injunction and straightforward communication, points out that it is high time she took her charges, Helena and Rosebud, back to the Nun's House (66). Very effective, too, are the lines in which she admonishes her pupils for gossiping about the 'fracas' between Edwin and Neville (83–4), as well as those in which she bids the pupils farewell for Christmas; the blending is always complete and perfect (143–4).

Part II

Dickens' Idiolects: the Chronological Development

6 Fictional Apprenticeship

Dickens began writing fiction in the 1830s, a period which, to some degree, witnessed the closing stages of the Romantic movement in English literature and simultaneously the beginnings of the Victorian age. There is, of course, no really clear-cut division, for, indeed, the Romantic approach remained deeply rooted in the work of many writers for a number of decades to come, running parallel, if one will, with the newly awakened desire for a more rational basis of life, for more down-to-earth attitudes in which the accent would be on continuous evolution and the superiority of man and his achievements in the more material sense. The continual forays into the country away from the dirt, crowds and crime of urban life, to be found so frequently in the novels of the early Victorians – and Dickens' first five novels, especially, provide examples in abundance – are a typical product of this tug-of-war between the two movements: Wordsworthian Nature was still written with a capital letter.

In the overlapping period – the 1830s and, to some degree if one includes Byronism, the 1820s – there was, correspondingly, a certain tension, a kind of restless exuberance which manifested itself in more walks of life than simply literature. During the rest of the nineteenth century, only some of the poetry of Tennyson, Browning, Arnold and Hopkins could be said to have even approached that of Wordsworth, Keats or Shelley; further, drama on a serious creative level was completely dormant until the 1890s. It was in the novel that the Victorians found their most lasting and effective form of self-expression through art. In this mode of fiction, the period 1832–42 was as active as any other decade but, apart from Dickens, no great heights were touched. Scott had died in 1832 and Lytton and Ainsworth were ruling the scene when, in 1836, quite literally out of the blue, *Pickwick* arrived, to be followed in rapid succession by four more novels from Dickens' pen during the time in question.[1]

With Dickens, however, a great many other influences (apart from the literary antecedents already mentioned) were also at work, one of the most significant of which – the theatre, whether serious, variety or melodrama – having already been referred to in these lines. Another very important one was the growing literary interest in lower-class culture, including its criminal aspects,[2] a reflection of which being the attempts of Surtees, Pierce Egon and others to reproduce the non-standard dialect of London. A further factor was certainly the shaky, uncertain state of social distinctions – the Victorian moneyed middle-class was just beginning to break through – a state which (indirectly) helped to pave the way for the rise of the cheeky, irrepressible Cockney of whom Sam Weller is the archetype.

Moreover, conflict in the Dickens of the earlier works was not the apposition of rational thinking and feeling but rather that between comedy and feeling or, more bluntly put, between laughter and tears. Sentimentality, otherwise drawn upon by Dickens to excess, is, for example, markedly lacking in *Pickwick*. Indeed, rather than being a novel in the more usual sense of the word, this book is a kind of extended fictional entertainment in the comic-picaresque tradition of the eighteenth century, the light-hearted, genial humour springing from a supremely vital and self-confident young genius, who did not even really know where he was going, but simply improvised from month to month.

As his own remarks in a later preface (1847) testify, Dickens fully realised the many weaknesses and immaturity of his first book, *Sketches by Boz*,[3] in which the provocatively original goes alongside the self-consciously derivative. In respect of the authorial voices, there is no really homogeneous style, but rather a complex mixture made up of the then prevalent ornate journalistic mode, with its pompous circumlocutions and a kind of high-flown literary potpourri manner full of flowery phrases, terribly heavy irony and the almost inevitable mock heroic, the whole occasionally and somewhat clumsily intermingled with legal jargon evidently picked up in his office-boy days. For the most part the humour, too, is ponderous and at times embarrassingly obvious, as in the mock heroic mode itself or in certain tedious plays on words: polysyllabic humour – a favourite pastime of many nineteenth century English writers – was, indeed, to remain with him some time. For all this, there are a number of bright exceptions, sudden splashes of colour which point to the future master, this being especially true as far as comic speech is concerned. In the passages in question, one already has the impression of an unusual vitality bursting out of all bonds, of an exceptionally inquisitive and observant eye ready to induce life into highly unlikely inanimate objects, of an equally sharp ear prompt to record the most outlandish language.

One of the very first extended passages of Dickens' version of the Cockney dialect is a pungent speech made by a mastersweep (173). There is also that inspired creature Mrs Bloss ('The Boarding House'), one of Dickens' first zanies, launching the reader on a dizzy trip down the rapids of her wildly erratic English (301–4). A companion zany in the content – or, rather, lack of it – of his utterances is that would-be-gentleman Mr Horatio Sparkins (in the tale of the same name), though his embryonic idiolect is otherwise fairly firmly rooted in the genteel register of the standard language (365). In a strident female inhabitant of the then notorious Seven Dials district, there is more than a hint of Mrs Gamp:

> Here's poor dear Mrs Sulliwin, as has five blessed children of her own, can't go out a-charing for one arternoon, but what hussies must be a-comin', and 'ticing avay her oun' 'usband, as she's been married to twelve year come next Easter Monday, for I see the certificate ven I vas a-drinkin' a cup o'tea vith her, only the werry last blessed Ven'sday as ever vas sent. I 'appen'd to say promiscuously, 'Mrs Sulliwin', says I – –. (70)

In 'Criminal Courts', we have the probable source of the Artful Dodger's unforgettable court scene, a young pickpocket who, when defending himself, 'asserts that all the witnesses have committed perjury, and hints that the police force generally have entered into a conspiracy "again" him' (199). Ikey, the factotum in the lock-up house ('A Passage in the Life of Mr Watkins Tottle'), who is 'neither very concise nor intelligible in his narratives', provides another non-standard gem in the vein of the mastersweep, though if anything he is more incomprehensibly long-winded – already it can be said that such speech is at its best when read aloud (450–1). The reader is also treated to the first of that long and lugubrious line of orators – and a prime example of pompous nonsense Mr Rogers ('The Parlour Orator') is – who were later, in satire both beguiling and biting, to fill so many pages in his works (236–9). In a story ('The Bloomsbury Christening') full of comic snippets, there is a letter (470–1) revealing how well, even at this point, Dickens could catch stylistically the very nature of the writer as if he were speaking (here pretentiously), and pointing toward the letters of, among others, Tony Weller (*PP*, 729–30) and Fanny Squeers (*NN*, 175–6). In whatever fictional speech there is to be found in the *Sketches*, then, there is enough which hints at future developments in general, but little, on the other hand, which prefigures the actual patterned complexity and brilliance of his uniquely stylised idiolects, the first of which were to burst into prominence in the very next book.

7 *Pickwick Papers* to *The Old Curiosity Shop*

Moving from the *Sketches* to *Pickwick Papers*,[1] Dickens' first attempt at an extended work of fiction, is moving into another world. Nowhere is this clearer than in the young author's use of language, despite the continued presence – above all in the authorial voices – of some of the negative aspects so apparent in the former book. That we gain such an impression is above all due to the marvel which is the actual speech of so many of the characters, and the resulting comic gusto of one richly inspired scene after another. It is these scenes, so completely dominating the book, that truly make it the (admittedly uneven) masterpiece it is.

With the notable exceptions of the Wellers, the most significant aspect of this novel's fictional speech is that, for all its verve, it is in the main very strongly and conventionally typified. It is an impressive tribute to Dickens' embryonic typifying abilities and concomitant rhythmic vitality that the speech of these subsidiary characters remains so utterly and convincingly readable, never letting up from the second chapter to the last but one.

It is, though, the two richly varied idiolects of Sam Weller and his father Tony Weller by which the novel stands or falls. They are both rooted in Dickens' fictional version of the Cockney dialect discussed above. Whereas Sam's idiolect, apart from occasional aspects of the domestic servant speech register, is otherwise not strongly typified, that of Tony is deeply imbued with the coaching register. Singly or together they appear in no less than thirty-five of the forty-one chapters between their entries into and exit from the novel. With one exception, Tony's appearances are always in company with Sam, the latter taking part, though, in about four times as many scenes as those involving his father. On the other hand, in the fourteen scenes in which the two are together, it is Tony's speech that almost invariably prevails; at such moments he uses nearly four times as many words as his son.

ZANY REALISM AND FACETIOUS LUMINOSITY: TWO TRIUMPHS OF THE IMAGINATION

As with many of Dickens' Cockney characters, the speech of the Wellers reveals certain phonological inconsistencies: 'gen'lm'n' and 'gen'lmen', 'ven' and 'wen', 'aggerawated' and 'aggrawates', and so on. Sometimes it may be the result of deliberate emphasis or rhythmic balance, but an additional cause could well be the undue haste and stress Dickens was subject to when producing the monthly numbers. An interesting point is the relative scarcity of the dropped or wrongly inserted aspirate, illustrating at this point already Dickens' highly selective method of presenting non-standard features. This also applies to the grammar and syntax of their speech: just enough non-standard detail to create a convincing picture and yet remain readable.

Far more interesting are the lexical distortions, above all the malapropisms. Sam, for instance, has a predilection for distorting the prefix of a word: 'except' (125) = accept, 'purwide' (154) = provide, 'perportion' (547) = proportion, 'perwent' (789) = prevent. This can become a genuine and effective malapropism as in 'a priory 'tachment' (551) = a prior attachment, or 'have-his-carcase' (609) = *habeas corpus*. However, in depth of ambiguity and breadth of fantasy, Tony's malapropisms can be far more amusing and apt. He is, moreover, very conscious of his own dignity when attempting a fine word, and does not lightly brook criticism. Such a situation arises when Mr Pell, his shady legal adviser, corrects him from 'prodigy son' to 'prodigal son' (612) and from 'probe it' to 'probate' (774), or his own son from 'dispensary' to 'dispensation' (736).

Both their idiolects are, however, truly individualised by a number of rhetorical features. The most obvious and perhaps best-known is the one beginning with a normal statement and then qualified by the construction 'as . . . said, when . . .', in other words a tagline invariable in form but always variable in content. With Sam, who resorts to the form again and again, they frequently involve a comic logic and far-fetched stretches of fantasy plus a great many macabre references (above all to death of a violent kind). Almost his first words in the novel, answering a request to get a pair of boots cleaned immediately, are as follows: 'No, no; reg'lar rotation, as Jack Ketch said, wen he tied the men up' (119). Tony's sallies are less macabre and, moreover, almost always tinged with his own singular moralising tone: 'It's all for my own good; vich is the reflection vith wićh the penitent schoolboy comforted his feeliń's ven they flogged him' (734). Dickens has sometimes been criticised for what have been considered implausible references in these Weller comparisons, references beyond the knowledge such persons could normally have been presumed to possess. However, the references to drama or history can be traced back either to the popular theatre of the day (which even attempted Shakespeare's tragedies) or to familiar legends. In the words of Sylvère Monod, 'there is nothing in the least learned, nothing exceeding the elementary level of knowledge that a young Londoner might be supposed to have acquired'.[2]

Father and son display, too, an amazing rapidity in picturesque impudence when making short, pithy comparisons typical of their cheerful, confident Cockney disregard of importance, personal or otherwise. 'Dumb as a drum vith a hole in it, sir', says Sam when Mr Pickwick asks him to be quiet at the magistrate's court (342). Tony has an equally sharp and ready tongue but, as usual, cannot avoid a zanily critical judgement, 'Wot's the good o' callin' a young 'ooman a Wenus or a angel, Sammy? . . . You might jist as well call her a griffin, or a unicorn, or a king's arms at once, which is werry well known to be a col-lection o' fabulous animals' (453). Here we can also observe a minor speech feature, also shared about equally by Tony and Sam, of pausing after the first syllable of a word containing two or more syllables. This feature, occasionally found in the speech of other Dickens' characters, is in both the result of strong emphasis. In Sam it may be brought about by sarcasm: 'gen-teel' (120), sheer enthusiasm: 'col-lecting' (166), seriousness of purpose: 'ex-tremities' (541) or stubborn desperation: 'ma-licious' (615). In Tony it generally – and typically – reflects a dignified belief in the morality and truth of what he is saying and is often coloured by deep indignation: 'ex-pressin' ' (783).

Three particular features differentiate Sam's speech from that of his father: his love of detail and anecdote, his extended use of adjectives, and his application of nicknames. Drawing regularly on his seemingly inexhaustible stock of anecdotes, Sam displays – like his creator – an extremely alert eye for detail. Some of his anecdotes are very long and any event or sight around him can spark off his lively inventive imagination. More often than not, Mr Pickwick forms the willing audience, as when Sam regales him with the story of the 'mysterious disappearance of a 'spectable tradesman' (423–4). It is, however, Sam's use of adjectives – especially of those expressing feelings and attitudes – which most clearly shows his development from a mere amusing sketch to a full-grown comic personality. It is not until about the middle of the book that he begins to blossom out in this respect. In relating the previously mentioned anecdote, he makes use within a few lines of 'tender young', 'lovely', 'most owdacious', 'melancholy', 'idle'. From now on it is made clear that Sam, despite his rough and ready exterior, is a man of sensibilities. Only when it is subordinate to that of his father is Sam's speech characterised by a certain dryness. Sam's application of nicknames, on the other hand, is aimed at deflating self-importance in others – he calls Job, for instance, 'a wolf in a mulberry suit' (345) and Mr Tuckle, the pompous footman, 'Blazes' (521) – or even in himself: in the exquisite Valentine-writing scene, he roundly refers to himself as 'a reg'lar soft-headed, inkred'lous turnip' (453). Again, only when speaking to his father, who comes in for a great variety, does he apply names of a familiar, affectionate nature: 'old Nobs' (369), 'my Prooshan Blue' (450), 'a perwerse old file' (606), to name a few. It will be observed that the adjectives 'old' and 'young' are used almost continuously.

Tony is a coachman, adapting the speech register of his profession to his everyday needs, whatever the society he is moving in. His usual manner of asking someone to continue, for instance, is 'Drive on' (453 ff.), and he calls the abrupt ending to Sam's Valentine 'a sudden pull up' (454). When together with his coaching colleagues (603–4), this typification becomes, naturally enough, even more pronounced. His letter informing Sam of Mrs Weller's death is completely in this register and is, too, a memorably apt, extended metaphor of life's journey itself (729–30). Indeed, Tony's use of the register goes far beyond that forced upon him when he is actually working. It infiltrates his whole life to such a significant extent that he cannot open his mouth in any situation without drifting into the idiom. That he does so naturally and with the greatest of conviction, remaining at the same time easily understandable, is a tribute to the young Dickens' typifying genius. The pointed, down-to-earth coaching terminology reinforces the weird originality of Tony's aphoristic moralising. His idiolect would be unthinkable without the register concerned.

Tony's language is perhaps more consistently convincing, for with it the reader never gains the impression that he is no longer being regaled by the true Dickens miming the character himself, that he is instead being lectured at by an out-of-storytelling-character Dickens bent on putting over a particular point dressed up in the linguistic and rhetorical idiosyncrasies of the character concerned. Such lapses in creative consistency are, unfortunately, sometimes to be found in Sam's speech. On the surface, maybe, it is difficult to give the reason why – both Sam and Tony each have a highly original, sharply delineated idiolect, with, as we have seen, certain very pronounced individualising and typifying features. But, even when unconvincing, Dickens seems to put exactly the same language techniques into use. Of course, it is not wrong in itself for an author to interpose a certain opinion, indeed he can hardly avoid doing so. It must be done, however, in such a way that the point in question is simultaneously related to the whole life, nature and background of the character as the miming author has conceived and realized him through his language in a particular work. Precisely this is true of Tony Weller, for instance, when he attacks poetry, especially when it is used to address a female (452). This attack is, within its context, completely persuasive, because it is being made by a man who, having had next to no formal education, obviously finds poetry difficult or impossible to understand, and who, moreover, within his very practical world (with the exceptions he himself names), is simply never addressed that way by anyone. He also senses very clearly the artificiality or hypocrisy behind the adoption of such a mode. The whole withering broadside is rooted in the world of his personality and hence, clothed in his caustic speech habits, is artistically satisfying. However, with Sam, in spite of the fact that his stock of knowledge is, as we all by now know, 'extensive and peculiar', it is sometimes difficult to avoid the impression that he is being manipulated to an extent beyond the role he can fit so convincingly. In other words, although it is clear that Sam at his penetrating best is an extension of the pert impudence and quick wit of his creator's own basically Cockney nature, his speech idiom occasionally reflects something else in Dickens, something less fundamental and acquired, rather. It is then that the result rings hollow. A good example of this is Sam's reply to Mr Pickwick in the Fleet, after the latter has commented on the fact that, for a great many prisoners, who are occupying themselves as they have always done in smoking, drinking, chatting and playing cards, 'imprisonment for debt is scarcely any punishment at all' (576). The reply reveals almost none of those rhetorical traits listed above except for the concluding Weller-type comparison, and even this, shorn of its linguistic features, reveals itself as weak and forced. We have none of the usual lithe rapidity of picturesque impudence, but only the unconvincing syntactic repetitiveness of four clauses beginning 'them ... as'; no 'unnecessary detail', no streams of aptly chosen adjectives, no examples of that emphatic pause so revealing of his true nature. No; Dickens is pointing – very rhetorically – the rather self-conscious finger of the as yet young social reformer determined to do his sincere best to make public intolerable evils, and (very temporarily) forgetting the true Sam, that extension of his own fundamental nature.

The true Sam always emerges either in a situation demanding immediate verbal action, giving rise with great naturalness to one of his serenely impudent comments, or at a moment deemed appropriate for allowing his fantasy free rein, resulting in one of his rambling, incident-studded anecdotes. It is when these comments or anecdotes spring directly from his own peculiarly honest – often metonymic – way of thinking, expressed in his own eccentric idiom, full of encyclopaedic and seemingly irrelevant detail, a conglomeration of knowledge picked up at random, misused or mispronounced words and eccentric comparisons, that the final picture is convincing. Sam's non-stop interpolations and the manifold language features which so irradiate them, have a two-fold function within the book as a whole: either that of providing, through their cheerfully luminous wit, a balming influence at genuinely serious moments, or that of off-setting, through facetiously ironic darker humour, the complacency of shallow, pompous philanthropy. Having, as he does, a foot in both of the book's two social worlds, and triumphantly supported by his wealth of effective language idiosyncrasies, Sam is constantly able to strike that balance without which the book would have been a failure.

Tony's expansively rounded speech idiom, especially with its symbolic application of the coaching register and obsessive variations on the theme of incurable misogyny, reveals nowhere a letting-up in inspiration or consistency. Admittedly, its role in the book is not as significant as that played by Sam's idiolect, but in itself, judged purely by the triumphant, unanswerable logic of its zany language structures, Tony's idiolect provides the first inkling in Dickens of the world of Nonsense, that strange world of order in disorder. Whether or not Dickens was in any way aware that his artistic realisation of Sam's language characterisation faltered on occasion, and that Tony's idiolect as such stands on a higher level, is not clear. It is a fact, however, that in the scenes in which the two appear together, Tony tends to dominate the conversation. This means that Sam becomes not colourless, but rather less loquacious, playing a kind of second fiddle to the overwhelming conviction and inspiration exhibited in the portrayal of his father. Perhaps we can do no better than to close with Tony's own reason for his superiority as, with characteristic gravity, he delivers it to his son: 'Vidth and visdom, Sammy, alvays grows together' (771).

Sandwiched though it is between two comic-episodic novels belonging virtually in the same literary progression, *Oliver Twist*[3] is in more than one respect a sidetrack. To begin with, the structure has in the main a firmness and precision lacking in the other two, and which Dickens was not to recapture until writing *Dombey & Son*. Further, the highly distinctive tone of the authorial voice – whether narrative, descriptive or commentarial – looks ahead in a way exhibited by neither of the other two. This distinctive tone is strikingly exemplified by the 'stop thief' episode (66–7) and by the description of Fagin in the dock (404–6). The whole novel is, too, essentially dramatic, or, rather, melodramatic in the Dickensian sense. It becomes very obvious, for example, that when the subject matter took Dickens by the throat, he was directly influenced by the language of contemporary melodrama, as in Oliver's plea (on his knees, of course) to Sikes to let him go (162); or even, indeed, by Shakespeare's *Macbeth*, both in Sikes' diction when being pursued after the unsuccessful robbery (203) and in Fagin's syntax: 'I've got that to tell you, Bill . . . will make you worse than me' (357).

In all respects, Fagin's speech is intriguing: although got up in the traditional rig-out and endowed with the greed, cowardice and sly, double-dealing manner so long typical, unfortunately, of the stage or fictional Jew, his speech idiom is almost invariably standard with only an occasional cant term or other non-standard detail. Moreover, judging by the absence of any unusual phonological features, it is obviously completely untouched by the very pronounced nasality which seems to have been characteristic of London Jews at least, and which Dickens reproduced in the case of Barney, one of Fagin's associates (320). Sikes' speech is equally intriguing: its measure of cant is little more than that of Fagin. With its theatrical vitality, surprising streams of vehement adjectives, scathing comparisons and brutally malicious humour, it radiates in all a peculiarly riveting quality. At times, it even exudes a faintly melancholy air verging on the poetic: 'It was Bartlemy time when I was shopped; and there warn't a penny trumpet in the fair, as I couldn't hear the squeaking on' (110).

Of the non-standard speech idioms not coloured by cant, far and away the most striking is provided by that worthy, Mr Bumble. He it is who, bitter satire, carries the image on his buttons of 'the Good Samaritan healing the sick and bruised man' (24); who, biting irony, calls the foundlings 'our fondlings' (8); and who, saving grace, is the possessor of a mini-idiolect which is not only in itself a pure gem, but which also plays an integral part in the novel's thematic structure. The unfeeling stupidity inherent in his self-important, pompous speech habits is, it would seem, a mirror of the same qualities to be found in actual officers of the state when operating under the mantle of the much hated Poor Law, a mirror of the crass weaknesses of the new law itself. His striving for genteel utterance leaves him struggling for the right word, as in his preposterous proposal of marriage to the infinitely more cunning Mrs Corney (197) or his hypocritical remark when re-meeting Oliver (398). It even leads him into completely zany statements, typical of which is his reply to Mrs Sowerberry's assertion that Oliver – turned defiant – must be mad: 'It's not Madness, ma'am . . . It's Meat' (46). Some of these have a touch of whimsical quaintness, such as his bitter comment on his disastrous marriage (268). He is a far more complex character than might appear at a first reading. Through the wide ranging variety and superlative invention of his speech, he is lifted above those around him, enabling him to assert a limited independence of a world that otherwise has him fast in its grip.

SPEECH AS SOCIAL CRITICISM – AN IDIOLECT ON THE ATTACK

Surpassing even Mr Bumble in rhetorical stature in this novel is Jack Dawkins, otherwise known in Fagin's gang as the Artful Dodger. His idiolect is rooted in Dickens' version of the Cockney dialect and is highly coloured by cant, the register of the criminal underworld he lives in. Dickens' occasional orthographical inconsistency in the presentation of this dialect comes more to the fore in this character's idiolect than anywhere else: 'niver' and 'never' (53) occur within a line of each other; for 'magistrate' we have 'madgst'rate' (53) and 'madg'strates' (334). Even the Dodger's substitution of 'W' for 'V' or vice versa – something done more consistently in the Wellers' idiolects – is just as inconsistent: 'very' and 'wery', for example, are about equally given. The same applies to the 'eye dialect' or lack of it: among other words, 'what' appears as frequently as 'wot'. All this, of course, particularly in Dickens' stylised world, need matter but little. Of far more import are the Dodger's inspired lexical distortions: he has a leaning towards highfalutin phraseology which leads him into amusing constructions, into genuinely successful malapropisms even. The famous court scene has several, of which the following makes a fine point to say the least: 'Oh! you know me, do you? . . . That's a case of deformation of character, any way' (334).

Despite moving for the most part among people with the same dialect roots and register, the Dodger's clearly defined idiolect marks him as rhetorically and rhythmically quite distinct from his companions. Perhaps the most striking rhetorical feature in his pugnacious tendency to shoot out a series of short, laconic, one might say staccato-like, phrases. These are often in the form of one exclamation after another, entailing continual use of such ejaculations as 'Oh!', 'Ah!', 'There!', 'Now then'. Here, for instance, are the closing words of his first scene: 'Oh no! Not in the least! By no means! Certainly not!' (54). Frequently, this same mode is also adorned with equally terse, equally aggressive rhetorical questions; indeed, he again and again asks all sorts of questions. Just as frequently he supplies his own impudent, sarcastic comments, these being rhythmically very pronounced and sometimes containing amusingly distorted quotations from nursery rhymes; 'What'll Fagin say? ... Ah, what? ... Toor rul lol loo, gammon and spinnage, the frog he wouldn't, and high cockolorum' (83). The defiantly unexpected negative is immediately apparent.

Whenever he opens his mouth for anything more than a terse remark, the Dodger almost invariably phrases in groups of three. These can be a series of three short phrases, as in his reaction to the fact that the police have witnesses against him: 'Ah! that's right ... Where are they? I should like to see 'em' (335). In turn, they can be in multiples of three – compound time, so to speak – with more often than not, especially when he is aroused, a concluding phrase which is more extended. There is a very extended coda, for instance, in his indignant outburst against the encroachment upon his 'priwileges' as an Englishman (334). A few lines later, a similar example has such a prolonged coda that he is finally interrupted by the clerk of the court, who wastes no time in committing him! However, even this does not quench him, and he ends the trial with a last torrent of impudence which falls naturally into three successive groupings of threes, concluding with a superbly defiant 'Here/carry me off to prison!/Take me away!' (336). Even the smallest of entries reveals the same pattern, as when Nancy goes into a faint, this showing, incidentally, how amusingly resourceful he is in his own laconic way, and how decorous even in the division of labour (289). To recognise such multiple 'threeings', which provide so firm an outline to his triumphant idiolect, requires the ability to hear the Dodger as if he were actually speaking, for few would recognise it on a fleeting reading.

The Artful Dodger rarely resists the temptation to voice his whole sceptical but pragmatic approach to the tyrannous life which forces him and his like into a life of crime. Two scenes – the one when he regales Oliver, who is cleaning his boots; the other the trial episode – give him ample opportunity to declaim at length on this theme, showing his character in all its hard, objective, shrewd lack of any kind of delusion. In the first of these scenes, he tries to persuade Oliver to knuckle under and become one of the gang. Oliver retorts that he would rather go if they would let him: 'Go! ... Why, where's your spirit? Don't you take any pride out of yourself? Would you go and be dependent on your friends?' (131). The splendid aggression of the Dodger's answer is reinforced by the three-fold rhythm of the syntax, and he continues to expound his philosophy in the same persuasive rhythms.

His belligerently sarcastic broadsides in the justly famous trial scene also cogently emphasise his whole scornfully defiant attitude to the people in authority who have forced him to develop the cynically amoral approach to life that rings through every impudent statement he makes. There is an appalling reproach in 'I'm an Englishman, ain't I? ... Where are my priwileges?' (334), or in 'this ain't the shop for justice' (335). G. B. Shaw's remark about the seditious quality of *Little Dorrit* – a novel written nearly two decades later – could as easily have been transferred to the earlier novel or, more exactly, to the character Jack Dawkins. It is in the form of fictional speech that such irony becomes infinitely more effective, particularly when it is in an idiolect such as this with its pounding rhythms, the irrepressible impudence of its rhetorical features and the significant ambiguity of its lexical distortions. This kind of speech stands in direct contrast, too, to the laboured results of some of Dickens' more lengthy authorial interpolations.

Through his utterances, the Dodger fills a vital structural role in the novel, in that his whole attitude to the Establishment, all his reactions to it, are an indictment of the same, laying bare its injustice, its weaknesses, and above all its omissions. This he does in a unique rhetorical manner at once knowing, sarcastic and as shrewdly artful as his nickname suggests, its boundless vitality enhanced by his irrepressible Cockney impudence and humour. Thus, it is no exaggeration to see in his idiolect the first signs in Dickens of fictional speech being imbued with more than a modicum of structural significance. His speech lives on its own and as part of the novel. Disregarding, then, such a minor blemish as the orthographical inconsistencies, we are left with the full wonder that is the Dodger's idiolect, one which, with the patterned variety, aggressive eccentricity and savagely impudent irony of its rhetorical and rhythmic qualities, lifts him head and shoulders above even such skilfully portrayed fellow characters as Fagin and Sikes. In the novel as a whole, only the speech idiom of Bumble can even begin to approach that of the Artful Dodger.

Of all Dickens' novels, *Nicholas Nickleby*[4] is the most clearly theatrical in theme and technique, but a theatricality less in what became the author's own vein and more a direct borrowing from the stage of that time, in particular from melodrama. The whole of the final section, for instance, is directly in this mode with all its trappings, and includes numerous, minutely detailed stage directions. Dickens had still not outgrown his ambition to write successfully for the theatre, and was trying his luck with various small pieces. The artistic uncertainty of the novel is primarily manifested in the general looseness of structure, but further major blemishes are the ever-nagging presence – as in all these earlier works – of awkward transitions from narrative to dialogue and back, plus the appalling number of blatant coincidences. However, on the positive side, this novel is 'remarkable for its random energies',[5] a fact triumphantly affirmed by the recent magnificent stage adaptation. As in so much of Dickens, an enormous amount of interest lies in the details – details through which the young author's genius shines with unequalled brilliance.

For the speech of this novel's characters, with the notable exceptions of the idiolects of Mantalini and Mrs Nickleby, Dickens still leans very heavily on the typifying process. There are, though, two contrasting usages of the melodramatic register: the one, satirically applied, covering Crummles and his troupe; and that, presented in all seriousness, as spoken by such leading characters as Ralph, Nicholas and Kate in moments of crisis. Says Kate (to the dastardly Hawk): 'Unhand me, sir, this instant' (241). Both the standard and non-standard forms of the genteel register are also on display, but with equal effectivity: on the one hand, Mrs Wititterly, whose gushing mixture of affected mannerisms and ostentatious phraseology clearly prefigures the absurd chatter of Mrs Skewton (*DS*), and, on the other, Mr Kenwigs' tortuous circumlocutions and pompous dignity of syntax and vocabulary when speaking to someone he considers rather lower on the social scale, plus his awkward, acutely realised servility towards those higher up (164–6). In the lower regions, Mr Squeers is the possessor of a speech idiom whose basically simple syntax, adorned with a startling variety of non-standard detail, accurately represents this greedy, repulsive man's brutally practical attitude to the people around him. His own peculiar version of the teaching register provides a comically exotic extension to his normal idiolect (90–1).

The divertingly preposterous idiolect of that 'idle profligate'

(xxix) Mr Alfred Mantalini is, in Professor Brook's words, a 'special variety of affected upper-class speech [with] a highly stylized manner of speaking',⁶ the operative word being 'affected'. In respect to his linguistic origins, Mantalini, like the later Mr Turveydrop (*BH*), presents teasing difficulties, the extreme affectation of his speech placing him in a category to which he otherwise does not belong. This affectation is shown phonologically in the raising of [ae] to [e], as in 'dem' for 'damn', and [ai] to [i], as in 'outrigeously' for 'outrageously'. Lexically, the affectation leads to three groups: firstly, those words stemming from his appropriation of upper-class usage ('demd' and its derivatives, 'infernal', 'cursed', etc.); secondly, those resulting from his effeminate baby-talk with women and reflecting, too, his extreme and fastidious social pretensions ('horrid', 'odiously', 'bow-wows', etc.); thirdly, those indicating a strong element of animal imagery which might possibly have to do with his randy nature ('dogs', 'fox', 'tiger', 'horse', etc.). On the face of it, though, his idiolect can be considered as rooted in the standard dialect with a coating, a highly personal aping, of the Regency brand of non-standard mannerisms found in the upper-class register.

Apart from the two speech tags, the ejaculation (one can hardly call it a laugh) 'Ha, ha' and the imprecation 'dem' (plus its derivatives), four other rhetorical features can be established in Mantalini's idiolect. When addressing his love of the moment, he displays an extraordinary variety of exaggerated terms of endearment: 'my sense's idol', 'chick-a-biddy', 'popolorum tibby', to name a few. He develops his persuasive powers by making love in the third person singular neuter form, talking to his wife, for instance, as if she were a helpless but lovable baby; at times, this topples over into delightful absurdity: 'How can it say so, when it is blooming in the front room like a little rose in a demnition flower-pot?' (258). In his selfish desire to impress or win over the other person, he piles up one adjective after another, crowning this with an occasional attempt at a far-fetched hyperbolical comparison: 'Not for twenty thousand hemispheres populated with – with – with little ballet dancers' (125). Sometimes, after vainly searching for a word, he ends up with nothing at all (433).

Mantalini's philanderings reveal pronounced rhythmical outlines. He is particularly prone to building up a series of short sentences, all more or less of the same construction and approximately the same length, giving them a simple but strong rhythmic impulse. The intention is obviously to overwhelm by accumulation of effect – a very common trick in the world of rhetoric. There is, too, a lexical repetitiveness about these sentences, rendering the overall effect (if one is susceptible) even more irresistible. The auxiliaries 'will' and 'shall', for example, appear over and over again. In one 'pathetic' approach he adopts when wheedling his wife into giving him yet another chance, he resorts to 'will' six times, and once, as a variation, 'shall' (430). There is something in this of Dickens' later highly developed accumulation technique, and it is one Mantalini does not discard even when down to the level of turning a mangle under the eyes of a scolding new mistress, who tells him he can enlist if the work is too much:

> For a soldier! ... For a soldier! Would his joy and gladness see him in a coarse red coat with a little tail? Would she hear of his being slapped and beat by drummers demnebly? Would she have him fire off real guns, and have his hair cut, and his whiskers shaved, and his eyes turned right and left, and his trousers pipeclayed? (820)

Very characteristic here, and a habitual feature in his idiolect as a whole, is the reiteration of the opening phrase.

Dickens seems to have found Mantalini's speech idiom – and hence Mantalini – from the first entry. There is, it is true, a slight and gradual increase in the application of the more elaborate rhetorical features as well as in the rhythmic patterns, this being an indication of the general lack of pre-planning. All in all, however, the overall effect of Mantalini's idiolect, with its mingling of affected upper-class dialect, effeminate fastidiousness and, on occasion, plain arrogance, is a convincing one. Despite the presence of some stock ingredients, the resulting language collage remains highly individual. What Mantalini says is, for all its emptiness, truly memorable and often extremely funny. This is all the more astonishing for its stemming from a character more foolish than intelligent, or, as Ralph Nickleby puts it, 'Half knave and half fool' (580). In a nutshell, his 'utterances show amazing resources of comic inventiveness ... and some of his phrases are all but proverbial'.[7]

PATTERNED IRRELEVANCIES AND THE WORLD OF NONSENSE

Far and away the brightest speech gem in *Nicholas Nickleby* is the idiolect of Mrs Nickleby. It is rooted in the standard dialect and coloured to some degree by the genteel register, her whole outlook (for what it is) being determined by unrelenting snobbery. For all that, she can, on occasion, resort to a non-standard feature: 'he'd take 'em for a pot of porter' (583), ''em' being used several times. Perhaps it can be put down to the clipped usage of those who belong to what is sometimes called the 'county type', as the Nickleby family obviously does to a degree. Referring to Nicholas' grief on Smike's death, she finds it understandable that he is 'cut up' (791).

Mrs Nickleby's very idiosyncratic 'never-ending' manner of delivery, one permeating her entire speech idiom, is, without a doubt, its most marked characteristic, and the one by which its owner is personally typified and for which she is best-known and justly famous. Most of her orations are far too long to quote, but it is worthwhile taking a look at a relatively short example, her first such venture in the book, in order to examine at first hand the rambling singularities of her speech manner. This particular disorganised outburst is brought about by Ralph Nickleby's proposal that Kate should work for a West End dressmaker. Cynically playing on that mixture of avarice and snobbery which forms the basis of his sister-in-law's ambitions for her children, Ralph points out that dressmakers are wealthy:

> Very true. ... What your uncle says, is very true, Kate, my dear. ... I recollect when your poor papa and I came to town after we married, that a young lady brought me home a chip cottage-bonnet, with white and green trimming, and green persian lining, in her own carriage, which drove up to the door full gallop; – at least, I am not quite certain whether it was her own carriage or a hackney chariot, but I remember very well that the horse dropped down dead as he was turning round, and that your poor papa said he hadn't had any corn for a fortnight. (120)

It will be immediately observed that, when in full flood, she pours out her disconnected recollections in one enormous circuitous sentence made up of a large number of clauses and subsidiary phrases. The result is an overwhelming jumble of items either barely related or seemingly unconnected, the whole often verging on utter nonsense as a result of sudden jumps to completely unexpected details, leaving adjectival clauses too far removed from the nouns they are supposed to be qualifying (728–9). Such sudden jumps almost invariably occur when Mrs Nickleby indulges in her frequent habit of correcting herself. Further, each train of thought is filled with scrupulous detail to a pathological degree, all this taking the speaker even farther away from the initial – usually just as trivial – subject.

In the excerpt given above, a number of rhetorical features can be observed that are habitually utilised by Mrs Nickleby, that serve as props, so to speak. Her 'retrospective moods' (446), these being endless recollections of her own (faded) past, give rise, for example, to ever-recurring vocabulary of remembrance: 'remember', 'recollect', 'recall', 'used to', etc. In addition, she shows a great fondness for epithets. These can be of a conventionally sentimental (even superficial) nature, as in the 'poor dear' applied to her departed husband, or of a downright unfavourable nature, especially when rebuking her children: 'how stupid you are', she says to Kate (220); and to her son: 'how *can* you be so ridiculous' (480). She allies this feature to a predilection for extreme exaggeration, as in such phrases of extremity as 'there never was', 'I never saw such' and 'if I said it once, I said it fifty times', as well as in her constant resort to the superlative. This latter usage occurs above all when she is talking *about* Kate and not *to* her: she becomes then the 'sweetest-tempered, kindest-hearted creature' (339), for instance. A – for her decisive – habit springing directly from her chaotic, uncontrolled way of thinking is that of irrelevant self-questioning. She will suddenly stop to question the validity of her own equally irrelevant statement or even to reverse it, this leading only to considerably greater confusion, if that were possible. Such a habit brings with it, naturally, the habitual use of constructions of doubt, hesitation and confirmation: 'Wait, though. ... Let me be sure I'm right. Was it ... or was it ... I declare I can't remember just now, but ...' (445–6).

Despite the apparent chaos, a certain consistency of outline is brought to Mrs Nickleby's speech by her habit of repeating either her own words or those of others. This would seem to be a kind of self-confirmation, giving her the necessary confidence to gallop on: 'She was always clever ... always' (219). In addition, she frequently confirms her own statement(s) with two, sometimes three, variations, as in the opinions she expresses concerning her 'lover', the madman: 'no encouragement – none whatever – not the least in the world', etc. (645–6). A variation of this rhythmic idiosyncrasy – and one directly theatrical in effect – is the repetition of the concluding word or phrase of the person with whom she is supposed to be conversing. Sometimes, for good measure, she does this twice. There is a neat reversal of this mannerism when Hawk's two toadies, Pyke and Pluck, take the words right out of the gullible woman's mouth, as well as repeating each other's. In this way, they are able, with great success, to work on Mrs Nickleby's snobbish weakness for titles and high society (344).

It is clear that Mrs Nickleby's idiolect is formed not only by her inability to exercise control over her thoughts and to differentiate qualitatively between any two of them, but also by her shallow, snobbish approach to life. Falling as she has on leaner times, she is led to dwell on days – more imagined than real – of former glory. As with all his successful characters, Dickens sees her (and hence her speech) clearly. In constructing her idiolect, he resorts to an increasing complexity throughout her appearances in the book; that is, we can distinguish an ever-growing and more distinctive use of the various speech features. This gradual growth in complexity can, once more, be put down only to the author's need at this stage to improvise.

Worse, he has not yet learned to let well alone, and sometimes gives in to the temptation to underline certain of Mrs Nickleby's personal qualities which her idiolect features make clear enough (642). On the other hand, Dickens often allows her to criticise others for the very faults she herself possesses. This lends a touch of ironic amusement, as in her impatient remonstrance with her daughter, Kate, who, embarrassed by Smike's obvious devotion, changes the subject suddenly and completely: 'Dear me, Kate ... what in the name of goodness graciousness makes you fly off to the time before I was married, when I'm talking to you about his thoughtfulness and attention to me?' (531). Between the lines, Dickens gives the impression of viewing his character, one based on his mother, with a curious mixture of amused affection and contempt.

Mrs Nickleby is certainly more than just a comic figure, crazily funny though her utterances often are. She is, as her idiolect clearly reveals, one who is out of touch with the world around her – a person who supplies her own questions and answers. The scenes with the madman – comic and horrifying at the same time – go a long way towards affirming this special form of alienation, the grotesque counterpoint of their speech patterns prefiguring the deeply, sometimes frighteningly, ambiguous nonsense language of Edward Lear and Lewis Carroll. Mrs Nickleby, like the actors in the Crummles troupe as well as a host of others created by Dickens, has withdrawn to such an extent into the only world she knows that her external and internal worlds have become one. Her stylised speech is a complex-patterned reflection of this peculiar form of solipsism.

In more than one respect, *The Old Curiosity Shop*[8] presents a divided world. To start with, it is built up around two clear-cut narratives about the adventures of two distinct groups of characters: the one constantly setting off afresh on purposeless journeys, the other endeavouring when possible to follow them. Dickens' technique in the handling of the double narrative is now sounder, however, than anything of a similar nature in *Pickwick Papers* or *Nicholas Nickleby*. Further, almost everything in the book seems to be depicted in black and white, giving it an aura of the fairy tale in which the malignant half bursts with demonically violent energy in its determination to corrupt the other half. Within this context, it is natural that most of the fictional speech is a stylised reflection either of the dark Quilp–Brass nether world, one riddled with baleful evil, or of the light Swiveller–Nubbles world, one full of honesty and cheerful optimism. Fittingly, the narrative voice is permeated to an entirely new degree of intensity with the impression of a supremely gifted storyteller directly addressing a listening audience, reacting to its wishes, pointing up the various effects, as in the engaging description of Astley's (293–4). Yet, as is the case in all these earlier works, the actual quality and consistency of the speech of this or that character varies greatly. Dick Swiveller's idiolect, supremely, and, to a lesser degree, those of Quilp and the Brasses, can be measured against almost any to be found elsewhere in Dickens. On the other hand, very little can be said in favour of the speech given to the more serious characters, Little Nell's standard English (Dickens' fictional version) springing at once to mind.

It is above all Quilp who, through the inhuman vitality of his parodic speech patterns, drives along with irresistible force the darker side of the novel. And yet he also serves a more positive though less apparent purpose: that of showing up the wishy-washy conventions of gentility. He is, after all, a *man*, one clearly of exceptional virility and prepared for anything in life. This is mirrored in the ruthless directness of his syntax and the brutal sarcasm of his choice of word (36). Close behind Quilp in virulence is his female counterpart, Sally Brass – 'That amiable virgin' (269) as Dickens, in rather bad taste, calls her. She, too, is directly, openly unpleasant, with her domineering, imperative manner glaring out of her sparse, abruptly aggressive sentences devoid of subordinate clauses (247). There is, at least, unlike her brother, nothing dissembling about her desire to irritate whoever is around. We find little of Sally's or Quilp's open, dynamic aggression in the speech of Sampson Brass. For all that, he is worthy of note for being the first of a series of characters in Dickens to possess a variety of sub-idiolects which, as befits his slippery, hypocritical nature, he turns on at will: obsequious to Quilp, defiantly and nervously spiteful to Sally, bullying to underlings, overfriendly and jocose to Kit, professional to Dick Swiveller (262). This is shown lexically, for his utilitarian syntax – a series of short sentences with next to no subsidiary clauses but smoother than his sister's – remains the same whatever the mode chosen.

PARODIC FANCY AND THE LOGIC OF 'CRUSHER' HONESTY

It is Dick Swiveller whose idiolect, in all its brilliant diversity, takes the palm in this novel, and its key-word is play-acting. He switches at will from one to the other of a variety of styles, often mixing them in addition. Only when he feels the occasion demands, which is seldom, does he relapse – if one may put it that way – into relatively normal standard English. In Dick's idiolect, this 'contrast manner' is characterised by sudden changes from the one mode to the other: from his 'scraps of verse' style to downright colloquialisms; from a preposterously exaggerated form of the genteel register down to vulgar slang; from the theatrical to plain straightforward English.[9] Unlike Flora Finching's profoundly complex divorce from reality, Dick is perfectly aware of the extent to which this play-acting dominates his contact with others, and can, if needs be, parody himself. A typically beguiling example is his description of his methods when writing to that irregular source of income, his rich aunt:

> I mean to blot it a good deal and shake some water over it out of the pepper-castor, to make it look penitent. 'I'm in such a state of mind that I hardly know what I write' – blot – 'if you could see me at this instant shedding tears for my past misconduct' – pepper-castor – 'my hand trembles when I think' – blot again – if that don't produce the effect, it's all over. (60)

Again and again Dick's histrionic leanings are able to find comic-parodic fulfilment in his dealings with others: whether, as 'Perpetual Grand' of the 'Glorious Apollers' (103), in his absurd badinage with Chuckster (415), or in his grandiloquent phraseology in general, or, best of all, in his delightful scenes with the Marchioness: 'Ha! . . . 'Tis well. Marchioness! – but no matter. Some wine there. Ho!' (429).

By now it will be clear that it is somewhat difficult to fix Dick's dialectal background. In his 'sanest' moments – and these are, from the language point of view, short – Dick speaks what is fundamentally the standard dialect. What we know about him would suggest that this ought to be the case, although the matter is complicated by Dick's showers of slang. Much of his slang is in keeping with the abrupt about-turns so typical of his speech, and exhibits a startling but effective brevity. This is specially so when used, after bemoaning his lot in this world (as he sometimes does), to sum up the various strokes of fate directed against him. He experiences, for example, a 'stifler' (67), a 'baffler' (161), a 'crusher' (374), and no less than seven 'staggerers' (254, 432). The matter is further complicated by the application – often simultaneous – of no less than four registers: genteel, melodramatic, legal and mercantile. In his opening scenes, especially, Dick slips into his own form of the genteel register, one as preposterously pompous as it is abundantly entertaining (24), and containing a hint of the 'contrast' mode of no less a personage than Mr Micawber (58, 67). From Dick's legal expressions and his own peculiar forensic manner (19–20), one gathers that he had, at some time or other in his chequered past, worked in a lawyer's office – there seems, indeed, much of the author himself in his creation's antics. In Dick's own words, however, 'The law don't agree with me ... It isn't moist enough, and there's too much confinement' (373). Another position he once held must have been of a mercantile nature, as is made clear by his terminology when treating Quilp to a 'shower of buffets' (99–100).

Dick's idiolect can be divided into three chief rhetorical categories. Structurally, the most significant is his love of reasoning, of building up logical arguments. This clearly stems from the above-mentioned legal training, and reaches proportions at once engaging and zany: 'a small party of twenty – making two hundred light fantastic toes in all, supposing every lady and gentleman to have the proper complement' (58). These private bouts of reasoning, often long, occur as frequently as his public flights of poetic fancy and gentility, and are equally spiced with abrupt colloquialisms (254) and trips into the exotic, as when he concludes that Sally Brass cannot be a dragon because 'they have a habit of combing their hair' (271). His calling Sally a 'dragon' is, too, just one illustration of yet another of Dick's richly imaginative speech habits: that of inventing nicknames for those around him. Among other names, Sally is also, for example, a 'Mermaid' and a 'sphynx of private life', her brother is 'Baron Sampsono Brasso', and Quilp a 'Bedlamite', 'deluding dwarf', 'evil spirit' and 'Salamander', to give some of the more apt. This is just one, the most original, aspect of what can be called the 'salutation urge'. Further, Dick either habitually repeats the name of the person he is addressing or simply throws in the appellations 'sir' or 'ma'am' when standing on his (theatrically) genteel dignity. The typical Swiveller contrast is supplied when the irrepressible Cockney wit of Dickens himself takes over. This metaphoric impudence is very much akin to the same quality in Sam Weller, as in Dick's response when Sally asks him if he has seen a silver pencil-case, allegedly missing: 'I didn't meet many in the street. ... I saw one – a stout pencil-case of respectable appearance – but as he was in company with an elderly penknife, and a young toothpick with whom he was in earnest conversation, I felt a delicacy in speaking to him' (433).

For many readers, perhaps the most obvious of Dick's many speech eccentricities is that which the author himself, in a typical Dickensian aside, calls his habit of 'running on ... with scraps of verse as if they were only prose in a hurry' (61). These 'scraps of verse' bring, of course, distinctive stylised rhythms, whether dramatic or satirical, to the fictional speech. A typical illustration is Dick's way of bemoaning the loss of his former love Sophy Wackles – once more with its interpolation of the remnants of a trivial popular song of the day, reminding one of the illimitable creator himself (414). A rhythmic feature of a rather different, more syntactic nature (though still bound up with his verse habits) is Dick's tendency either to repeat phrases or words: 'What is the odds so long as the . . .' (17), or 'miserable orphan' (171); or, like many other Dickens characters, to build up a series of sentences on the same basic construction, as in his 'shall I' (253) or 'I hope' (374) series. These delightfully varied rhythmic patterns are always breaking through; virtually his last words in the book – his imagination incorrigible to the end – are: 'Strew then, oh strew, a bed of rushes. Here will we stay, till morning blushes' (488).

Basically, and above all initially, Dick indulges in his pseudo-poetic or genteel fancies either for the sheer fun of it or as a necessary antidote to the bleak failures of his everyday life. The rather ridiculous first impression he makes covers a very real, down-to-earth, logical, at bottom good-hearted man. Gabriel Pearson has drawn attention to the structural importance gradually extended to this character, seeing his speech as a 'subversive commentary' against both Nell and Quilp.[10] If correct, this would imply less a change in the kind of speech habits Dick uses and more one in the content and in the extent to which he uses some of them. This actually does prove to be the case. His soliloquising bouts of reasoning increase as the plot develops, and although the rhetorical – one might say 'bardic' – element still exists, it is far less emphasised. The genteel manner is also turned on only at specific moments. But, if anything, there is an increase in the play-acting element.

The turning point, that moment when Dick not only begins to regard his destiny with something more than shallow facetiousness, but even begins to mock himself openly by means of his own fantasy, is the scene – almost the exact middle of the book – when, having just been installed through Quilp's agency in Brass' office and previous to which he had been made hopelessly drunk by Quilp, he begins to ponder on the moment of truth experienced in that state and on his general fortunes:

What shall I be next? Shall I be a convict in a felt hat and a grey suit, trotting about a dockyard with my number neatly embroidered on my uniform, and the order of the garter on my leg, restrained from chafing my ankle by a twisted belcher handkerchief? Shall I be that? Will that do, or is it too genteel? Whatever you please, have it your own way, of course. (253)

This tone is new, frankly questioning, even sarcastic, tending to self-mockery. After this point, his 'snatches of verse' become rarer and shorter (twelve in the first five of his scenes, five in the following ten), and his play-acting less frivolous, now containing a distinctly wry, more pithy tone. Note, for instance, how he gravely tells Quilp that he (Dick) is not cut out for the law and that he is considering 'running away. ... Towards Highgate, I suppose. Perhaps the bells might strike up "Turn again, Swiveller, Lord Mayor of London." Whittington's name was Dick. I wish cats were scarcer' (373).

More frequent, too, become the 'saner' passages, those in which he reasons or talks sensibly. Now his reasoning is a search for truth in the everyday world and in himself, whereas in the initial scenes he is always calculating, and fairly cold-bloodedly at that. In the above scene with Quilp, this more serious strain begins to underline his better self, that warmer, more sensitive, more compassionate side. Whatever fantasy, theatricality or zaniness remains is put, now, to effective structural use. One chapter, for instance, ends with Little Nell turning from gazing into a deep and murky well in the crypt of the old church to look at the setting autumnal sun: the well symbolising her future grave, the setting sun her early death. The succeeding chapter, in stark contrast, presents us almost at once with the following banter between Dick and Mr Chuckster, one of his 'Glorious Apollers':

'Won't you come in?' said Dick. 'All alone. Swiveller solus. "'Tis now the witching —"'
'"Hour of night!"'
'"When churchyards yawn,"'
'"And graves give up their dead."' (415)

This is an unconscious (perhaps even conscious) parody of the Nell passage; the more so as Dick begins the scene by applying 'black crape' to his hat as a symbol of mourning for the loss of his Sophy. His preceding remark, if seen in the light of the above juxtaposition, is directly derisive: 'And this ... is life, I believe Oh, certainly. Why not? I'm quite satisfied. ... Ha, ha, ha!' (414). In a similar manner, his card-playing with the Marchioness and the attendant pseudo-dramatic speech (429–31) burlesque the card-playing scenes, with their stiffly melodramatic language, of Nell's grandfather. Dick's speech is still the comic mixture of scraps of verse and colloquialisms, but the tact and tender feeling reflected in it is a whole world removed from the Swiveller roistering with Fred Trent in the opening pages.

Thus, the change in Dick Swiveller's role in the novel is reflected very distinctly in his actual speech. And what two more different purposes could be served by a single idiolect form than the diverting though shallow rhetoric of the initial Swiveller and his later idiom, equally diverting but now of a structural significance which is at times profound? Indeed, of all the people in this somewhat lop-sided book, he is the only one – with the marginal exception of Quilp – who develops into more than a mere cipher, more than an exotically genteel flash-in-the-Dickensian-pan. His is a complex character – a thinking person, honest and upright, filling significantly and memorably the oversimplified gap between the two poles of the novel; or, rather, providing the Quilp–Brass nether world with a far richer, far more satisfying counter-pole than that of Nell and her like. Better still, as with all Dickens' greatest idiolects, we can also pluck Dick's idiolect, as it stands, from the novel; for, in all its teeming variety and happy fusion, it must be counted one of the most engaging simply to be read aloud and listened to.

The Old Curiosity Shop brings to a close Dickens' first great flush of spontaneous enthusiasm for the writing of fiction. Although the first four novels contain many pages of expressively eloquent writing and a number of brilliantly variegated idiolects, they also show obvious signs of that haste and improvisation already pointed out in these lines. In these early novels, the ebullient young author was – albeit with irrepressible self-confidence, unlimited energy, youthful high spirits and a rare talent for improvisation – drawing primarily on his prodigious natural gifts without allowing himself time to harness them. For all that, and as I have already attempted to indicate, there are more than a few traces of the developments to come, particularly those of a structural nature. In the discussion of the next two novels, *Barnaby Rudge* and *Martin Chuzzlewit*, I shall try to make clear that now

Dickens was obviously beginning to reflect more seriously – more consciously, if one will – on the whole direction and purpose of an art which has remained unique in English fiction; further, that these reflections later led to a fundamental reorganisation of his language techniques as a whole and of his fictional speech in particular.

It may seem odd to pair in such a way the two novels now to be discussed, but it is to be emphasised that they occupy a transition phase for the following reasons: *Barnaby Rudge*, although belonging chronologically to the novels just discussed (it was begun exactly one week after the last episode of *The Old Curiosity Shop*), had been planned years previously and again and again taken up, thus, inevitably, forcing Dickens to give it more thought. This is not to say that the novel is better than those preceding it, but that more signs of care are apparent, especially in the development of its thematic structure, and these allow the reader to draw certain conclusions. *Martin Chuzzlewit*, on the other hand, was begun after a break from novel-writing of over a year (a period that included Dickens' first trip to America), a break which enabled the author not only to fling himself back into work refreshed, but also presented him with the opportunity of fully digesting the greatly varying experience of the first five novels.

8 *Barnaby Rudge* and *Martin Chuzzlewit*

Barnaby Rudge,[1] one of Dickens' two historical novels, is on[ly] partly in the 'Newgate' tradition popular at the time. It manifes[ts] much, though, of Carlyle's influence as well as that of Scott. O[f] more importance for this discussion is the fact that for the fir[st] time in his fiction, Dickens consciously set out to stabilise h[is] methods. A close examination of the two sections of the boo[k] taken together with the two plots, shows that they evince con[n-] siderable skill in their interweaving. In addition, the narrativ[e] voice is in many ways now more distinctive, less self-consciou[s.] New, for instance, is a beautifully applied poetic mode. Howeve[r,] in this voice it is the superb, powerfully dramatic descriptions [of] the mob violence in the anti-Catholic Gordon riots of 1780 whic[h] form the high point of the novel. The reader is carried along [–] overwhelmed is a better word – by a rhetorical technique whic[h] achieves its combination of frenzied activity, terror and tensio[n] through the accumulation of sickening effects, through relentle[ss] syntactic repetition, and through a cinematographic techniqu[e] focusing now here, now there, now from afar, now close u[p.] Moreover, we can also find Dickens' first tentative, often ver[y] effective attempts at symbolic writing. This is apparent not on[ly] in the narrative passages, but also, strikingly, in the speech [of] some of the characters: that of Dennis, the dehumanised hang[-] man, personifying what has become corrupt in the people; that [of] Hugh, the 'natural man' forced into evil by an uncomprehendin[g] world; and that of the dark world of Barnaby and Gordo[n] standing for a future still striving to be born.

With the exception of Miss Miggs' idiolect, and, to a degree, of Ned Dennis', there is in this novel a pointed absence of those inspired bursts of unforgettably vivid fictional speech that so often regale the reader of Dickens' works. In this respect, only *A Tale of Two Cities* is more subdued. That unusual and repulsive character Ned Dennis does not make his first appearance till halfway through the book; from then onwards, however, he plays a dominant structural role. His minor but effective idiolect is completely rooted in Dickens' version of the non-standard dialect of London. Furthermore, besides his ugly professional tag 'to work off' – meaning to hang someone – his speech is personally typified by his euphemistic phraseology which images the overweening and perverted pride he has in his repulsive occupation. It is primarily and fittingly composed of short, brutally abrupt sentences, many in the form of the imperative or the interrogative, rhetorical or otherwise. He is directly in the Sikes–Quilp succession, but now the sadism is officially sanctioned. An appalling commentary on the corruption he has undergone is his reprimanding of those Newgate prisoners pleading to be released from the death cell. Dickens, typically, enhances the grotesqueness of Dennis' response by the use of epistrophe, five clauses ending with 'a' purpose for you' (501). The occasional blending of dramatic irony into the speech of Dennis as well as of others is a further indication of the author's new, more thoughtful, methods: 'You'll be the death of me' (283) says Dennis to Gashford, Gordon's dissembling secretary, these being almost his first words in the book. Dennis' idiolect becomes unconvincing only when Dickens – again typically – slips in a longer, syntactically very uncharacteristic oration, as in Dennis' account of how he hanged Mary Jones (284).[2]

THE RHETORIC OF OBSESSIVE PATTERNS IN HYPOCRISY

Miss Miggs, that 'sour and shrewish woman' (xxi), is the domestic servant of Mr and Mrs Varden, around whose family a great deal of the book's plot revolves. She aspires to the affections of Mr Varden's apprentice, Sim Tappertit, and is, therefore, intensely jealous of the Varden daughter, Dolly. Miggs is also bound up with the Gordon riots by being an ardent supporter of the anti-

Catholic cause. It is worth noting that of all Dickens' fictional characters, what she says is reported most frequently in free indirect speech. This lends considerable authorial irony to her vindictive, hypocritical outbursts. Like Dennis', her idiolect is firmly rooted in Dickens' version of the Cockney dialect. She has a particular fondness for the substitution of 'w' for 'v' ('wessel', 'wanities') and for the use of 'as' as a relative pronoun – the 'irrelevant pronoun' (546) as the author calls it. Both phonologically and lexically, her speech indicates even more individuality. When telling the rioters how to get up to her attic prison, her non-standard pronunciation also serves to draw attention to Dickens' below-the-surface vulgarity: 'the two-pair bedroom ... which do not bear, but the contrairy' (482); the same applies to her malapropism 'aperiently' (388), also found, more appropriately, in Mrs Gamp. Her blend words reveal considerable imagination: 'prenounce' (483) from 'pronounce' and 'renounce'; 'relude' (313) from 'refer' and 'allude'; 'repeal' (148) from, ironically, 'appeal' and 'revoke'. A sardonic comment on her own character is her remark 'titiwate theirselves into whitening and suppulchres' (546), almost certainly a corruption of 'whited sepulchre' (Matthew xxiii: 27), meaning hypocrite.

Without a doubt, Miggs' most personal, unusual and distinct linguistic idiosyncrasy is her tendency, when aroused, to pour out streams of words ending in 's'. It will be found that these are mostly nouns, regardless of the validity of accidence or not; indeed, when her indignation rises to fever pitch, she will add an 's' to almost anything, as is proved by the hysterically vindictive outburst she directs against her arch-rival, the pretty Dolly Varden (546–7). Here there are no less than twenty instances showing a particular predilection for adding an 's' to words ending with the suffix '-ion'. Even more outrageous is her concluding variation in this example: 'pinching ins nor fillings out'. It is interesting to note that the first half of the book – comprising six of the total of twelve scenes in which she appears – contains barely a hint of what is to come in this respect: we have only 'intentions' which occurs three times (105, 169, 205), and of which variations are to be found in the second half. It would seem that this linguistic device did not occur to the author until the weekly episodes were well under way. Thereafter a progressive increase in its application is to be observed, rising gradually from eleven instances in her seventh scene to as many as twenty-four in her final one (617–18). When it appears, it undeniably adds to the intensity of Miggs' excitement as well as being comical in itself.

Apart from the 's'-adding obsession, Miggs' idiolect is chiefly individualised by means of certain well-defined rhetorical features. Six main groupings can be distinguished, one of which, her Cockney sharpness, pervades practically everything she says. Like the Wellers or the Dodger, she is never at a loss for an apt, cheeky comparison or remark, even when taken by surprise: 'Why I wish I may only have a walking funeral, and never be buried decent with a mourning-coach and feathers' (70). Also typically Cockney is her eye for detail, this coming out especially in her continual references to her sister.[3] This last-named feature prefigures Mrs Gamp's references to Mrs Harris, for Miggs' sister never actually appears. There is much, indeed, that generally hints at that idiolect queen, Mrs Gamp: Miggs' frequent resort to religious imagery, for instance, especially from the Bible, a usage closely bound up with her fanatical intolerance and hypocrisy ('potter's wessel', earthly wanities', 'base degenerating daughters', etc.). A further product of her intense but perverted emotions is the extreme exaggeration manifested in her speech. This comes out above all in streams of passionate, often wildly hysterical, adjectives: Mrs Varden is 'the mildest, amiablest, forgivingest-spirited, longest-sufferingest female as ever she could have believed' (170), as well as in the habitual application of 'so', 'such' and the auxiliary 'do'. In Miggs' later appearances, there is a definite falling off in the usage of these last-named words: the ruling tone becomes one of jealousy and bitterness rather than hypocrisy. The intensity of her feelings is also very apparent in the inordinate number of exclamations, ejaculations or variations thereof, usually repeated two, three or more times, one after the other, and rising in intensity: 'Gracious! ... Goodness gracious! ... Goodness gracious me!' (70). Once more in the later appearances, there is a gradually increasing application of rhetorical questions with a whole flood in her final say (615). Finally, her overweening egotism comes out again and again in her persistent recourse to the first person singular pronouns, these often being followed by the conditional or by such verbs as 'hope', 'believe', 'think', 'know', 'hate' and 'love', all invariably hypocritical in their application (55, 56 ff.).

In Miggs' speech there is a habitual verbal or phrasal repetition that shows an almost paranoiac determination to be heard, a determination clearly springing from a deep-rooted inferiority complex (71). Closely related to this rhythmic pattern – one that imposes a fairly marked framework on Miggs' floods of rhetoric – is her habit of immediately confirming any statement she herself has just made (71). These repetitive rhythmic patterns occur with fair regularity right through Miggs' appearances, revealing just a few fluctuations in their application. Such a feature is of further interest in that it contains a hint of some of Dickens' later, more pronounced developments in this line, in particular those connected with anaphoric sequences and the like.

As the above has underlined, Dickens conceived many of Miggs' more important speech mannerisms as he was going along. In this particular, Miggs' whole characterisation receives a stimulus in the second half of the novel, during which, both linguistically and rhetorically, she grows considerably in stature as a literary character. However, two features of the idiolect – Miggs' use of the first person singular pronouns and of religious phraseology, both rhetorical aspects of her vindictive, selfish hypocrisy – arise constantly on each of her appearances in the novel. Thus, it is evident, in this respect at least, that Dickens had a clear conception from the very beginning of the kind of figure he wished to set before the public. It must be remembered, that he had a deep distrust of the fanatical kind of Protestantism practised by such as Miggs and her mistress Mrs Varden.

It is not enough to say that she forms the basis of yet another of 'Dickens's easy, cheap jokes against women [although] the humours in which the joke is clothed are, for once, good enough to dispel distaste'.[4] She can be seen, it is true, as a rather more complex successor to that frustrated middle-aged spinster, Rachel Wardle (*PP*). But, as the highly imaginative, passionately obsessive rhetorical devices show, she has a deep need, one as valid as that of any other person, to resist what is in fact tyrannous, unjust and, indeed, cruel – for her life of subjugation is nothing else. Unpleasant, then, though she may be, she deserves – and by the last scene extracts – more than a little of our sympathy.

Thus, all her idiolect features, particularly the rhetorical ones, are not only singularly ingenious and, frequently, forcefully humorous in themselves, they also very effectively serve an important and not immediately obvious role in the novel. In her final bitter outburst, as James Kincaid points out, 'The laughter has been turned back on us.'[5] An additional aspect of her speech –

one shared to a degree by other characters in the novel – which is of no little structural significance is supplied by the continually recurring images of breaking in or bolting in (69–74). Finally, a number of Miggs' idiolectal features can undoubtedly be seen to prefigure many to be found in the great idiolect of her justifiably famous successor, Sairey Gamp. It is safe to say that without Miggs, the latter's richly variegated speech would not have occurred in quite the form in which it does.

As the opening chapters (excluding the very first) so bountifully prove, Dickens set about work on *Martin Chuzzlewit*,[6] his sixth novel, relatively refreshed, full of both a renewal of his old high spirits and a consciousness of ever-growing powers. Indeed, as one critic points out, this book is remarkable for 'the delight Dickens takes in exploiting language with the skill of a performing artist'.[7] The author spared no pains in the construction of a novel more artistically satisfying all round than any he had produced until then. It is, for instance, through the underlying theme of selfishness and greed, and the results thereof, the first to be consciously endowed with at least a skeleton of unity in respect to subject matter. To aid him in his new approach, Dickens for a second time turned to what seems to have been limited use of memoranda or working plans, although it is not clear how far this went for two sheets only have survived. All this and other signs scattered throughout the novel, plus many remarks in letters written at this time, make it very clear that the novelist is now thinking ahead and is constantly preoccupied with problems of construction. That he was only partially successful – for there is in the novel a superabundance of disconcertingly varied characteristics – is another matter.

To start with, the writing in the authorial modalities reveals some of the best of these new aspects. A poetic element, for example, frequently breaks through: sometimes in a sombre vein, sometimes impressionistic, sometimes tragic with symbolic allusions. This often beautiful mode is also applied, on a significantly solemn note, at the end of many chapters as well as at the conclusion of the novel itself. But over and above the poetic suggestiveness and confident lack of superfluity, there is a further quality, one peculiar, in this intensity at least, to Dickens only, and by which 'the language itself seems an organ of perception, shaping the experience almost as soon as it is received'.[8] This is reflected in the fictional speech as much as in the narrative prose, and is obviously crucial in imbuing both modalities with more structural and universal significance than had previously been the case. Above all, the great idiolects of Mrs Gamp and Mr Pecksniff are paradigms of the new mode. But not only these: to varying degrees, the speech idioms of both Jonas Chuzzlewit and Bailey Junior have also been successfully woven into the general thematic texture, the one mirroring, the other countering the novel's central theme of soul-warping egoism and greed.

Jonas Chuzzlewit is completely and utterly his speech. Although obviously not uneducated, his abrupt unfriendliness renders him deliberately slovenly in what he utters – making it brief, to the point, and interspersing it with colloquialisms, abbreviated or otherwise ('t'other', 'ain't', etc.), slang expressions ('ecod', 'gals', etc.), and terms of abuse ('stupid', 'perverse old file', etc.). In his rudeness, he frequently emphasises a word very strongly, this being indicated by italics (392). In short, his idiolect shows him at every turn following absolutely the motto drummed into him by his father: 'Do other men, for they would do you' (181), a course which leads him finally into murder, in intention into two. After the murder of Montague, Dickens heightens the effect of Jonas' characterisation either by expressing the thoughts of the tortured man through a dramatic form of narrative prose or by presenting his words in the form of free indirect speech, thus very effectively maintaining the mounting tension (773–9).

Bailey Junior is an uninhibited, precocious youth directly in the tradition of the 'Artful Dodger'. Despite the vicissitudes of his external fortunes, his mini-idiolect, thoroughly rooted in Dickens version of the non-standard London dialect, remains throughout defiantly impudent and irrepressibly lively. He is, indeed, the eternal Cockney, forever indulging in cheeky antics when not actually making pert remarks – not for nothing is he a 'a conspicuous feature' (141) of Todgers'. With this young man is taken to an extreme the non-standard feature of doubling negatives, what the author himself calls Bailey Junior's 'redundancy of negatives' (170). Typically, his idiolect bristles with imperatives and interrogative phrases: 'It *is* my gracious, an't it? Wouldn't I be gracious neither, not if I wos him!' (170). Bailey's first disrespectful words to Pecksniff also incorporate that very Dickensian touch, the personalising of inanimate objects (123). His transference to the nefarious world of Tigg Montague gives him, if that is possible, even more precocity and self-possession, plus a ridiculously funny, patronising air – something only the streets of London could throw up: 'a breeched and booted Sphinx' (422–3). Like the Artful Dodger's, Bailey Junior's idiolectal aggressions are a suit of armour donned to protect what is at bottom a more generous nature from the onslaughts of the ruthlessly egotistical city life surrounding him.

COMPLEX PRAGMATISM AND ZANY VERBOSITY IN THE NON-STANDARD MODE

Mrs Sairey Gamp[9] – 'a professional nurse' (xxiv) as she is euphemistically termed – is the possessor of what is probably the most individual, certainly the most complex, idiolect in the whole of Dickens. Of the idiolect's overwhelming mass of non-standard detail, a number of features are either unique to Mrs Gamp or so often used by her that they can be considered completely personal. Phonologically, for example, in addition to the peculiarity of Mrs Gamp's monophthongisation of [ju] to [u], as in 'doo' (due), 'dooty' and 'constitooshun', we can also observe what seems, for the time, a highly personal application of the earlier pronunciation of [oi] as in 'pizon' (poison) and 'jints' (joints) – it will be remembered that the initial inspiration for Mrs Gamp came from a 'nurse' of the older generation who was looking after a friend of Dickens' acquaintance, the rich benefactress Miss Coutts. A further very personal feature, one obviously stemming from her pugnacious personality, is Mrs Gamp's forceful tendency to add an extra syllable to certain words ('gold*i*an', 'mort*i*al', 'serp*i*ant'). Without a doubt, however, the most idiosyncratic of Mrs Gamp's non-standard pronunciations is the use of a sibilant-like consonant usually indicated by Dickens with a [g], as in 'roge' (rose), but sometimes with [dg], as in 'parapidge' (parapets) or just [j], as in 'topjy' (topsy). The source of this sound is probably hinted at in the use of 'indiwidge' (individual) and 'perfeejus' (perfidious), the pronunciation of which was once considered high class; by Dickens' time, it was to be found only from time to time among the lower classes. It would seem likely that Dickens extended its application here to underline a certain thickness of speech on the part of the drink-sodden Mrs Gamp. In view of the mass of detail involved, it is not surprising that there is an occasional inconsistency, 'satigefaction' – 'satisfaction' – and 'rouse' – 'rouge' – for example, appearing in both normal and distorted versions.

In respect to non-standard grammar, three chief categories can be determined: Mrs Gamp's irregular syntax, accidence and freedom with parts of speech. In her seemingly confused syntactic wanderings, she personalises one feature particularly – the use of 'nominativus pendens'[10] – to such a degree that it becomes, as Fowler puts it, its 'most familiar and violent instance':[11] 'which fiddle-strings is weakness to expredge my nerves this night!' (779). Another highly personal syntactic irregularity is her Chiverian 'breathe it never did (814) plus that quaint mix-up 'when the money was declined to be give back' (704), both aspects of what I have termed the 'backward manner'. One inflectional feature – her irregular comparisons – occurs so frequently and reveals such weird flights of the imagination that it can only be called Gampian: 'betterer', 'favouritest', 'smilinest', 'awfullest', etc. Finally, quite apart from her free use of adjectives as adverbs, Mrs Gamp manifests a flexibility in her application of other parts of speech which is almost Elizabethan – or modern! – in effect: 'Whether I sicks or monthlies' (406) or 'as ever any one as monthlied' (462).

In her patterned meanderings through the English language, Mrs Gamp often distorts not only the shape of a word but also its meaning, the results being peculiar to herself. It may be a genuine and significant malapropism, as in 'torters of the Imposition' (464) or 'witness for the persecution' (626), or an unconsciously ironic manipulation, as when she stoutly affirms her willingness to 'certify afore the Lord Mayor and Uncommon Counsellors, if needful' (466). Her lexical eccentricities seem to know no end, for, 'owldacious' to the end, she wears no 'marks', is afraid neither of 'lunacies' nor the 'pelisse', and is able to 'reconize' her 'mortar' with the fact that a 'Punch's show . . . may do it' (i.e. bring on the labour pains). She has, not surprisingly, a marked liking for building up her own exotic constructions: 'disregardlessness' (626), 'proticipate' (625), which is probably a blend word from 'propagate' and 'anticipate', and 'indepency' (631) are just a few. She will, perversely, reverse the normal order: 'contrairy quite' (631), or join two words where one would be sufficient: 'directly minnit' (777) and 'widder woman' (317); sometimes, in fact, this linguistic doubling is carried out to the length of two full phrases following each other: 'which is a certain loss, and never can repay'

(317). This marvellous flow of lexical distortions, of which the foregoing are just a few, highlights Mrs Gamp's startlingly vivid and pointed imagination, putting her on a linguistic level shared otherwise only by Sam and Tony Weller.

Mrs Gamp's idiolect is typified both professionally and personally. Her speech is dotted, for instance, with words and phrases from as well as references (often vulgar) to her 'nursing' profession (406). With these one can also include all those – and, again, there are many – connected with life and death. Far more eye-catching, though, is Mrs Gamp's 'never-ending' manner, one made up of an endless stream of haphazard recollections from the past (some of doubtful validity), mixed at random with completely irrelevant details concerning the present. The length of some of these 'runs' – her regaling *seven* others during afternoon tea at Jonas Chuzzlewit's house is a classic illustration (704–5) – forces one to imagine that Mrs Gamp speaks at great speed and that those around her are endowed, at least while she is speaking, with infinite patience. Apart from two relatively short appearances, Mrs Gamp indulges at every opportunity she can in such long sustained outbursts. She is incurably garrulous, with an extraordinary eye for 'unnecessary detail', pausing only occasionally for breath and brooking no interruption.

By far the most striking of the many and varied rhetorical features which go to make up Mrs Gamp's star-studded idiolect is simultaneously one of Dickens' most original inventions: a lady who is, in fact, a purely mythical person existing in the mind of Mrs Gamp only, but to whom she refers again and again: 'I knows a lady, which her name ... is Harris' (704). So much of Sairey's extravagant love of detail is lavished on this figment of her imagination that the reader finally feels he knows more about Mrs Harris than about many an actual character in the world of novel-writing. The introduction of such a 'person' is, rhetorically, all gain, for 'Thus does every incident narrated by Mrs Gamp assume the form of conversation on a quasi epic scale'.[12] It is important to note, though, that she quotes her fictitious friend always for the most realistic of purposes: with a view either to direct monetary profit, as in the recital aimed at Mr Pecksniff (314), or to ensuring future work, into which category comes her grotesque address to Mr Mould, the undertaker (404–8). More work means more money and hence the possibility of gratifying her never-latent desire for alcohol. To further her purposes, she persuasively practises excessive but indirect self-flattery: and this is where Mrs Harris comes in. Sairey's character – and this is borne out by practically everything she says in the book – is essentially pragmatic, amoral rather than immoral, and in this she resembles the Artful Dodger. She lives completely for personal gain, never experiencing any personal doubts about her behaviour. Not for her the soul-searching soliloquy – Mrs Harris is invention enough.

Less immediately striking, but of profound general significance, is Mrs Gamp's recourse to religious phraseology. Not one of her scenes passes without her making some such reference or other, much of it, naturally, very distorted or jumbled, and the major part stemming directly from the Bible. In Mrs Gamp's eyes, the 'land of the living' (425) is 'a wale of grief' (318), a 'Piljian's Projiss of a mortal wale' (404), or a 'walley of the shadder' (462) in which we must do 'our painful dooty' (410) towards our 'feller creeturs' (314) and 'seek not to protcipate' (625), but go 'like a lamb to the sacrifige' (626), to which end we need all 'our religious feelins' (462) to appreciate 'the sufferins of other people' (463) and to live without 'bearin' malice in our arts' (749), even if 'led a Martha to the Stakes for it' (425); then all the ''torters of the Imposition' (464) will never, 'till death' (631) – that 'happy releage' (705) – allow the 'twining serpiant' (759) to gain entry. And 'that's the sacred truth' (705), in 'Bible language' (716); so we must 'be joyful' (778) and not such who are better banished to 'Jonadge's belly' (624), if 'this tearful walley would be changed into a flowerin' guardian' (704), for 'Rich folks may ride on camels, but it ain't so easy for 'em to see out of a needle's eye' (407).

There are, in fact, two aspects of this form of speech which make it exceedingly diverting as well as generally significant. Firstly, the conspicuous mixture of biblical with very non-standard colloquial language, and, secondly, the weird, one might say imaginatively pregnant transformations of otherwise familiar passages from the Bible. Mrs Gamp is not a hypocrite; she is too pragmatic for that. This language falls quite naturally from her lips, and she is not at all conscious of anything unusual in the phraseology she uses. Nor is she, it follows, mocking the religious attitudes of those with whom she comes into contact – for this she has too little time, patience or interest. If anything can be detected behind the words, it is more a kind of resigned but realistic fatalism. Be that as it may, this rhetorical feature in all its fascinating variety underlines perhaps more than any other the rare extent to which Dickens' genius was in contact with the very roots of English culture to its basis in the common people.

There is a marked figurative power in much of Mrs Gamp's speech, and this picturesque quality, reinforced by the down-to-earth expressiveness of the colloquial idiom, has clearly gone through the same Gampian filtering processes as the abovementioned religious element: 'we never knows wot's hidden in each other's hearts; and if we had glass winders there, we'd need keep the shetters up, some on us, I do assure you!' (464). About Jonas, 'All the wickedness of the world is Print to him' (424), and Mrs Harris' father sings 'with a voice like a Jew's-harp in the bass notes' (715). Her lapse into the melodramatic mode is pure theatrical comedy: 'never shall you darken Sairey's doors agen, you twining serpiant' (759). Indeed, her 'wild flights' are sometimes so wild that they verge on the zany, as in her description of Mrs Harris' husband's brother who, as a result of his mother being allegedly frightened by a bull into a shoemaker's shop while pregnant for him, is 'marked with a mad bull in Wellington boots upon his left arm' (704). Others move in a logic obscure to those around her if unfamiliar with the midwifery branch of her profession, and which also reveal Dickens' tendency to indulge a covert vulgarity (627). The weirdness of her imagination and innate impudence colour even her complete indifference to the fate of others: the delirious Lewsome, for example, would 'make a lovely corpse', and, glancing out of his sick-room window, this ungainly old alcoholic is 'glad to see a parapidge, in case of fire, and lots of roofs and chimley-pots to walk upon' (411).

Another feature of these richly imaginative Gampian asides – asides Dickens also delighted in distributing so freely in his role as narrative voice – is the sudden stark objectivity, often sharp with sarcasm, which imbues so many of them, coming like a dash of cold water. These are, of course, yet another aspect of that now familiar pragmatic nature of hers with its relentless materialistic purposefulness (320). As is shown by her curt dismissal of Bailey Junior's supposed death, the fatalistic indifference of her objectivity can verge on the frightening. Hence, for all her ignorance and the fact that she spends a great deal of the time in a drunken haze, Mrs Gamp is supremely clear-sighted and to the point when needs be. She plainly realises that 'facts bein' stubborn and not easy drove' (786), they must be utilised with care if she is to put them to her own use; but not before she submerges them in the great ocean of her imagination. Well could she present herself simply and incontestably thus: 'Gamp is my name, and Gamp my nater' (425), this meaning nothing in normal human terms and yet everything in Mrs Gamp's.

Three other, less important, rhetorical features remain to be noted: Mrs Gamp's self-vindicatory phraseology, her partiality for terms of endearment, and her use of 'but'. Mrs Gamp is excessively fond of introducing or linking her floods of persuasive rhetoric with such self-vindicatory expressions as 'I'll not deceive you' or 'I will not denige'. These protestations of honesty – invariably fake – crop up when Mrs Gamp is busily whitewashing herself, a frequent occurrence! Closely allied to this fawning approach to those around her is the flood of honeyed appellations she releases when bent on flattery; Mercy Chuzzlewit alone, for example, comes in for 'pretty dear', 'sweet thing', 'my little bird', 'my darling dovey of a dear young married lady', and 'my precious chick'. When infiltrated by the religious element discussed above, such an approach becomes a blessing invoked by an apparently benign Mrs Gamp: 'blessed is the man', 'Bless their precious hearts'. Her 'Wishin you lots of sickness' (468) is for Sairey identical with a blessing anyway. Finally, probably no single word – not excepting her use of 'which' as a conjunction – falls so frequently from Mrs Gamp's lips as the word 'but'. As a rule, she applies it conjunctionally, on occasion, though, as a preposition. It will be established that either she is hypocritically emphasising the humbleness of her position in such a way that a 'but-clause' (or series of such) is demanded, a classic illustration being provided in her aggressive reaction to Jonas on the wharf (631), or, typically, she is bent on flattery, piling up sentences to round them off with a 'punch-line' beginning with 'but' – the rambling, obsequious discourse she directs at Mr Mould (the undertaker, hence a source of business) contains several such punch-lines, to all of which he ignominiously succumbs (404–8).

The very pronounced rhythmic patterns of Mrs Gamp's idiolect come under two general headings: the schematic patterns stemming from syntactic repetition and the metrical patterns that transform much of her speech into blank verse. The first category embraces Mrs Gamp's singular habit, when in company, of addressing each person in turn. Her three-fold 'To think as I could see ...' (703–4), for instance, casts such a spell over the listeners that they are struck dumb. It is a speech idiosyncrasy which provides an underlying pattern of strong regular rhythms, making her idiolect ideal for reading aloud; it became, indeed, one of Dickens' most successful public readings. Of course, the egotistical, material reasons alluded to above lie at the root of this mannerism, too. It is one which, subjecting the recipients as it does to a kind of rhetorical fusillade, is eminently suitable for silencing, overwhelming or convincing them, as needs be (424–5). Moreover, it imposes an ordered framework on an otherwise chaotic collection of idiolectal incidence.

A more subtle and artistic development of complex rhythmic patterns is to be found in the iambic pentameters of Mrs Gamp's non-standard speech. The following are the chief observations that can be made: firstly, deliberate stress of non-standard words, a procedure that even involves alliteration:

But Í will nót deníge
that Í am wórritéd and wéxed this dáy,
and wíth good réagion, Lórd forbíd! (624)

Secondly, a varying choice is continually made between 'this here', 'that there' and 'this' or 'that', depending on the metrical or auditory needs: 'hold that there nige of yourn, I beg you, sir' (812). Thirdly, a similar choice is exercised between the standard and non-standard past tense forms: 'I thought I smelt her wen she come' (758). Fourthly, standard and non-standard features are mixed for the sake of rhythmic symmetry, as in the following:

Excúge me íf I mákes remárk, that hé may néither bé
so wéak as péople thínks, nor péople máy not thínk he ís
so wéak as théy preténds, and whát I knóws, I knóws;
and whát you dón't, you dón't; so dó not ásk me, Bétsey.
(755)

Fifthly, adverbs are applied both regularly and irregularly, the choice, again, being made on metrical grounds: 'performing beautiful upon the Arp' (814) and 'There she identically goes!' (626). Lastly, the incorporation of archaic usage to increase rhythmic stress: 'Say not the words, Mrs Harris' (404) and 'seek not to proticipate' (625). The wonderful poetry of the resulting blank verse, with its surety of tone and irresistible energy, is far removed from the uninspired monotony of the kind of blank verse that Dickens fell into for (say) the unduly prolonged decline of Little Nell. In the words of W. J. B. Owen, 'Mrs Gamp is a poet ... [She] has two Englishes, if not three – standard, non-standard and archaic – and draws upon them all to answer the exigencies of her poetic daemon.'[13]

In the miraculous *tour de force* which is Mrs Gamp's idiolect, Dickens was working with a prodigious variety of material and on several levels at once. Basically, there are the 'three Englishes' into the blending of which the author fused the strikingly personal linguistic and rhetorical features already discussed, imprinting on the whole symmetrical rhythms of staccato stridency or poetic expressiveness – Sairey's idiolect being 'perhaps the greatest triumph in literature of verbal collage'.[14]

To judge her by her language alone – and more completely than any other character in Dickens, she *is* her language – this 'nurse' from the lower reaches of nineteenth century Cockney society is the possessor of an incredibly exotic imagination, a head chock-full of an infinite diversity of facts, and a heartlessly pragmatic nature. All this is fired by a selfish, aggressively verbose determination to impress on her listeners qualities which are as non-existent as that sublime creation Mrs Harris herself, and which inevitably lead to those wild verbal flights into zany regions of which there are so many examples and for which she is so justly famous.

One cannot expect Sairey Gamp to 'develop' in the Jamesian sense, to spend her time questioning her motives, for she is eternally and marvellously fixed in a way which renders the label 'flat character' meaningless. As a character, she is so successful artistically just because all her vocal gestures – each eloquent enough in itself – are a reflection of her essential self. This is the chief reason, perhaps, why it is so difficult with this character and her memorable language to avoid that impression of timelessness common to all the greatest characters of fiction. Time does not pass Mrs Gamp by; she has long overtaken it. Through the manifold rhetorical and linguistic flights of her uniquely imaginative idiolect, she can be considered the actual personification of the desires, the feelings, the attitudes, the way of life – of so much, indeed, right down to the more sordid aspects of Victorian society of which she is an undeniable and potent part, and on which she is such a bitterly satirical comment. It is here that her importance lies and not, as a reader of fiction might justly expect, in her structural role in the novel as a whole, a role which is very flimsily based, anyway. For Sairey and her idiolect, the book is simply the backcloth.

On her every entrance, then, she goes on her own inimitable verbal wanderings, standing and falling by the stylistic triumph that is her multi-faceted idiolect, one that is, to take her own words, like 'gold as has passed the furnage' (755). It is a monumental illustration of the extent to which Dickens now possessed the ability to create a mode of fictional speech that, although on the one hand stylised to the artistic extreme, extracts, concentrates and exaggerates on the other enough of the 'echoes' of the dialect in which it is rooted to be convincing, and even, as Amy Cruse has pointed out,[15] to be quoted and imitated by many of the author's readers at the time. As a person, it is true, Mrs Gamp does not deserve the following commendation from Mr Mould, the undertaker, but when one considers the imaginative wonders of her idiolect alone, it is hard not to agree: 'She's the sort of woman ... one would feel disposed to bury for nothing: and do it neatly, too!' (408).

SPEECH AND MR PECKSNIFF: SELF-PARODIC BURLESQUE AND AUTHORIAL UNCERTAINTY

In creating this 'moral man' (12), Dickens makes it clear in his initial description that he was concerned with presenting a person who aimed to hold up to the world a certain image (in the modern sense of the word), an image embodying middle-class respectability. In Victorian society, particularly, this image often bore little comparison with the reality beneath the surface. Further, such persons – continually obliged to bolster up the shaky foundations of this image – are genteely and excessively verbose with special emphasis on the religious register; such respectability, as George Gissing puts it, 'cannot hold its tongue ... the language it affects is wont to be nauseous'.[16] Here a distinction must at once be drawn: nauseous Pecksniff's nature may well be, but not his brilliance of language – 'his style is his salvation'.[17] There is, indeed, above all after the opening scenes, a dichotomy between the two. More often than not, the later Pecksniff seems to be standing outside himself, considering himself with what could be termed wry detachment and an amused, self-questioning air. But, for the reader there is 'no deception' (13) about the initially presented Pecksniff, in respect of whose speech the author remarks 'that if they were not actual diamonds which fell from his lips, they were the very brightest paste, and shone prodigiously' (12). Here one must contradict Dickens, for the words we have from Pecksniff really are, in the main, 'diamonds' and nothing else.

Pecksniff's kaleidoscopic idiolect is rooted, dialectally, in his own singular version of the standard genteel register. Besides being highly ornate, with an excessive utilisation of the complimentary salutation, it is governed by a pseudo-dramatic manner of delivery which, although redolent of the oratorical register, is mainly applied, with few exceptions, by Pecksniff throughout his private life, even to those closest to him. This is drawn out exquisitely in his fondness for his own high-flown 'architectural academy' advertisement, which he quotes both when sober (15) and drunk (151).

It is clear, then, that Pecksniff *is* his 'soft and oily' manner, whether in public or private. In this respect, furthermore, he remains constant throughout the book, despite the gradual addition of other idiolectal features, additions which confirm the author's somewhat vacillating attitude towards his own creation. Pecksniff's high-flown circumlocution leads him into deliciously banal phraseology or platitudes: 'to pursue the giddy round of pleasures that revolves abroad' (86) or 'when regaling on my humble fare' (121). The hypocrisy which is second nature shows itself primarily in Pecksniff's habit of impugning the motives of others at the very moment when his own motives are questionable in the extreme. The platitudinous remarks Pecksniff makes invariably serve as an overtly ironic comment on his own behaviour: 'Horde of unnatural plunderers and robbers' (802) he cries to the assembled characters in the preposterous concatenation scene.

Pecksniff makes it obvious that he revels in the very sound of the words he chooses, and to underline the resulting emphasis they are often written with a capital letter: 'Hope', 'Bounty' (80). But, right at the beginning (15), Dickens adds that Pecksniff indulges in this love of the sound of a word to the detriment of actual meaning. After his initial misuse of 'warbler', though, there are just two more such solecisms in the whole book: 'almanack' for 'calender', a word he confuses with 'calendar' (87), and 'metaphysically' for 'metaphorically' (302). In other words, either Dickens forgot to pursue the mannerism, or Pecksniff's character developed so strongly in the author's imagination during the writing of the monthly instalments that other idiolectal features simply sprang 'fully armed', shall we say, from the personality itself. With an eye on the unforeseen developments undergone at the time by both Pecksniff (who was originally based on a person from real life) and Mrs Gamp, Dickens himself, in a letter to Forster, wrote that it was to him 'one of the most surprising processes of the mind in this sort of invention. Given what one knows, what one does not know springs up; and I am as absolutely certain of its being true, as I am of the law of gravitation – if such a thing be possible, more so.'[18] An extension of the 'right-sound' habit, and equally short-lived, is Pecksniff's inability to find the right word. There are two examples in the opening scene, but only two thereafter (59, 163), the final one occurring as early as the middle of the fourth number – the habit dying virtually at birth, so to speak.

Far more interesting, and a permanent feature of his idiolect, is the vocabulary of Pecksniff's ingrained hypocrisy. Certain words crop up again and again, above all 'humble' or its variation 'lowly', but also 'hope', 'trust', 'heart', 'bosom', 'moral', 'virtue', 'truth', plus 'universe', 'society', 'humanity', 'mankind' and 'duty' – Pecksniff is constantly harping on the fact that he has such. To sugar the pill, he sprinkles his genteel admonitions with a gentle shower of archaic poeticisms: 'perchance', 'may' (20), ''Tis the voice of the sluggard', 'slumber' (150). It is just their very hackneyed quality which makes them so delightful from Pecksniff's lips.

Occasionally there are whole passages, even scenes, when Mr Pecksniff suddenly, for nefarious reasons of his own, moves into an objective mode of speaking which is in stark contrast to the ornate gentility of his customary fawning manner. He does so, for example, very lewdly and with an astonishing directness, in his unwelcome proposal to the impossibly straight-laced Mary Graham (484), and also, hilariously, when shaking his discontented daughter, Cherry, rejected by Jonas Chuzzlewit: 'None of your nonsense, Miss! . . . I'll do it again! (471–2) . . . if you dare to talk in that loud manner'. This 'contrast manner' of delivery is not, however, carried to the lengths found in the idiolects of Dick Swiveller or Mr Micawber, nor is it applied in a way resembling theirs at all. With them it is an integral feature of their idiolects as a whole; with Pecksniff, the move into plain language is undertaken only for the definite purposes referred to above. Moreover, it takes us away completely from that language upon which the originality of this character is based.

An off-shoot of this contrast manner, and one more integral to the idiolect as a whole, is Pecksniff's distinct and frequently occurring tendency to interpolate into his speech explanatory or self-justifying remarks, always with the intention of enhancing the impression he is trying to make. These parentheses usually preserve the ornately genteel style of the main flow. He may, however, slip in an aside in down-to-earth, unadorned English, normally to gull information out of someone softened by the preceding gentility, but sometimes doing so for no obvious reason, albeit the effect remains startlingly amusing. If such an abrupt move into the colloquial comes after a great burst of oratory – as the 'You had better be off' (802), which follows a lengthy diatribe in the concatenation scene – we are reminded, perhaps, of Mr Micawber, though there the real resemblance ends. At times, some of the asides have a whimsically, even regretfully self-questioning air about them that is, I would suggest, somewhat out of character: 'Well, well, what am I? I don't know what I am, exactly. Never mind!' (473).

Pecksniff's highly figurative use of language serves to underline the three fundamentals of his nature: his hypocrisy, sexuality and greed. Of the various categories of imagery which can be specified, two of them are determined by his hypocritical, selfish nature. Firstly, his idiolect is coloured by a conspicuous religious element, one which is resorted to very deliberately and not, as in the case of Mrs Gamp, unconsciously: 'fatted calf' (87), 'sainted parent' (157), 'Oh Calf, Calf! ... Oh, Baal, Baal!' (168), and many others. Secondly, and more subtly, there is the 'silent tomb' (481) image, one recurring directly and indirectly on a number of occasions. The ostensible reference is to his late wife, 'In honour of her memory. For the sake of a voice from the tomb' (150); in fact, it has a significant bearing on his hypocrisy. The reader will remember Miss Miggs' 'whitening and suppulchres' and that it is a probably corruption of 'whited sepulchre' (Matthew, xxiii: 27), meaning 'hypocrite'. It is not difficult to see the connection between Pecksniff's 'silent tomb' references and the biblical analogy for 'hypocrite', and that not only is it an ironic comment that boomerangs back on himself, but also one that signifies an obsession with two things he cannot face: death and, even worse, eternal silence.

Less subtle, but extremely characteristic, is the animal imagery. Not surprisingly, perhaps, this comes especially to the fore when he is excited, an emotional state which leads him to mix the varieties indiscriminately. A very amusing illustration of such confusion is his last tremendous outburst in the book – a long, rather disjointed metaphor aimed at underlining the greed of old Martin's friends and other relatives (802). Much of this animal imagery is, of course, a product of Pecksniff's simmering sexuality – as in 'rampant animals' (116) – though this characteristic comes out far more stridently in those images that are directly sensual. His lascivious nature is laid utterly bare, for instance, in the whole of his avowal of love to Mary Graham (480–4). In this respect, his addiction to the bottle only intensifies his randiness, as Mrs Todgers is forced to find out: 'I should very much like to see Mrs Todgers's notion of a wooden leg' (153). The sexuality of his oft-repeated 'serpent' image is fairly obvious, perhaps a little less so in his persistent reference to the top of Salisbury Cathedral, though the phallic associations of church steeples have been hinted at in at least one modern novel.[19] 'I wouldn't have believed it,' Pecksniff says to Old Martin, 'if a Fiery Serpent had proclaimed it from the top of Salisbury Cathedral' (496). About his late wife and his state of widowhood he even goes so far as to maintain, '*My* Eve, I grieve to say, is no more, sir; but ... I do a little bit of Adam still' (384). Knowing what we do of Victorian conventions, it is a marvel that Dickens went so far, doing so more directly in Pecksniff's speech than, even, in the symbolism of Quilp's smoking through the night (*OCS*, 37–8).

However, the rhetorical feature most likely to endear the average reader is Pecksniff's proclivity to glide into the ridiculous or zany. When attempting, for example, to illustrate through metaphor, he sometimes so overreaches himself that he figuratively lands on his back, creating what Sylvère Monod calls 'graceful ... incongruous metaphors'.[20] Young Martin is a 'leper and a serpent' (210), and with John Westlock, Pecksniff has 'nourished in [his] breast an ostrich, and not a human pupil' (86), meaning obviously 'serpent', a word of which, as we have seen, he was otherwise excessively fond. But, with one exception – 'wolves and vultures, and other animals of the feathered tribe' (802) – all these comic absurdities stem from the first third of the novel. This is also the case with a related feature: a peculiarly inventive quality plunging the reader into a zany world. It is gift Pecksniff shares, of course, with all Dickens' greatest comic characters, and we are not surprised to hear that he used to think 'pickled onions grew on trees' (86). Indeed, allowing for surface differences, Pecksniff is already moving in the bizarre world of Sairey Gamp (87–8).

In Pecksniff's idiolect there are three different kinds of syntactic patterning. Most commonly, he has a tendency to repeat either what he himself has just uttered or the words of the person speaking to him, sometimes very slightly varied. In the former case, it serves to add emphasis to his own statement: 'I am not sorry . . . I am really not sorry' (56). In the case of words of others, it serves a variety of purposes, embracing a peculiar mixture of inquisitiveness, ingratiating hypocrisy and sheer pleasure in the sound of words. His appropriations from the mouth of Mrs Lupin in an early scene strikingly and bountifully fulfil all three purposes (32–4). Thereafter in the novel, this idiosyncrasy, although consistently present, is considerably modified.

Closely related to such confirmative repetitions are Pecksniff's echoes in the form of choral comment. In the scene in which young Martin tries to effect a reconciliation between himself and his grandfather, Pecksniff, acting as the 'Chorus in a Greek Tragedy, delivers his opinion as a commentary on the proceedings' (667). The impact of the iambic pentameters of Pecksniff's echoic interpolations, of the well-chosen, pointed words, reveals, rhetorically, a somewhat unusual Pecksniff. Here, while moulding and directing his language to the definite effect he has in mind, he is keeping a clear eye for beauty of metrical line. Irrepressible to the end, he supplies repetitive interpolations of a rather different nature in the final unravelling scene when, humiliated, he is submitted to interminably long, melodramatic explanations and primitive abuse (in a way, incidentally, that shows the more cruel, juvenile side of Dickens' idea of comedy and justice). The imagination which lighted upon the short, simple syntax of the interjected comments lifts them triumphantly above old Martin's laboured rhetoric, showing it up in all its shallow artificiality. Despite his surface defeat, it is now Pecksniff who, rhetorically speaking, is the real victor in this final scene (805–6).

At first sight there would appear to be but little resemblance between the Artful Dodger, the engaging pickpocket, and Mr

Seth Pecksniff, the 'moral man', yet they do share, in form at least, a tendency when excited to phrase in syntactic groups of three. Moreover, Pecksniff also frequently concludes such a 'threeing' unit with a coda, a kind of rhetorical 'squiggle', so to speak. It becomes clear, too, that he has a distinct fondness within this pattern of ringing the changes on auxiliary verbs, or for building up each line by use of contrast: 'My duty is to build, not speak; to act, not talk; to deal with marble, stone, and brick: not language. I am very much affected. God bless you!' (554); happily, the most far-fetched untruth Pecksniff ever utters. Such schematic patterns prefigure Dickens' almost obsessive use of the same in later life. Here they not only allow Pecksniff to keep talking, but also exert a mesmeric influence on the person to be gulled.

With Pecksniff's idiolect – that 'prodigious achievement of imaginative energy'[21] – the reader swims in a whole ocean of language features whose variety is rivalled by that of Mrs Gamp's idiolect only. But, as his persistent use of parenthetical remarks reveals, he is well aware of the effect his speech is making; he is a man who is able to see through himself and what he is doing. This becomes clearer as the novel gathers momentum, bringing with it a significant move away from the author's original conception. Indeed, almost from the beginning, as the speech discrepencies prove, Dickens found himself gliding between that conception and a tendency to parody the same. With this parody, one gains the impression that Pecksniff is directing it against himself as much as against those around him. The whole world must be made a joke of through language, and, as can easily be guessed, it is Dickens the mimic who is doing so.

It is worth pointing out that after the fourth number (which contains the marvellously funny Todgers episode), although many amusing scenes remain, the zany quality tends to fall away. There is one exception – a scene of high theatrical comedy in which Pecksniff, receiving a surprise visit from old Martin at a moment when embarrassing chaos rules in the house, resourcefully reacts by quickly donning his garden hat and seizing a spade before he opens the door to greet the visitor with a deliciously ambiguous remark. (384). At such moments, Pecksniff's speech, like that of so many Dickens zanies, merges into the Victorian nonsense tradition which began to make itself felt around this time. It is a form of writing that almost defies analysis – certainly such a discussion would go well beyond the limits of these lines.

It must be admitted that the uneven development of some of Pecksniff's speech features has led to a certain lack of general structural balance in the novel as a whole, for it must not be forgotten that Pecksniff is one of its dominating characters. This criticism is virtually nullified, however, when he and his idiolect as a whole are abstracted from the work within which they are found; for, as G. K. Chesterton has so typically put it, 'while Pecksniff is the best thing in the story, the story is the worst thing in Pecksniff'.[22] Here one must add, of course, that Mrs Gamp, Pecksniff's great counterpole in idiolectal brilliance, is just as much 'the best thing in the story', if not more so; certainly she and her idiolect can be abstracted from the novel with equal success, and, indeed, this was actually done. Be that as it may, taken together Mrs Gamp and Mr Pecksniff mark a turning point in Dickens' idiolectal techniques, forming the artistic summit of a series of extraordinary solo achievements of the inventive imagination, achievements which, in this respect, he was never to surpass. With each succeeding novel, from *Dombey & Son* onwards, the emphasis was to be on ever greater structural integration of the fictional speech. Thus, of necessity, Dickens was forced to set limits to his wide-ranging powers of spontaneous invention; the gradual gain on the one hand balancing the gradual loss on the other.

It will now be clear that *Martin Chuzzlewit*, to an even greater extent than *Barnaby Rudge*, is to be considered a transitional novel. This is true not only of its fictional speech – though here, as a comparison with *Dombey & Son* makes clear, the change is at its most apparent – but also of the obvious and for the most part strikingly successful attempts to forge a more functional, a more homogeneous prose style. When John Lucas writes that *Martin Chuzzlewit* is 'a crucial novel in Dickens's development ... a crisis novel',[23] he is underlining a point as significant as it is undeniable.

9 *Dombey & Son* to *Bleak House*

Generally speaking, despite the joys offered by Mrs Skewton and Captain Cuttle, *Dombey & Son*[1] is not the novel in which to look for lavishly varied idiolects full of wide-ranging eccentricity and humour. In his desire to achieve a well-formed integrated structure, Dickens had perforce to put the reins on the spontaneity of his easy-going, natural joviality and comic fluency. This in turn gave him less scope for exercising, in his highly stylised fiction, his unique talents as a theatrical storyteller. Moreover, in spite of Dickens' determined efforts to balance the novel's structure, it somehow managed to get out of control after the death of young Paul at the end of the fifth number. For these reasons, then, *Dombey & Son* must be considered a relative failure.

On the positive side, however, considerable technical strides can be registered, especially in the search for greater structural integration of the fictional speech and a more homogeneous style for the narrative voice. Foretokens of the magnificent stylistic fusion of all the prose modalities arrived at over a decade later are to be seen, firstly in the use of free direct and indirect speech to smooth the transitions between the dialogue and the narrative prose; further, in the way the author now advances plot essentials through the dialogue (the brilliantly executed opening chapter providing an excellent illustration), an economical technique first consciously applied in *Barnaby Rudge*. Then, very importantly, there is the broad dramatic scale of the reiteration at regular intervals of certain key-phrases ('what the waves were saying') which act, in effect, as rhetorical *leit-motivs*, as well as isolated passages of that more concentrated syntactic repetition later to become so obsessive (769–74). A very Dickensian technique now freely resorted to is the so-called 'pathetic fallacy' together with its reverse, people being 'reduced to thing-like characteristics'.[2]

Pervading all these stylistic developments is a deeper, more poetic approach, one that seems to have been determined by the subject matter of the novel – it is a pathetic-sentimental tale based primarily on the workings of pride. This poetic mode brings a beauty of line and insight above all to the depictions of Mr Dombey's inner life (838–43),[3] with their peculiar blend of direct authorial point-of-view and free direct speech. All in all, therefore, Dickens' stylistic techniques in *Dombey & Son* are more mature, more consciously artistic. Comedy, although deliciously present, is merely an incidental feature; pathos is the dominating characteristic of the book's style.

Apart from the considerable idiolects of Captain Cuttle, Major Bagstock and above all Mrs Skewton, there are just two further speech idioms of any note: those of Mr Toots and Susan Nipper. Mr Toots – 'that Innocent' (250) as Susan, his future wife, calls him – is a loveable character: simple-minded, good-natured but permanently embarrassed and tongue-tied. 'Oh, it's of no consequence', his own speech tag, succinctly expresses his actual nature. He is probably one of the most inarticulate creatures in all Dickens, constantly falling into 'a deep well of silence' (251). Yet, for all that, he is a very Dickensian figure, serving as a structural counterpoise to the rhetoric of pompous pride and effusive hypocrisy. A character similar in nature and in relationship to the respective heroine as John Chivery (*LD*), Toots also has his own little private but useless whim: that of addressing letters to himself.

The lady he finally turns to, Susan Nipper, although basically good-natured, is otherwise quite the opposite: ever-suspicious, quick-tempered and very loquacious. Her mini-idiolect is just slightly tinged with non-standard deviations: 'it don't', ''em', etc., but her general manner of delivery – that of shooting everything out in one breath – is very appropriate to her character. Springing from her aggressive self-defence mechanism is Susan's obsessive resort to the peculiar (in intensity and imaginative variety of content) syntactic construction 'I may ... but ...' which appears very frequently, as in 'I may not be Meethosalem, but I am not a child in arms' (614). She has, indeed, an inordinate fondness for the word 'but' almost rivalling Mrs Gamp in its usage. Her speech is also, at all times, coloured by a weird turn of phrase: 'I'll call in them hobgoblins that lives in the cock-loft to come and eat you up alive' (51), tautology (324–5) or quite simply quaintness (606). Although her aggressive honesty can be viewed as part of the vital force opposing the phony (for all their glitter) utterances of the Skewton–Bagstock–James Carker group, the impression is given that her idiolect has been developed more for its own innate qualities rather than for structural reasons.

INVENTIVE BANALITY, PLAIN TALK AND APHASIC MUDDLE

With the 'Hon. Mrs Skewton', playfully known as 'Cleopatra', the reader is, idiolectically, in another world. Her daughter, Edith, marries the widowed Mr Dombey, thus enabling the mother-in-law – from her entry in the seventh number to her exit in the thirteenth – to hold the stage during those scenes in which the novel's action shifts from old Sol's domain back to Dombey's world. As all her speech forms make clear, she is one of Dickens' 'upper-class grotesques' walling out other people with their peculiar eccentricities and their obedience to stale conventions'.[4]

'Cleopatra's' major idiolect, the one she constantly turns on when in public, is a mannered, eccentric aping of the once fashionable Regency register of the upper-class dialect. In private, when alone with her daughter, her manner could not be more different: aggressive, plain and down-to-earth. Perhaps no Dickens character exhibits greater speech dichotomy than Mrs Skewton. It seems, incidently, that the author toyed with developing the bridge 'in short', used twice in her opening scene (289, 294), but decided to drop it, to take it up in the following novel (*DC*) in Mr Micawber's famous idiolect. In addition to the two contrasting idioms, there also exists a fragment of another idiolect: the grotesque aphasic idiom she uses after her paralytic stroke. In this very clever merging of remnants of her two other speech idioms, the bizarre mixture of blend and shortened words is a ghastly commentary not only on her now completely addled brain and inability to articulate, but also on the flimsy values upon which her affected public idiolect had been based (570–1). This public idiolect, however, with all its joys, is the one that will chiefly concern us here.

In her choice of vocabulary, Mrs Skewton's imagination knows no bounds, two categories being discernible: firstly, the general vocabulary of affected speech, this manifesting itself particularly in her superfluous use of adjectives and adverbs qualifying the same. Besides the various derivatives of 'charm', which occur again and again, she reveals an almost equal fondness for 'positively', 'extremely', 'dreadfully', 'excessively', 'perfectly' and 'delightful' (out of which she twists 'delightfullest'). This affectation is also reflected in an equally excessive application of certain verbs ('dote', 'rave', 'adore', 'reproach') and auxiliaries (above all 'must'), as well as in innumerable phrases ('be mute' is one delicious example). Secondly, in her countless variations on the complimentary salutation, Mrs Skewton extends her fawning powers of invention to all around her in public. Each of these persons is regaled with a whole range of hypocritically endearing adjectives that sometimes take on significant undertones. Edith can, for instance, be 'my dearest love' but also 'Wicked one'; Florence 'my darling' or even 'our extremely fascinating friend';[5] 'my dearest Dombey' is simultaneously the 'falsest of men', 'wicked guesser' and a 'cunning man' – the final insult, after her stroke, being 'Grangeby' and 'Domber' (her first husband was a Granger). Ironically, 'My dear Mr Carker' is 'That very sensible friend'. But it is her 'friend' of old, the repulsively sycophantic Major Bagstock, who comes in for broadside after broadside of arch, semi-insulting 'endearments': 'perfidious goblin', 'shocking bear', 'insupportable creature', 'naughty Infidel', 'barbarous being', 'coarse person', and so on. Their obvious brutality (tinged with animal imagery) goes beyond showing up the ridiculous affectation of Mrs Skewton's public manner. They reveal Bagstock's nature in a light not perhaps intended by the speaker, nor interpreted so by the actual recipient.

Empty-headed and foolish old worldling that she is, Mrs Skewton never gives up trying to impress her listeners – if they listen – with a kind of 'get-away-from-the-degeneration-of-modern-times-back-to-the-simplicity-of-Nature' talk. Her outbursts in this vein can be so comically idiotic that without a doubt it is her most individual and entertaining claim to fame. Take the scene at Warwick Castle, for instance, in which Mrs Skewton's sublimely idiotic rambling is theatrically set off by Carker's drily sarcastic interpolations, and of which the following is just a part:

'Those darling bygone times, Mr Carker ... with their delicious fortresses, and their dear old dungeons, and their delightful places of torture, and their romantic vengeances, and their picturesque assaults and sieges, and everything that makes life truly charming! How dreadfully we have degenerated!'

'Yes, we have fallen off deplorably,' said Mr Carker ... (387).

This is her very own speech manner, her unique mode of approach to the world of Society. Above all, it is the actual vocabulary which typifies her as nothing else does – to this extended degree, at least: besides 'Nature' (or 'natural'), 'Soul' and 'Faith', all of which she eternally reiterates, she brings in 'Being', 'Arcadian', 'simplicity', 'seclusion', 'contemplation', and a host of others, each repetition being a further nail in the coffin of her dishonest aspirations. When she informs us that 'Cows are my passion' (289), we are once more reminded that with Dickens' best comic speech we are never far from the zany. Moreover, her expectations in life, so expressed, are more than just good comedy; they are – as so often in Dickens – an unconsciously ironic comment on her own gushing (to use her word) 'poses'.

For 'Cleopatra', the impression being made by any one of her sparkling 'runs' of affectation is the chief purpose of life (even though, with an eye ever on the main chance, she may simply be marking time), so much so that in the process she often simply forgets names. This means that, to fill in space, the speech tag 'what's-his-name' (or a variant) comes up again and again like a musical refrain. This tag alternates with 'and all that' (again with variants) which crops up with equal frequency when she either suddenly loses interest in continuing the flow of affectation or simply cannot find the right word. Sometimes one of those around her – usually her long-suffering daughter Edith – fills the gap, or she just carries straight on, or (again) she finds a word herself. The habitual 'what's-his-name' is the only remnant of her public idiolect to be found in the private, unaffected speech idiom to which she reverts when alone with Edith. It is also, logically, a mainstay of her aphasic speech – she seems to be able to say nothing else to Mrs Brown and her daughter (575).[6] This grasshopper-like quality so characteristic of her garrulous nonsense is intensified both by the continual interpolation of unexpected, often irrelevant, asides and by her fondness for posing questions whether of a rhetorical, 'fill-in' nature or, more likely, to indulge her overweening inquisitiveness. She moves into the book on a question (287), and moves out of it and life in the same way (584).

Unlike those of Mrs Nickleby, Mrs Skewton's parenthetical remarks almost invariably leave the main stream undisturbed. When one also considers that, over and above this, she indulges in a great number of elaborate, over-descriptive relative clauses, the full extent of her rhetorical hopping, skipping and jumping will be appreciated. That she does not lose herself, as Mrs Nickleby does, stems from her determination to keep her eye (and hence her tongue) on a number of matters at the same time. This is structurally significant, for it emphasises the extent to which she has no simple, sincere attitude to life – she merely reacts (in public, and before her stroke) as the plenteously gifted rhetorical opportunist she is.

In addition to those created by the refrain-like interpolations discussed above, even clearer patterns are forced upon Mrs Skewton's idiolect by her manifest preference for the anaphoric mode. We have already experienced an illustration of this mode in her comments on the Middle Ages. Being a more dramatically arresting structure, it enables 'Cleopatra' to hold her audience with greater ease. It also allows her to avoid the necessity of forming complicated sentences requiring serious thought – something of which she is incapable. Thus, a semblance of order is imposed on an otherwise fatuous jumble of gushing effusions. Despite its flimsiness, this order is still able to supply a stinging commentary on the emptiness lying behind the façade, and it is indicative of Dickens' care with language that the habit falls into disuse after her stroke.

Mrs Skewton's fascinating public idiolect is resounding proof of the miracles Dickens could perform with the most banal material when moulding it to the thematic needs of the character concerned. Its immense vitality has as its chief source of energy the 'Heart-Nature-Soul' manner, in which she has been personally typified, as well as the vocabulary of affectation and hypocritical endearment. In the main, the rhetorical features serve to draw out just how time-bound this mincing grotesque is – that her mind is going and that the further she withdraws into the degrading fancies of her artificial youth, the closer she moves to that stroke which must inevitably mow her down. Through her exotic use of the out-of-date Regency register, she becomes a forcible image of a decaying aristocratic order which is fighting a losing battle against the encroaching mercantile class of early Victorian England – a class in itself also ruthlessly satirised in the same novel – to which the older, impoverished order is forced to sell itself in marriage alliances. Moreover, it is not only her actual speech, in all its forms, which is so eloquently effective; the same can be said with equal truth about the prose describing her (521) – the success of the two aspects together being a sure sign that the peculiar genius of the author was at one with the character. Mrs Skewton's public idiolect is, then, an extremely engaging reflection of her refusal to accept time and change. Its contours are, too, thrown into even sharper relief when abruptly contrasted with the aggressive, unadorned straight-from-the-shoulder idiom she reverts to when alone with her daughter. Further, her aphasic idiom after the stroke is a savagely expressive censure of the flimsiness of the tawdry values previously adhered to – her references to herself in the past tense being of a significance not to be ignored. In all, it would be no exaggeration to see her public idiolect as one parallel (only higher up the social scale) to that of Mrs Gamp.

'CATECHISM' CUTTLE AND 'BALMY' BUNSBY

With the simple, good-natured, honest Captain Cuttle, ever admonishing friend or foe to 'overhaul their catechism', the reader is at the other extreme from the Skewton–Bagstock–James Carker pole, and every rough-and-ready word of the captain's complex theatrical idiolect is meant to counteract the moral turpitude behind the phony rhetoric of the other side. It is very firmly rooted in the seafaring register of the non-standard dialect already discussed within these lines, but goes far beyond the mere transference to private life of the professional terms and non-standard detail of a retired sea captain. Of the rhetorical features, the best known is perhaps the speech tag 'when found, make a note', one usually preceded by 'overhaul the book' or some variation thereof, the whole succeeding some outlandish misquotation or other: 'Train up a fig-tree in the way it should go, and when you are old sit under the shade on it. Overhaul the – Well ... I an't quite certain where that's to be found, but when found, make a note of' (267). When carried away by his moralising, he can at times sail right into the zany, as when he talks of 'garden angels' (545) and 'the askings' (= marriage bans, 783). His strong moral convictions frequently bring a touch of the imperative into his speech, especially towards Rob the Grinder, whose slimy nature obviously disgusts him; but it also comes out in his manner of introducing people: 'Here is (are) ...'. This imperative touch, however, is but one side of that pugnacious will of his never to give up without a fight and which also finds expression in his choice of word or phrase.

Cuttle's sincere, unaffected goodness is mirrored in the vocabulary of cheerful morality ('dear', 'poor', 'cherry', 'joy', 'heart', 'love', etc.), as well as in the manifold variety of his affectionate way of addressing Florence and Walter ('Hearts-delight', 'Beauty', 'bright di'mond' and 'brave lad', 'gallant', for example). Indeed, the depth of his tender-feeling for them both can prod him into a rhetoric of solemn rhythms full of poetic overtones in which the non-standard elements, far from jarring, movingly enhance the intensity and sincerity of his utterance. Such a passage as the one beginning 'There's perils and dangers on the deep' (690), with the overwhelming power of its lyrical beauty, makes it doubtful whether any other writer in the English language can rival Dickens in the poetic genius he brought to the fictional presentation of the speech of the lower classes. For all that, as when Cuttle expounds to Toots on Walter's virtues (462-3), an outburst full of a rhetoric that is not the captain's, there are some less convincing moments, but these only slightly mar an idiolect both entertaining and structurally well-integrated. As the captain himself puts it: 'I never wanted two or three words in my life that I didn't know where to lay my hand upon 'em ... It comes of not wasting language as some do' (42).

A miniature yet, for all that, richly rewarding idiolect is the gem of nonsense given to Captain Cuttle's mate, that profoundly taciturn philosopher of nonsense, Jack Bunsby, about whom it is certainly no surprise to hear from his friend that he 'took as many spars and bars and bolts about the outside of his head when he was young, as you'd want a order for on Chatham-yard to build a pleasure-yacht with' (335). Only this could have been the cause of the sheer idiocy of Bunsby's rhetorical questions, nonsensical interpolations and meaningless conclusions: 'Whereby ... why not? If so, what odds?' (338). Cuttle and Bunsby are, as is often the case in Dickens, companion figures such as reach their height in the telling contrasts of that ill-assorted pair Flora Finching and Mr F's Aunt (*LD*), and whose speech idiosyncrasies are considerably enhanced when contrasted in a stylised theatrical manner, one with the other.

THE IDIOM OF BRUTISH TOADYISM

Major Bagstock's obscenely brutal speech idiom, replete with apostrophising incriminations, hypocritical sycophancies and vituperative epithets, lays bare a personage who is, in a sense, even more frightening than any in that line which goes back through Jonas Chuzzlewit, Ned Dennis, Quilp and Squeers to Sikes. Pride, sexual vanity and utter selfishness – all fundamental to the darker thematic structure of *Dombey & Son* – are bound up, one with the other, in the harsh, apoplectic explosions which govern the syntax of this mean, cold-hearted, social parasite. His utterances are, in the main, simply a string of canting variations on his own name, through which he chiefly aims at creating an impression of bluntly candid, rough-and-ready honesty. As in what is his initial declaration in the novel, however, his incorrigible sexual conceit is continually seeping through: 'Joey B., Sir . . . is worth a dozen of you. If you had a few more of the Bagstock breed among you, Sir, you'd be none the worse for it. Old Joe, Sir, needn't look far for a wife even now, if he was on the look-out; but he's hard-hearted, . . . tough, and de-vilish sly!' (85).[7]

The basic callousness of his nature is frighteningly illustrated by the off-hand way he throws off the tragedy of the death of Edith's only child (291). Yet about himself he is sensitive to the extreme, and if someone has pricked his overweening self-esteem, this monster of vindictiveness heaps abuse on him or her by means of an apostrophe shot through with the idiolectal characteristics of his normal speech idiom. The harmless Miss Tox, for example, is subject to a particularly blistering attack of this kind (125). It is very much in keeping that he is a past master in the application of derogatory adjectives and names, Miss Tox, again, coming in for a great many: 'Lucifer', 'scheming jade', 'ridiculous old spectacle', and more in the same vein. This command of epithets is, moreover, horribly flexible, and he is able to turn them to equal account even when flattering. In his approach to Mr Dombey, for instance, he is revoltingly sycophantic, calling himself among other things 'a smoke-dried, sun-burnt, used-up, invalided old dog of a Major' (125). But the final irony is that so much of what he says about others, whether to their faces or behind their backs, is strictly and truly applicable to himself most of all, and vice versa. Take the following words of his to Mrs Skewton: 'A man never heard of Bagstock, Ma'am, in those days; he heard of the Flower – the Flower of Ours. The Flower may have faded, more or less, Ma'am ... but it is a tough plant yet, and constant as the evergreen' (367). And when one considers that in the same novel the simple, kind-hearted Toots calls himself 'a Blighted Flower' (876), the irony is complete! Small wonder that some of Bagstock's best scenes are those with Mrs Skewton or the slimy James Carker, with whom he pursues gruesome duals with no hypocritical holds barred on any side.

With *Dombey & Son*, for all its failings, we are in a newer Dickens world, one that looks forward to the fictional mastery of the later works, and what we have examined above confirms this. In both the authorial modalities and the fictional speech, the process of integration and development have begun to make great strides forward: in the one moving in the direction of a unified though complex prose style, in the other towards a representational use of fictional speech which, in spite of a loss in the original verve and brilliance of touch, proves an invaluable gain for the structure as a whole. It remained to be seen only whether the speech idioms of the characters would be able to recapture their former magic without dispensing with the new structural qualities.

David Copperfield,[8] Dickens' next novel, is without a shadow of doubt 'one of the masterpieces of English narrative prose'.[9] There is nothing less than inspired genius in the almost naive freshness and spontaneity of the impressions of childhood that pervade its opening numbers. These impressions are, in fact, a deeply artistic blending of truth and fiction, of the child-like and the sophisticated. This has been greatly aided by the fictional form chosen – the *Bildungsroman* imbued with fairy-tale elements – one allowing Dickens to unveil hidden aspects of both his early life and present troubled inner state without running the risk of detection and eventual censure.

The narrative voice, continuing recent developments, reveals a kaleidoscopic variety of distinctive, flexible modes ready to be applied with a purpose in mind that is above all both of artistic and thematic moment. The passing of time – structurally of vital importance in this novel – is, for instance, conveyed through subtle variations in tempo arrived at by presenting a series of impressions from the past slowed down by the utilisation of certain carefully selected words; the description of David's second half-year at school is just one illustration of this technique at work (105–6). On a more extended scale, it is also evident in the four 'Retrospect' chapters, in which striking use is made of the present tense and participial constructions, the whole adding up to a style closer to free direct speech than anything else. A great deal of the writing displays, too, a lighter, more detached tone, in which it is possible to detect the influence of the incomparably elegant style of Thackeray, who rose to ascendency at this time. As a result, authorial comment is now far less embarrassing or portentous, being fused with greater skill and less obtrusiveness into the writing as a whole. Two particularly impressive episodes exemplifying Dickens' increasing sureness of narrative touch are the portrayals of Dora's death and of the great storm. There is, in the former, a masterly economy of means, delicate tact and a poignantly effective move into the present tense. This is writing that lifts the scene above even that of Paul Dombey's death (768). At the same level of excellence is the urgent word painting informing the remarkable description of the great storm, with its emphasis on the darker, more turbulent colours (786–95).

In its variety and expressive quality, in the artistic balance achieved between Dickensian flamboyance and structural requirements, the fictional speech of this novel remains as a whole unequalled in the author's canon. If, apart from idiolectal integration, Dickens made any truly significant step forward, it is manifested in the speech idioms of such 'straight characters as Dora, Steerforth and Traddles. In contrast to the stilted technique of the previous novels (and even here, unfortunately, in the speech of Martha, Agnes, Mrs Steerforth and Little Emily), theirs are idioms in which the rhythms are now of considerable flexibility and ease of flow, and whose rhetorical features are not only less trite and more subtle, but fulfil a more clearly defined functional purpose. Even minor characters in the non-standard mode satisfy this multi-purpose standard, and that 'good plain creature' (139) Barkis, the carrier, is such a person. He is one of that legion of Dickens characters who achieves immortality though uttering scarcely more than a dozen lines in the book, all of which are torn out of his own inarticularity. His constantly repeated 'Barkis is willin'' is not just a reversion to former comic grotesqueness; his basically warm and generous nature really *is* willing, despite the suspicion and 'nearness' thrust upon him by the world of Murdstone and his cognates. His willingness is as much a moving commentary on their frozen world of 'firmness' as it is on David's nagging preoccupation with self.

It is as well to take a closer look at the speech idioms of the three 'straight' characters mentioned above to see what it actually is that brings them to life. The deceptive lightness of Steerforth's idiom, for instance, with its easy grace and apparent vitality of utterance, covers a profoundly world-weary manner. This is admirably revealed in his quick, knowing comment on David's naive enthusiasm for the trivial play both had seen, a comment that also includes the name 'Daisy', one full of suggestive overtones, that he henceforth attaches to his old school friend (288). His airy charm is dangerous and hence of considerable import, for when David succumbs to it, it becomes fatal to others, extending its evil influence in ever-widening ripples.[10] Of incidental interest is the extent to which this idiom prefigures the increasingly polished upper-class register forms of Harthouse, Gowan and, finally, Wrayburn with whom they reach their peak.

Dora's speech also possesses deceptive charm and lightness, but with her these qualities reflect naive ignorance of the world rather than sophisticated weariness. In the droll innocence of her comedy of logic, she is of the unspoiled world of the Micawbers, whereas Steerforth belongs irrevocably to the forces of evil. Through the disarming artlessness of her comic candour she fulfils the further purpose of showing up David's somewhat equivocal nature. The genuine individuality of her speech idiom makes her, perhaps, the first Dickens heroine worthy of serious linguistic attention.

The speech of David's sincere and modest friend, Traddles, aptly reflects its owner's nature, it being syntactically and lexically of emphatic straightforwardness, manifesting no ostentation whatsoever and interspersed with sudden splashes of whimsical humour. In all it is a true expression of the 'serio-comic' (593) good nature of this 'simple, unaffected fellow' (877), right down right down to the obsession of his 'dearest girl' tag. More directly than Dora, he helps to expose the evil heartlessness of the 'other side' as well as David's less amenable traits.

MR MICAWBER AND THE TRIUMPH OF RHETORIC OVER REALITY

More even than Mr Pecksniff, this character (modelled, in part, on the author's own father) has an extraordinary 'relish in [the] formal piling up of words' (754). His brilliantly realised idiolect is basically genteel rooted in the standard dialect, but his penchant for long-winded, highfalutin vocabulary is, even in Dickens, unparalleled. Indeed, taken alone, the sheer preposterousness of his genteel circumlocutary manner is enough to justify his fame; sometimes, too, it can be very funny, as when he puts down an over-hasty reaction to 'the momentary laceration of a wounded spirit, made sensitive by a recent collision with the Minion of Power – in other words, with a ribald Turncock attached to the waterworks' (412). This rambling is constantly interrupted by the bridge 'in short', a bridge to sudden, down-to-earth colloquialisms ('floored', 'Collar him', 'Shove') that in the context are both dramatic and humorous. More significant, though, are his equally frequent reiterations of 'until something turns up' plus 'which I am, I may say, hourly expecting', for they reflect both his deep-rooted resilience and his sanguine expectations in respect to future success. To avoid direct mention of the word 'debt' ('pecuniary difficulties' is a particular favourite), he will go through any genteel linguistic contortion – as long, of course, as the resulting euphemism is long and ornate enough. However, it is only when the reader considers the flood of supporting detail that goes to make up this idiolect – the mannered interpolations of futile but well-meant advice, the fragments of poems, popular songs, the sayings, the pseudo-poetic utterances, the stagey innuendos, the melodramatic villification of self – that the full artistry behind its miraculously fused complexity becomes overwhelmingly apparent.

A special feature of Micawber's characterisation is his letter-writing – in Dickens, he is without a doubt the most ardent devotee of this epistolary mode, forcing Betsey Trotwood to comment twice on the habit (750, 774). The mode can be considered a part of his idiolect, for he writes exactly as he speaks, capitalising significant words and phrases for emphasis. Of his eight lengthy set pieces in this form, four are written from the depths of despair and the other four in cheerful optimism, mirroring very aptly the ups and downs of his ever-changing moods as well as supplying him with a dramatic forum ideal for his stagey mode of self-expression. Moreover, despite the ornate complexities of the style, they hold the reader's attention right down to those elaborate complimentary closes that creep down the page like the poetry of Lewis Carroll's crocodile – but, in this case, no one could weep to see such quantities of words. Mr Micawber feels so at home in this mode that he uses it even in his theatrical unmasking of Uriah Heep, although he is actually present. Thus, in this scene, being in his element, he is at his most effective – he is far more interested in the triumph of his style than in any worldly triumph over Heep.

Despite the alarming vicissitudes of his life, Micawber's genteel circumlocutory style, initially at least, follows a measured, stately tread. Later, however, when inner doubts stemming from ever-recurring setbacks rise to the surface, there are occasions when the syntax becomes shorter, more abrupt, and, in moments of despair, often concludes in short, defiantly explosive, staccato-like predications. This is interesting for it shows a Dickens adapting the idiolect to functional purposes. Previously, any such change – Pecksniff is a classic example – was the result simply of haste and lack of a clear concept from the outset. Even more than the set rhetorical features does this suggestive flexibility underline Mr Micawber's undying resilience and sanguinity. But whatever aspect of his marvellous speech one wishes to take, Mr Micawber can be seen beating back at an adverse world with language, giving no quarter and expecting none. Through his richly imaginative theatrical rhetoric, he triumphs over what is for him a baleful reality and in this unique way asserts his own freedom. Thus he is able to protect the essence of his nature from the never-ending assaults of the world at large, a world seemingly relentless in its bids to crush all true individuality. Without question, Mr Micawber is one of Dickens' most complex comic images, not only furthering the great idiolectal tradition of such as the Wellers, Swiveller, Pecksniff and Mrs Gamp, but in fact bringing many of their attributes together in structurally significant speech of impressive strength and artistry.

MRS MICAWBER: LOGIC AND LOYALTY

Mr Micawber's loyal spouse is very similar in register and outlook. On the whole, she is given considerably less to say than her husband, yet when they appear together she, if anything, dominates in quantity of utterances. With her husband, she shares letter-writing (though only two against his eight) and two speech tags ('difficulties' and 'something turning up'). In addition, after a lengthy verbal outpouring, she often resorts to 'in fact', to all intents and purposes fulfilling the same function as her husband's 'in short', although it is not followed by the abrupt, down-to-earth colloquialisms that he uses. However, 'I never will desert Mr Micawber' is the tag she most frequently employs – one could say, over-employs – it being the one which illuminates that essential quality of her nature: her loyalty to her husband. Far more individual, though, is the logical manner in which she persistently reasons on behalf of her husband: of his abilities she is utterly convinced, whether it is to do with the Custom House, coals, corn, brewing, banking, the law or the lofty position of governor of Australia! Like much more in her husband's idiolect, this feature shows her rising above the sordid facts of their everyday life and actually defying them. She will embellish all this with an immense variety of asides, plus quotations, both supposed or actual, from the speech of others, but above all – and to the chagrin of her husband – from the lips of her deceased 'papa'. The asides are quaint and highly imaginative, displaying much of the typical Dickensian detail. Her speech as a whole being less ornate, more prim and precise, the resulting rhythmic patterns are more regular, even and concise. Like the Artful Dodger and Mr Pecksniff, she has a fondness for presenting sentences in groups of three, occasionally adding, as they also do, a kind of coda which in her case is usually her favourite speech tag: 'He is the parent of my children! He is the father of my twins! He is the husband of my affections . . . and I ne-ver-will-desert Mr Micawber!' (172).

Taken together, as they must be, the justly famous idiolects of that resilient duo, Mr and Mrs Micawber, especially of the former, undoubtedly form the idiolectal high spot of this novel, in both individual brilliance and structural significance. For the novel is not simply David's story: from the entry of the Murdstones right down to the short reappearance of Creakle, Heep and

Littimer, it is simultaneously a more effective continuation of the parodic criticism of society and its dehumanising influence first attempted on an organised level in *Dombey & Son*. As has already been indicated in respect of Mr Micawber, the importance he and his wife have is that they are in opposition to this inhuman system. Every word they say is a parody of it – they actually seem to enjoy their 'downs'. Moreover, they so act on them through language that a transmutation takes place: the horrors are swept away, and in their place there is a world of rhetorical delight, complete in itself. They are like a double act in variety, hamming their way through the trials and tribulations of this world, and emphasising thus the precious humanity that has not yet been torn away from them.

BETSEY TROTWOOD AND THE RHYTHMS OF PLAIN SPEAKING

There are two chief driving forces behind the well-delineated speech habits of this aggressive but basically kind lady: her determination to make people do what she, in all sincerity, feels is right, and her deep-rooted contempt for most members of the male sex. So many Dickens characters have an obsession, and this contempt is Miss Trotwood's. As a result of an unhappy marriage, she has little time for men and 'the imbecility of the whole set of 'em!' (197). It would be argued that her other obsession – the incessant war she wages on donkeys (and their owners) who dare to trespass on the patch of green before her cottage – is really one and the same as that involving the male sex: in other words, that all men are donkeys! Be that as it may, it is this trespassing which gives rise to 'Janet! Donkeys!', her speech tag when down at Dover (Janet is her servant). In conformity with her direct, honest, down-to-earth nature, her standard speech is not adorned with any highfalutin terms, Latinisms or the like. As a consequence, the scenes in which she is together with the Micawbers afford a dramatically arresting contrast. For all the consistency of her bare straightforwardness, however, a certain quaintness can creep in, as in her peremptory remark to the slimy Heep: 'If you're an eel, sir, conduct yourself like one. If you're a man, control your limbs, sir! Good God! ... I am not going to be serpentined and corkscrewed out of my senses!' (517).

Perhaps the most salient feature of Miss Trotwood's idiolect is the manner in which she extemporises on people's names, providing a bountiful supply of variations as the mood suits her: Murdstone is (obviously) 'a Murderer' (197); Peggotty 'that out-of-the-way woman with the savagest of names' (274); the newly married Dora and David are 'a pair of babes in the wood' (639); Dora herself is given 'Little Blossom', that 'fatal name' (700). This mannerism is obviously part and parcel of her determination to mould people to her way of thinking, and, to a high degree, of her antipathy towards the opposite sex. Springing from the same roots is her fondness for giving advice – in this case one could almost liken it to a desire to indoctrinate – a fondness which she indulges almost every time she opens her mouth. In her admonition to David when he leaves her for the first time, there is a touch of Polonius, through far less superficial or fussy: 'Never ... be mean in anything; never be false; never be cruel. Avoid these three vices, Trot, and I can always be hopeful of you' (224). So convinced is she of the rightness of her views that it can sometimes lead her into wildly arbitrary though downright positive generalisations, which for all that have something of that quaintness mentioned above: 'a Quaker flying a kite is a much more ridiculous object than anybody else' (205). Part and parcel of this overriding conviction is the strong emphasis she attaches to many words (indicated by italics) as well as the frequency of her hefty though pious ejaculations. Finally, there is a solid, four-square rhythm about all these utterances that precludes any doubt about who is speaking. This comes above all to the fore when she refers to men, for she is, as one of that sex avers, 'gruffish, and comes down upon you, sharp' (189).

With the speech of this abrupt but worthy lady who, in the best sense of the word, 'seldom conducted herself like any ordinary Christian' (4), we are moving along the new paths Dickens was taking in respect to structural purposefulness in fictional prose modalities. In her idiolect, he dispenses completely with rhetorical fireworks, yet succeeds in presenting a thoroughly convincing picture of a character who, despite her grimly austere exterior and uncompromising attitude to the world, is at the bottom unexpectedly warm-hearted, generous and loving to those who win her affection. Every single feature of her idiolect reflects her plain-dealing nature and determination to do the right thing without flinching, as well as to teach (or bully) others into doing the same. Although on the 'right' side too, Miss Trotwood remains at the other end of the language pole from the Micawbers, but is almost, if not quite, as effective, rhetorically, in countering the inroads of evil self-interest.

MISS MOWCHER – BEFORE AND AFTER

Going solely by this character's speech in this novel, there are *two* Miss Mowchers, each clear and distinct from the other: the one appearing before Steerforth's elopement with Emily, the other afterwards; the one endowed with the makings of a noteworthy idiolect rooted in the non-standard dialect and full of easy, impudent familiarity, slang, pert rhetorical questions and imperatives, the other completely and colourlessly standard, subdued, with forced slides into the stale rhetoric of conventional melodrama: 'Trust me no more, but trust me no less' (465). What happened was that Dickens had, after the appearance of this character's first episode, received a heart-rending letter from a certain Mrs Seymour Hill, a chiropodist and manicurist, and a tiny dwarf upon whose exterior the author had deliberately modelled the first Miss Mowcher. Deeply affected by the fact that Mrs Hill obviously suffered greatly from the picture he had drawn (and also, perhaps, by the threat of legal proceedings), the remorseful author, determined to make amends regardless of the artistic cost, submitted his idiolectal portrait to such a radical change that in effect a completely new character was born – or rather the other was 'killed'. The loss, artistically, is ours.[11]

The initial speech idiom indicates a bounding vitality chiefly reflected in the highly-personal rhetorical features of which the most penetrating is a vulgar, even disgusting turn of phrase. This feature is made to bristle with an undercurrent of disrespectful sarcasm, as when she takes out and comments on scraps of fingernails belonging to one of her aristocratic customers (330). She seems determined to arouse disgust by hammering home the word 'nail' six times on the one page, suggesting that young ladies collect the 'Russian Prince's nails' and 'put 'em in albums!' The vulgar sarcasm even shines through her euphemisms: 'Oh my stars and what's-their-names!' (328). She is altogether fond of being suggestively euphemistic, as again becomes apparent in her habit of showering names of various kinds (sarcastically derogatory for the most part) on those she is talking to or about: 'flower', 'my blessed infant', 'my chicken', and so on. Coupled with this is an excessive habit of adding emphasis (shown by italics). She will even extend this by running off a series of emphatic statements each followed by a shorter, pert qualification, thus bringing a certain rhythmic symmetry to her outbursts. Delightful in another way, though foreboding for the plot, is her play on the letter E (for Emily). In her pert, sarcastic, sometimes meaningful comments, she is more than a little akin to the later, profoundly realised Jenny Wren (*OMF*).

And so this flash of verbal brilliance comes and goes. Her initial idiolect is confined to just eight pages, but the impact she makes is out of all proportion to the limited extent of her appearance. Developed in the normal Dickensian way, her embryo idiolect could have taken its place with the best, and, further, could have supplied the 'other', worldly side with invaluable idiolectal support. To turn to the forced, lifeless pathos of the second Miss Mowcher is to move down – or rather back – in the Dickens world (465).

URIAH HEEP AND THE SMOOTH MODE OF HYPOCRISY

The key-word connected with this slimy character is 'humble' (or, as he pronounces it himself, ''umble'), its incessant use underlining Heep's extreme hypocrisy – rather too much, one could add. The conception of such a character, driven by external circumstances to dissembling of this intensity, began with Rob the Grinder in the previous novel. Dickens had obviously become obsessed by the conviction that charitable institutions often brought up children in a way leading inevitably to such hypocrisy, and he gives Uriah perhaps his most extended speech in order that he may, with considerable bitterness, be able to defend himself by explaining his upbringing (574–5). One cannot help having mixed feelings about him: on the one hand repelled by the false humility of his speech idiom with its strong undercurrent of insolence – at times barely concealed (this is certainly the chief reason why he comes in for such excessive abuse from the characters around him);[12] on the other hand, not only convinced that he cannot really be held responsible for his own twisted nature, but also impressed by the fact that he shows no little courage and resilience under the circumstances, even flashes of wit: 'A strait-waistcoat' (758), he says, like a shot out of a gun, when, after his unmasking, Miss Trotwood asks him if he knows what she wants. In his conversations with David, there is more than a hint of Dostoevsky's Smerdyakov and this character's knowing insolence to his half-brother Ivan Karamazov.[13]

Basically, Heep's speech is fairly standard, but Dickens adds a sprinkling of non-standard deviations, above all (and untypically) when he wishes to create a somewhat more negative effect. The most prevalent such feature, especially when Uriah is excited, is the absence of the aspirate. In general, however, the author creates an atmosphere of less educated speech by inserting colloquialisms more common, perhaps, to the lower classes. A far more personal – and very apt – feature is Uriah's syntax, which in general seems to slide along with a smoothness dictated by the use of an uncomplicated sentence structure, aided by the continual repetition of certain words chosen for their inherent ''umbleness' and the even simplicity of their sound ('lowly dwelling', 'meek and umble', 'sinful', 'follies', 'worthy', etc.). This 'smooth mode', as it can be called, governs practically all his speech. But underlying this mode is a deliberate intention to annoy, this breaking out on occasion in direct insolence. When unmasked, the very devil comes out, 'Master Copperfield' becoming 'a puppy with a proud stomach' (747), Mr Micawber the 'scum of society' (748) and Mr Wickfield the 'old ass' (748). If such an outburst is of a lascivious nature, the effect being even more unpleasant, it takes the form of the vulgar lyricism common to the popular song (382). More subtle, because hypocritically disguised, is his habit of interjecting deeply wounding comments while others are conversing. This is especially evident in the scene with Mr Wickfield and Dr Strong (617–9) in which Uriah acts like a kind of malicious chorus without the benign humour Pecksniff can add under similar circumstances.

It is through the fiery insolence of his speech in the unmasking scene that the true Heep emerges from under the smooth surface hypocrisy, a Heep who – in the sense already indicated – demands more respect. Here his vindictive hatred burns with genuine passion, the same passion which must have made him long for Agnes. However, as he stands — that is, as he is revealed to us through the major part of his idiolect – Heep is a paradigm of hypocrisy. Dickens has depicted, with uncommon psychological insight, that peculiar mixture of unctuous servility, simmering sexuality and barely concealed insolence so often thrown up, apparently, in the Victorian world. Equally important, Heep is yet another – probably *the* person – who shows up David's character in many unlooked-for lights, not all of them favourable, thus bringing out the structural subtlety of Dickens' portrait of the narrator. Whichever viewpoint one takes, Heep remains a considerable artistic achievement.

In more ways than one, *David Copperfield* occupies, as Professor Fielding among others has pointed out, 'a special place in Dickens's works. Just as it stands in a central position in the succession of his novels ... so it unites the ease of his youth with the greater sense of design of his maturity.'[14] This Janus-like position leaves a very distinct mark on Dickens' prose in the novel, for here he not only turns previously applied language techniques to even more polished account, but also – both through the new modal variety and poetic depth of many passages in the authorial voices and through the individual brilliance, greater structural cogency and disciplined variety of the fictional speech – prefigures the consummate poetic-dramatic masterpieces of his artistic maturity. *David Copperfield* testifies to an extent that none of the previous works had done, that it is primarily the surpassing felicity of Dickens' command of language, the sheer ability he possessed of shaping words into deeply expressive poetry – of delighting in creative play with language itself, a gift shared at this level with Shakespeare alone – which raises his greatest works to the pinnacle of nineteenth century fiction. For a full understanding of this peerless novelist's work, it is of fundamental importance to recognise just how much language was for him more than simply a tool; that during the act of creation it was in fact the beginning, the means, the end, one and indivisible with everything else entailed, dominating the entire creative process.

That panoramic triumph *Bleak House*[15] is a tremendously intricate, thematically highly topical but devastatingly critical study of Victorian society at all its levels. In a structural sense, it is Dickens' first really successful attempt at such. In its main narrative, alternating between the first and third person, are interwoven both the moral ingredients of a social fable and the typical pattern of the emerging nineteenth century detective story. But, over and above all this, it displays a copiousness of inventive genius such as is to be found in no other novel in the English language, not even in the author's own *Little Dorrit* or *Our Mutual Friend*. In other words, the special stylised qualities of Dickens' creative thought are presented here to unsurpassed all-round advantage. The result is a masterpiece.

Many of the undeniable stylistic achievements of *Bleak House* were almost certainly forced upon Dickens by the novel's sheer complexity, a factor which led him into seeking new means of

> bringing his huge *dramatis personae* into some kind of order, of bridging the gap between the two voices of the novel, and of fusing the various forms of which the novel is composed ... Its elements are made to reflect upon and alter one another by a glittering virtuosity of style.[16]

However, style in this book – as rather differently in *David Copperfield* – still embraces both old and new techniques, but so intertwined that it is difficult to write of them separately. The authorial voices – and by this is meant the prose devoted to the narrative itself, to descriptive elements, and to direct authorial comments – now exhibit a confidently evolving modal variety plus a distinctive artistry manifest in the way one mode flows into another. From the famous opening, with its adroit structural utilisation of present participles and present tenses, to the lovely prose description, at once poetically beautiful and dramatically sinister, of the coldly brilliant silence of the moonlit night that witnesses Tulkinghorn's murder (663); from the ever-recurring alliteration, which enables the author to achieve a profound unity of tone and atmosphere (8–9), to that extension of the poetic mode developed in the previous novels and which at times reaches an elegiac serenity (181); from the now polished – and sparing – use of blank verse, at times touched with a mellow beauty (151), to an even more adroit and satirically telling application of the pathetic fallacy (and its reverse), as in the descriptions of fashionable and slum streets which exploit to the full the possible grammatical variations of verbs and participles (653).

However, what was startlingly new – and was beginning to make itself apparent here, there and everywhere – was a certain rhetorical quality, a 'creeping oralisation', of the authorial modalities. Mention has already been made of how, at about this time, the fictional speech and authorial voices were beginning to display similar characteristics. This must have been, of course, a major factor in holding the various components together, in creating that modal web which gives this book its inclusive unity.

A less obvious though considerably more far-reaching stylistic development of this middle period – the metonymical evolution of the fictional speech – is now complete. To put it another way: the characters will be found to exist far less for their own sake, or rather for the sake of idiolectal brilliance, than for their ability through their speech to personify, to incorporate, at least a part of the world within which they find themselves. Now they actually represent this world, and through this representation they are also made to comment on it in a variety of essentially ironic ways, even to parody it. In turning thus to structural use his own peculiar method of characterisation through stylised speech forms, Dickens in *Bleak House* comes close to artistic perfection. The majority of the characters are still seemingly fixed in eternal gestures and idioms, pursuing their course in each case through the complexities of plot with an apparently never-ending number of subtle idiolectal variations on their own individualising and typifying ground themes. But, in any single analysis, it is now virtually impossible to discuss this or that speech feature without at once referring also to its structural function within the novel as a whole. Certainly a mere listing of the surface characteristics will be of little value, bringing indeed far less in volume and interest than the leading idiolects of the early novels.[17]

Before turning to the novel's major idiolects, let us glance at the speech of Mr Snagsby – a subordinate though none the less important figure – to see how even at such a minor level, the new procedure can be made to work both artistically and convincingly. On a first reading, his speech idiom is but a shadow of the lively, irresistible brilliance common to so much of Dickens' earlier fictional speech. Yet, a closer study reveals how finely, how consistently and how much to the structural point this cleverly realised speech idiom is. Nevertheless, this much Dickens has retained of past methods: that Snagsby *is* his speech and virtually nothing else; further, that for all the penetrating effectiveness of the extended series of subtle idiolectal variations, his speech remains basically unaltered from his first appearance to his last. One has only to compare his manner when addressing

Tulkinghorn early on (132) to that towards Allan Woodcourt much later (645). The deferential, naively pretentious circumlocutions in the colloquial manner, continually broken by an apologetic 'sir' or cough, plus the interspersions (usually in the wrong places!) of sudden short-lived outbursts of timorous indignation or weak, half-hearted attempts at pert humour – all these are the varied ingredients which together make up the never-changing ground base of Snagsby's mini-idiolect. In all it is a carefully balanced reflection of the narrow-horizoned yet warm-hearted nature of this brow-beaten 'little man', one for whom, in the limitations of his tongue-tied helplessness, a half-a-crown slipped into some poor wretch's hand is the one desperate panacea. Above all, though, he acts through his speech not only as an ironic comment on and a parody of the society with which he occasionally comes into contact, but also as a rhetorical manifestation of the deadening influence of the cruel, heartless world around him. It is this which is his vital structural niche.[18]

THE REV. MR CHADBAND: THE SELF-INDICTMENT OF DRONING UNCTUOUSNESS[19]

Preachers of the nonconformist order who propagated evangelical humbug in inflated canting terms were, it appears, a peculiarity of the English scene over the whole of the nineteenth century and even later. Chadband is one of Dickens' satirical characterisations of the kind of preacher so many people were forced to endure. The author obviously had a deep loathing for this type of 'bringer of the Lord's word', a loathing which developed into a near obsession. Despite this, however, he was not led to present a distorted rhetorical picture, for, astonishing though it may seem, the language mode used really was typical.[20] In this respect, it is also important to stress the role played by social differences in producing the Stigginses, the Howlers, the Little Bethels and the Chadbands. The Anglican body (especially those sections referred to very generally as the 'High' and 'Broad' Churches) being on the whole identified with only the upper classes, these sermonisers filled a vacuum which undoubtedly existed among the lower orders of society. By the time of the writing of *Bleak House*, such a man as Chadband could freely pour out (and this was the horror of it) his pompous, pseudo-religious nonsense with little fear of strong contradiction – gone were the days when a Stiggins could be ducked!

In a sense, every word or phrase, every linguistic or rhetorical trick Chadband uses, typifies him, for each and every one of these features plays its part in his 'profession' – if one can term it that. However, the majority of the features which go to make up his speech idiom are, in various ways, shared by others who tune into the Dickensian oratorical register. It is just one in particular that really sets him apart (in Dickens), this being the chief tool of his trade, so to speak: his manner of regaling the audience with extended comparisons that are, from beginning to end, utterly meaningless and ridiculous. The author himself calls it 'piling verbose flights of stairs' (264). Within the mere three scenes in which he is present, Chadband 'treats' his listeners – both willing and unwilling – to no less than eight such rambling, empty comparisons; dangerous because misleading, indeed nonsensical. The most striking – and lengthy – illustration is provided when the hapless, inarticulate street-crossing sweeper, Jo, is forced to sit on a stool at Snagsby's and endure the unfeeling Chadband in full flood (358–9).

This personal typification is strengthened by a characteristic application of biblical and other religious phraseology plus a habitual use of the pronoun 'we' or peremptory appeals involving the objective case 'us'. The latter characteristic is very typical of Chadband's slimy approach, the irony being that he belongs to that group of characters in the novel which shuts out any true identification with and sympathy for those around them. Closely related to this last feature is a pernicious and disrespectful switch to the pronoun 'you' (269), as well as the anaphoric application of the auxiliary 'may' in the subjunctive mood: 'may it grow, may it thrive, may it prosper, may it advance, . . .' and so on *ad nauseam* (269).

Chadbandism expects no answers from others, so it is no surprise to learn that this glib hypocrite absolutely revels in posing nonsensical rhetorical questions, following them with his own equally nonsensical answers, thus filling out the gaping emptiness of his long-winded comparisons. He further underlines the smug hypocrisy behind the droning repetitiveness of his rhetoric by invariably addressing anyone within reach as his 'friend' or a slight variation thereof (the sceptical Inspector Bucket becomes 'my brother'!). Another method he has of holding attention to his verbal posturing is that of anaphoric repetition, whether of sentence and clause structures or simply words and phrases. One typical example, mentioned already, starts with a repetition of the whole sentence 'May this house ...' (269), continues then with a mere catalogue of shortened predications – thus, the initial rhythms are of a leisurely smoothness, the later ones more drummingly repetitive. Semantically, the verbs are also repetitive, showing up the true emptiness of Chadband's oily variations on what is, basically, nothing. As is obviously intended, such accumulative patterns succeed in creating a monotonous, deadening effect, one that is all-pervasive and, for some, all-persuasive.[21]

It was a stroke of genius to confront Jo, the wretchedly poor outcast of society, twice with Chadband's futile unctuousness, thus dramatically and uncomfortably drawing out the sins of society towards the ignorant crossing-sweeper. The reader is made to see a society that does not care, that will not mend, that is heartless in its short-sighted selfishness; and it is the moral falseness of Chadbandism that makes him see all this. Yet, as so often before, Dickens achieves startling interest with the tawdriest of boring material, for Chadband's idiolect, as George Gissing, adopting Keats' phrase, has put it, 'is a joy for ever'.[22] In effect, Dickens has made it operate on three levels at once: as a biting indictment of society in general, as a very effective structural tool in this particular sub-plot of the novel, and, simply, as an extremely entertaining speech idiom, one so artistically finished that it really is a joy in itself.

WILLIAM GUPPY: THE SPEECH OF A SOCIAL CLIMBER

This comically pretentious, rather foolish, thick-skinned lawyer's clerk is the possessor of an idiolect whose dialect roots and register colourings present a puzzling picture. The idiom is rooted, more or less, in Dickens' flexible version of the non-standard dialect of London, but in addition moves (often simultaneously) within the legal, genteel and cheaply-sentimental registers. A most engaging illustration of this complex mixture is provided by the preposterous proposal of marriage he makes (on his knees, of course!) to the impossibly priggish Esther Summerson. It is full of sentimental phrases from cheap novelettes interspersed with colloquial expressions straight from the lawyer's office plus occasional non-standard detail:

> Miss Summerson! Angel! – No, don't ring – I have been brought up in a sharp school, and am accustomed to a variety of general practice. Though a young man, I have ferreted out evidence, got up cases, and seen lots of life. Blest with your hand, what means might I not find of advancing your interests, and pushing your fortunes! ... Cruel miss ... hear but another word! ... I could not forbear a tribute to those charms when I put up the steps of the 'ackney-coach. It was a feeble tribute to Thee, but it was well meant. Thy image has ever since been fixed in my breast. (125)

All this, of course, typifies his character as that of one bent on rising in the professional and social world, and appropriately fixes him within the novel's thematic structure as a whole.

The sentimental or professional registers, whether mixed or not, are always used against a general background of the genteel register in which the inadvertent application of everyday colloquialism points to non-standard origins. When he either forgets himself or considers the occasion unimportant, he slips into truly Cockney idiom, his very first entry showing this clearly: 'This is about a London particular [=dense fog] *now*, ain't it, miss?' (35). A singular intermingling of the professional and genteel – one in which he avoids the sentimental mode, speaking more to the point rather than meandering pompously – follows in his episodes with Lady Dedlock. His speech here exhibits, moreover, a curious mixture of nervous servility and professional confidence, made all the more outlandish when, knowing he has information of importance to her, Guppy transforms one such private interview into a court scene (404–9).

By adding more of the genteel to the professional register plus a touch of the sentimental, Guppy arrives at yet another diverting mixture in his discourses with his friend Jobling. In their delightful exchanges, there is a touch of the combination Chuckster–Swiveller (*OCS*), especially in the extensive use Guppy makes of his speech tag 'there *are* chords in the human mind' when referring to his unrequited love for Esther (273–84). Finally, Guppy can, when he so wishes, concentrate entirely on his version of the genteel register, such a case arising when he sets out to impress Mrs Chadband that he knows Esther – in other words, that he moves in 'high society' (269).

It will be clear to just what extent Guppy – like Inspector Bucket – has an idiolect of wide-ranging flexibility, varying the profusely quaint mixture of registers according to the situation he is in. However, there is more to this complicated speech idiom than just comedy: its flexibility, strengthened by the clumsy investigations Guppy conducts into Esther's past, can be viewed as a significant parody of Inspector Bucket's controlled selection of sub-idiolects and key role in the novel. In everything he does, in fact, Guppy is a living parody – primarily as Bucket's narrowed-down fictional shadow, but also through his petty legal ambitions, his put-on manner (whether condescending or servile) towards those with whom he comes into contact, and his ridiculous courtship of Esther. It is true even within this last-named role; his later retraction, for instance, of his previous proposal – one made after he has seen Esther's now pock-marked face – is nothing less than a parody of the first (542–4).

With respect to both idiolectal interest and his fully-realised role in the novel's structure, Guppy is an undeniable success. It is unfortunate, then, that Dickens, when getting rid of this character towards the end of the novel, feels it fit to show the cruel side of his humour; for, despite all his pretentious faults, Guppy is basically kind-hearted. The scene is the least necessary in the book, and one cannot help feeling that the author is only dragging him back to give him a last kick. So when, in his renewed offer of marriage to Esther, Guppy asserts, 'I do not consider. ... I am by any means throwing myself away' (862), one can only feel that he would be doing just that!

HAROLD SKIMPOLE: SURFACE GLITTER AND THE IMPRISONING MODE

This personage is, by all accounts, Dickens' only too devastatingly obvious portrayal of the still-living Leigh Hunt, erstwhile friend and confidant of Keats, Byron and Shelley, now notorious for his financial irresponsibility. Skimpole's idiolect, rooted in the standard dialect, is a subtly varied version of the genteel register, one which has been lexically and syntactically simplified, hence the superficial lightness and misleading charm that make him such a dangerous social parasite. In Chapter 4, I pointed out how skilfully Dickens has made structural use of this character's speech, using it to show how cut off he in actual fact is from the people around him, that in society he is as much a systemised prisoner as those he would fain despise.

The speech idiom used by this character to propound his dangerously attractive, seemingly harmless attitude to life is expertly conceived, its surface glitter and ease corresponding exactly to the true nature of the egotistical fancies he strews around him. The sentences are practically all very short, in most cases not at all developed – Skimpole merely makes a series of airy springs from one simple predication to the next, thus adroitly avoiding any commitment which might embarrass him. A good example of this kind of syntax is the passage beginning 'It's only you, the generous creatures' (71). The words Skimpole chooses are invariably of a positive and optimistic nature and this, together with a persistent application of the present tense, succeeds in lending a false sense of plain-speaking as well as a misleading air that he is expressing an eternal truth.

The appalling egocentricity of Skimpole's pseudo-argumentation is underlined further by both his unbridled use of the first person singular and his partiality for 'speaking of himself as if he were not at all his own affair, as if Skimpole were a third person' (70). One of the longest speeches – a plea to 'let Harold Skimpole live' (69–70) – is an exposition of what Dickens on a later page calls Skimpole's 'Drone philosophy' (93), and by presenting it in free indirect speech, the author places it in a starkly ironic light. A shorter excerpt – a subtle play on the indefinite 'Somebody' – probably goes farther than any other passage in drawing out this character's heartlessly indifferent de-personalising of those who help him out of money difficulties: 'Somebody always does it for me. *I* can't do it, you know, for I never have any money. But Somebody does it. I get out by Somebody's means; I am not like the starling; I get out. If you were to ask me who Somebody is, upon my word I couldn't tell you. Let us drink to Somebody. God bless him!' (523).

There is much in Skimpole's idiolect that is reminiscent of Oscar Wilde and the aesthetic movement – of the utterances and general style of, say, Dorian Gray – revealing thus a Dickens well ahead of his time. It was a mode that, in the mouth of Eugene Wrayburn (*OMF*) over a decade later, was to move even closer to

Wilde's manner. For all that, Dickens makes it quite clear that he utterly repudiated the self-centred kind of romantic aestheticism implicit in Skimpole's 'Drone philosophy'. In a novel so much concerned with avoidance of responsibility by society and the individual, Dickens, significantly, makes Skimpole a recreant doctor – one who not only denies all help to a seriously ill Jo, but even clandestinely turns him away. Thus, the reader's initial amused incredulity in the face of Skimpole's glittering, airy nonsense is turned sour, until the final reaction becomes one of complete disgust. It is worth pointing out, perhaps, that this is not the feeling left by Pecksniff's final exit, and as such is a pointer to the vast strides Dickens was making in the development of his art and of his sense of artistic responsibility. By any standards, Skimpole's idiolect is a consummate achievement.

INSPECTOR BUCKET: THE SERVANT OF AUTHORITY AND IDIOLECTAL ADJUSTABILITY

The idiolect of this formidable officer of the law is, of professional necessity, the most flexible in the book, if not in all of Dickens' fiction. It is made to serve a multitude of purposes, Bucket having an almost magical 'adaptability to all grades' (720). This is, of course, only to be expected from a person 'to whom it is on an emergency, as natural to be groom of the ceremonies as it is to be anything else' (316). Although his speech is grammatically standard, his easy flow of colloquialisms indicates non-standard roots. Be that as it may, at least eight sub-idiolects can be discerned.

Much of Inspector Bucket's 'adaptability' comes out to striking advantage in the ever-mounting tension of the search for Lady Dedlock. Here it becomes clear that when swayed by urgency, his phrasing becomes short rapid and factual, as in his miraculously quick reaction to the attempt of the speechless Sir Leicester to indicate that he wants his wife found at all costs: 'Certainly. The littlest key? *To* be sure. Take the notes out? So I will. Count 'em? That's soon done' (763). The brief, to-the-point questions and answers serve a very different purpose from Skimpole's sterile condensations. More, the unaffected colloquial manner adds, under the circumstances, a rather piquant air. Otherwise towards Sir Leicester, his address is – from motives of deference and tact – more expansive and rhetorical, tending if anything to repetitive, even rather pompous, constructions: 'Sir Leicester Dedlock, Baronet' (725). This is true only when actually speaking to the stricken aristocrat, for, despite Sir Leicester's continuing presence, there is a pointed difference in Bucket's manner when he turns to that nefarious group made up of Mrs Snagsby, Smallweed and the Chadbands. Now he moves into an apparent joviality (under which he is as cold as ice) that is, in fact, a curious mixture of bullying and coaxing, the Inspector twisting the scheming band round his finger when bargaining about hush-money (732).

In the third of this swift succession of scenes, we have Bucket unmasking the murderess, Mademoiselle Hortense. His idiom now, once more different, is a teasing amalgam of playful threats and sober determined objectivity, the brief sentences shorn of everything but the plain facts. At such moments, the Inspector's power is nothing less than awesome, even to the fiery Frenchwoman. This effect is heightened by a sudden change back to his 'Sir Leicester mode' when he respectfully informs that worthy of details about Tulkinghorn's murder, this, in turn, being continually interspersed with warnings to Lady Dedlock's former maid in the 'Hortense mode'. The following, for instance, is part of his reaction to her when she calls him a 'Devil': 'Angel and devil by turns, eh? ... But I am in my regular employment, you must consider. Let me put your shawl tidy ... Anything wanting to the bonnet? There's a cab at the door' (743).

A further mode in Bucket's intriguing speech compound is one he turns on when craftily weedling information out of the Dedlock's butler about the movements of his Lady on the night of Tulkinghorn's murder. By making use of a grossly exaggerated, but in manner very Dickensian, white lie, the ever resourceful Inspector is able to play both on the butler's credulity and on his vanity. He begins with a series of apparently harmless questions and little anecdotes; then, the butler completely in his hand, he suddenly pops the leading question, this being in the form of the answer he has already guessed but wishes to have confirmed (720–3). However, when the end in view demands the exertion of fine feeling, Bucket is quite capable of producing a kind of amiable verbosity, as in his drawn-out but tactful method of arresting George, the old soldier. Here, too, the Inspector begins with one of those white lies that seem second nature to him, this ending with a grouping of three similarly constructed clauses which exert a mesmeric influence on his listeners (672). If, as here, he is determined to buy time, nothing can put a stop to his verbosity; even children fall under his spell, and just to keep the ball rolling he will stoop to anything – a quaint form of sententiousness, for example: 'So it is, and such is life. The cat's away, and the mice they play; the frost breaks up, and the water runs' (736).

Yet another and somewhat unexpected mode is applied at George's shooting gallery where the ubiquitous Inspector suddenly turns up to arrest Gridley, the ruined suitor in Chancery, only to find him dying. To a surprising degree, this rather disconcerts Bucket, and his short, emphatic, down-to-earth syntax takes on a clumsily embarrassed tone through a well-meant but unhappy choice of words – particularly his final words: 'I shall take you on a score of warrants yet, if I have luck' (352). Finally, towards Mr Snagsby when they make their way to Tom-all-Alone's, his manner becomes much more matey, more informal, and a shade more colloquial (308–17). He takes this colloquial manner to an extreme, besides adding a typical touch of the admonitory, when questioning Jo in the same scene.

In every sense of the word, Inspector Bucket is one of the key figures in this complex novel. His manner of controlling completely through his singular speech flexibility the scenes in which he appears, his redoubtable powers, his frightening ability to turn up at the most unexpected moment and without being heard, his amoral adjustability (the ideal servant of authority) – such qualities hint strongly at those representing the law in the nightmare world of Kafka, and point up the same kind of very serious moral.

With this great novel it would seem that Dickens had finally reached a summit beyond which there were no new peaks to conquer. Nevertheless, a phase was to come as a result of which he was to forge out of the multifarious fictional modes within which he was now working, an artistic homogeneity of style – that 'oral style' already discussed in these lines – which has remained one of the supreme achievements in the world of English letters.

10 *Hard Times* and *Little Dorrit*

The step from *Bleak House* to *Hard Times*[1] involves a radical transition – one has only to compare the respective opening chapters. To begin with, Dickens had returned – after a gap of thirteen years – to weekly serialisation. This resulted, untypically, in an astonishing economy of means, and it is no surprise to hear that the author had heartily complained about the restrictions imposed upon him: 'The difficulty of space is CRUSHING'[2], he writes. For all that, the process obviously imprinted on Dickens a greater awareness of a taut, tightly-knit structure. His new novel – a moral fable whose form and content, right up to the basically *un*happy ending, can be viewed as ironic twists of the fairy tale – confronts the reader with a background utterly unlike that previously met with in Dickens' fiction: industrial unrest in the north of England. This has led, unfortunately, to a certain lack of intimacy between subject and author which, more perhaps than anything else, accounts for the book's limitations and relative lack of success; for here will be found far less both of what is popularly considered Dickensian and of not so obvious but more valuable artistic qualities. Furthermore, despite the author's undeniably intelligent attempt to be rational in his approach, the book reveals him as still governed far more by feeling than by thought.

The controlled application of key-words – the most decisive technical advancement displayed in *Hard Times* – and its relationship to the repetition technique, has already been discussed within these lines. One of the most conspicuous and well-known illustrations of this method is to be found on the very first page –

comprising the whole of the first chapter! – in the description and speech of Gradgrind. Mr Bounderby's idiolect, as well as the description of his appearance, his house and his bank – in fact all the language connected with him – reveal similar links. The mode may, at times, be too obvious or become mannered, but its unifying qualities give it clear structural advantages.

In the sense of syntactic rather than lexical reiteration, the new stylistic approach is seen to caustic effect in the telling satire of the descriptions of Coketown – that 'triumph of fact' and hence the 'Keynote'. One need only glance at the very first of these, where the recurrence of certain words, especially of the connectives, is immediately obvious. Far more effective, however, is the syntactic and phonic repetition, out of which is created a truly depressing atmosphere of droning, never-ending, utterly soulless monotony, the frightening impression of a world that has lost its balance being cogently reinforced by the suggestive elephant simile (22). In a passage that begins 'They were ruined ... when ...' (110), a bitingly sarcastic attack on the callousness of the Coketown millowners, the satirical effect of such a method is heightened to a striking extent. Here the repetition takes the form of a syntagmatic sequence: the gradual intensification in rhythmic emphasis, brought about by the determined reiteration of the basic syntactic structure, continually leads the reader to the threshold of a temporal-conditional clause where his expectation of a brutal thrust is countered each time by relative clauses characterised by a propitiatory neutrality of tone. The very slight but effective variation of the last indicative strengthens the climax of the repeated structure to the same degree that the perfect understatement of the final clause consummates the ironic contrast Dickens was aiming at.

For all the obvious effectivity of such and other passages, it will be generally found that the old inspired turn of language lurks beneath the surface, rather, with only an occasional breakthrough, this being especially true of the fictional speech. It is obvious that, for structural, thematic or a variety of other reasons alluded to above, Dickens' pen became more inhibited than at any other time in his career. There is certainly less verbal humour than in any other of his novels except *A Tale of Two Cities*. The otherwise more prominent idiolect technique encompassing a string of scintillating or subtle variations on what are fundamentally the same idiolectal ground patterns is, then, scarcely allowed to come into its own. Even the basic speech devices themselves strike one as less inspired than the usual run. Limited exceptions can be made of the speech idioms of Sparsit and Harthouse, particularly when they converse together.

Nowhere does this uncharacteristic lack of surety come out more clearly than in the speech of Stephen Blackpool in which Dickens made one of his rare forays into a regional dialect outside that to be found in London and its surrounds. The fault lies in the author's rather self-conscious and uncertain application of local Lancashire idiom and pronunciation,[3] as well as in the impossibility of a rhetoric which is 'laboured and stately'.[4] The stylisation is off on the wrong track, this being nowhere more apparent than in the long drawn-out sentences, embarrassing simplifications and class comparisons that make up Stephen's homily to Rachael after he has been rescued from the disused coal pit (272). All this is a great pity, for he has been allotted a role of substantial structural significance in the novel.

The jealous, petty, vindictive Mrs Sparsit, whose staircase image and relentless pursuit of Louisa provide perhaps the most powerful dramatic writing in the book, is otherwise the possessor of a minor, somewhat scantily decorated idiolect. It is a long way from the exotically crazy utterances and lush imaginative variety of, say, that other snobbish parasite, Mrs Skewton. Further, Mrs Sparsit's private listing of Harthouse's physical characteristics (119) prefigures a far more successful assay in this mode by Lady Tippins (*OMF*, 119). For all that, though, it is in such unheard speeches as this private listing that she rises, rhetorically, a little above her normal efforts, the explosive apostrophes directed either at the absent Bounderby (for whom she has the greatest contempt) or at her great enemy Louisa (incorporating the splendid staircase image) being cases in point.

The languid, basically disinterested (except when aroused by Louisa) nature of James Harthouse is reflected in half-finished sentences and tiredly polite ejaculations. His speech, especially when he is supremely bored (128–30), reminds one forcibly of the Society manner of the later Eugene Wrayburn (*OMF*). Harthouse also resembles this character in the deceptive turn his idiom takes when concentrating on the woman who has captured his interest. His careless, apparently disinterested ease when questioning Tom about his sister, slily prodding him with a minimum of means into revealing volubility, is an excellent illustration of the considerable progress Dickens had made in mastering the off-hand manner of the upper-class register. Not only that, the author provides in this scene, as so often elsewhere, dialogue worthy of the theatre, in its artistically contrived concentration, rhythmic vitality and dramatic tension (132–6).

This Dickensian theatricality of the dialogue comes out to even greater advantage in two memorable scenes both involving Louisa, a character otherwise linguistically colourless in the worst Dickens hero–heroine tradition. The first of these scenes is that ironically drawn, very factual interview between Louisa and her father, in which it is decided she should marry Bounderby (97–102). With its simmering undertones of feeling and dramatic subtlety, it is one of the artistic successes of the novel. The second such scene pairs the innocent (in the ways of the world) Louisa with the glibly experienced Harthouse, who has been slowly but steadily worming his indolently cunning way into her confidence (172). The bare formality which is her normal speech is here shown in a different, more positive, light when held up against the 'genteel listlessness [and] assumed honesty in dishonesty' (166) which provide the foundation of Harthouse's idiolect. Louisa's admission that she had sold some of her jewellery to get her worthless brother out of debt shows a very gradual progression; this is capitally conveyed by the subtly varying syntax, from hesitating indecision to a series of short, to-the-point statements, all bristling with dramatic tension. Here it is less the words she uses and far more the structure of the sentences which indicates the extent to which Harthouse has broken through her normal reserve. All in all, a magnificent piece of writing.

'Nobody's Fault', the title originally intended for *Little Dorrit*,[5] though perhaps less felicitous than the final choice, tells us a great deal more about Dickens' implicit and explicit intentions in this his most profound social satire. The word 'Nobody' is, in fact, as significant an item in the general structure as 'Facts' in the previous novel, and forms the basis of what can be considered Dickens' most tragic novel, one whose searching pessimistic mood stretches right through to the gloomy tones of the subdued ending. This cathartic work has the elements of a moral fable in general or, more specifically, of the morality plays of the 16th century: there is frequent generalisation (which seems as strong here as the more typical Dickens particularisation), emblematic usage, ritualistic patterns, allegorical presentation of characters (Bar, Physician, Bishop), the ever-recurring image of life as a pilgrimage. In this context, the unchangeability of the characters, of their speech, takes on an added significance.

However, *Little Dorrit* is far too complex in its probings into the human psyche to be classified simply as a morality play dressed up in Victorian trappings. It makes up for what little definite plot and detailed incident it contains by concentrating on the development of theme and mood as reflected in the multitude of characters representing society. For Dickens, it is a society the whole of which is enclosed in a prison of its own making – what Edmund Wilson called 'imprisoning states of mind'[6] – a prison in which rulers and ruled alike are confined, in which public and personal relationships are inextricably and tragically mixed, in which the chief object of each person's private worship is basically 'nothingness'. Mrs Merdle expresses this directly when remonstrating with her husband for creating such a bad impression in Society, and her words can be taken as the key-note of this dark, bitterly pessimistic novel: 'I simply request you to care about nothing – or seem to care about nothing – as everybody else does' (397). It is this image, presented with remarkable variety and depth of perception, which from beginning to end dominates each and every one of the book's stylistic modalities, above all those animating the fictional speech.

Other words closely related to the key-note and to which considerable significance is also attached are 'shadow' – the very real one hanging over all our lives is 'a deeper shadow than the shadow of the Marshalsea Wall' (650); 'secret', which expresses man's essential isolation brought on by innate selfishness; and 'gentleman', which is satirically rendered in a variety of meanings. There is humour present, of course, but it is somehow so absorbed in the general gloom-ridden structure that it takes on a peculiar aura of its own, beneath which sadness and despair are forever lurking. All is integrated, and it is the consummate artistry of this integration that lends the novel its unique character, not only in Dickens' canon but in the context of the Victorian novel as a whole.

Despite the general thematic gloom, many passages confirm that the descriptive prose does not always wallow in over-sombre regions, but remains rather at a slightly subdued, beautifully rounded poetic level, with a new delicacy of touch achieved through lexical simplicity and syntactic symmetry (27, 200). More extended is the lovely description of an Autumn evening in the Alps, one displaying an irresistible poetic felicity, its effectiveness increasing when we view it as a pendant of the prison image (431–3). A summer evening in London evokes a similar feeling of tranquillity (793).

However, these expressive passages in the older, more 'set-piece' style, beautiful as they can be, are of secondary importance when viewed against the remarkable modal flexibility that now affects all aspects of Dickens' prose style. It is that flexibility which enables the author to fulfil within the same mode a variety of intentions simultaneously, thus enhancing as seldom before the suggestive quality of whatever mode is concerned; Mr Dorrit's idiolect is a classic case in point. Further, the greatly expanded flexibility also facilitates the moves from one mode to another, being aided in this by the highly stylised rhetorical patterns of the repetitive mode (28) and the occasional but adroit use of free indirect speech (142). Finally, and of paramount importance, Dickens had now attained near perfection in the structural integration of the fictional speech, although – and this is the price to be paid – the accent is even less on idiolectal fireworks. Where he still succeeds in combining old and new – as so strikingly in Flora's idiolect, or rather in those of Flora and Mr F's Aunt taken together – the effect can be overwhelming.

Characterising much of the fictional speech in general – and, in this measure, peculiar to *Little Dorrit* – is a kind of syntactic waywardness, a waywardness which can be taken as emblematical of the arbitrary ways of Society in its dealings with others. The most original form concerned is what can be termed the 'backward manner', one shared to a great extent by John Chivery and his mother: 'sure and certain as in this house I am. I see my son go out with my own eyes when in this house I was' (258), and to a lesser degree by other members of their circle – the conversation of Mr Plornish and Mr Nandy, for example (579). Richard Stang has related this eccentric syntax to the needs of the thematic structure as a whole: 'The same kind of reversals of ordinary expectations that pervade the structure of the book can be found in ... syntactical patterns that run backwards like a crab.'[7]

It is possible that Dickens struck upon the 'backward manner' when working out Cavalletto's Anglo–Italian speech idiom: 'The last time when it I have heard' (676) – although such syntactic patterns seem to have more in common with those found in German.[8] Be that as it may, the idiolects of Mr Casby, Mr Pancks and especially Flora Finching also reveal, each in their different ways, unusual syntactic freedom. Nor must one forget Mrs Plornish, whose speech becomes riotously free when she resorts to what she fondly imagines is a foreign tongue: 'E ope you no ight. ... What appen? Peka Padrona! ... Ow you know him bad? ... E see you? ... why ope bad man no see?' (577).[9] Such harmless linguistic pretence on a non-standard level can be viewed as a parody of the affected, empty, verbal monstrosities falling so glibly from the lips of those attached to the Circumlocution Office, a world in which 'any words will do, since everybody is nobody and nothing is to be done'.[10]

MR WILLIAM DORRIT AND THE DRAMATIC NUANCES OF GENTEEL CONDESCENSION[11]

As is evinced by its extraordinary flexibility and expressive artistry, the idiolect of this character has been evolved with considerable care and subtlety. Within the framework of the genteel register of the standard dialect, it has been made to mirror his benign condescension, his pompous though not (normally) unpleasant manner, the ridiculously exaggerated sense he has of his own dignity, and the twists his weak mind has undergone during his long, degrading term of enforced imprisonment. Fascinating in itself though this idiolect is, the full impact of its wide-ranging but subtle flexibility can be appreciated only directly within the context of this or that scene, where in pregnant dialogue the full extent of its structural integration and the dramatic nuances of Dickens' satirical intentions become plain to the reader. Three decisive scenes come to mind, two of which occur while he is still in the Marshalsea and one in Rome shortly before his death, each being crucial to a full understanding of the novel.

In the first of these scenes, William Dorrit is trying simultaneously to bolster up the spirits of his brother Fred, who is *not* incarcerated in the Marshalsea, and to keep up face before the other inmates of the debtors' prison (221–5). The narrative

comment and dialogue in this bizarre scene are beautifull
pointed and balanced, one against the other, pursuing parall
strands of meaning. The whole is as full of deep psychologic
insight and subtle shading of dramatic effect as anything i
George Eliot or even Henry James, and put over, too, with
flexibility, breadth and expressiveness of language of which the
were only seldom capable. Practically every word Dorrit uses is
parody of himself; further, in the grotesque homily directed at th
assembled company in the prison lodge, beginning 'Gentlemer
whoever came ...' and ending 'Gentlemen, God bless you!' (225
there is a certain ritualistic quality about his delivery, as if he
aware of his own twisted nature and is acting it out in prescribe
forms. It forms the conclusion of the scene under discussion, an
Dickens reinforces the irony by presenting the passage in fre
indirect speech; in the last juxtaposition of 'gentleman/Gentle
men' as well as in the suggestive hesitation on the word 'and
Dickens shows how even the tiniest detail can play a significar
part. Dorrit's speech in this scene ironically underscores his ow
tragi-ridiculous situation in a manner impossible, it would seem
to better.

Yet, if anything, the piercing satire of the second of these scene
is even more effective, almost causing the reader direct hurt in th
way it strips Dorrit down to the sorry essence of what he has nov
become: a living image of nothingness. In his shabby Marshalse
room, surrounded by his family and Mr Clennam, he is 'enter
taining' that poor, weak old man from the workhouse, Mr Nand
(372–4). Dickens leaves Mr Dorrit's words to speak mainly fo
themselves, adding little comment. Again, it is in languag
consummately applied, as in, for instance, the simplicity of synta:
in Dorrit's two-way speech as he addresses the old man and th
onlookers in turn:

> 'Not ready for more ham, yet, Nandy? Why, how slow you are
> (His last teeth ... are going, poor old boy.) ... No shrimps
> Nandy? ... (His hearing is becoming very defective. He'll b
> deaf directly.) ... Do you walk much, Nandy, about the yar
> within the walls of that place of yours?'
>
> 'No, sir; no. I haven't any great liking for that.'
>
> 'No, to be sure ... Very natural ... (Legs going.)'
>
> Once, he asked the pensioner, in that general clemenc
> which asked him anything to keep him afloat, how old hi
> younger grandchild was? ...

'How old, sir? Let me think now.'

The Father of Marshalsea tapped his forehead. '(Memory weak.) ... Don't distress yourself ... (Faculties evidently decaying – old man rusts in the life he leads!)' (374–4)

[Th]e entire episode is a wonderful manifestation of the author's [su]btlety of humour and delicate realisation of dramatic possibili[tie]s. Dorrit's whole approach to Mr Nandy is at bottom a parody [of] his very own position and nature.

The third of these crucial scenes is that embracing his stroke at [a] banquet in Rome and, his mind now giving way completely (his [de]ath is soon to follow), the subsequent reversion to the world of [th]e Marshalsea (647–9). As a result, he falls back into the speech [re]gister peculiar to that prison, asking Amy 'if Bob is on the lock?' [an]d continuing – embarrassingly, for it is before a gathering of [En]glish 'Society' in Rome – in the same vein. There is consider[ab]le (again, directly painful) depth of irony here, especially in the [dr]amatically charged repetition of the blessing previously [in]voked at the actual prison lodge in the first of the scenes [di]scussed above, and (in plural form) of the key-word 'gentle[m]an'. The subtly controlled language of this highly charged scene [un]derlines, in particular, the extent to which twenty years in [pr]ison had warped Dorrit's soul, and, in general, the message that [all] human beings, to varying degrees, are in prisons of their own [m]aking. This is the primary message of the book, and it is fitting [th]at the book's most fully realised character should be instru[m]ental in delivering it.

[FL]ORA FINCHING AND MR F'S AUNT: TWO SIDES [O]F THE SAME RHETORICAL COIN

[In] respect of surface interest, no other idiolect in *Little Dorrit* [co]mes anywhere near that of Flora Finching – or rather that of [Fl]ora taken together with the tiny, brutally direct speech idiom of [he]r *alter ego*, Mr F's Aunt. Dickens somewhat unkindly based [Fl]ora's idiolect on the manner of a gushing, elderly matron by the [na]me of Mrs Maria Winter, née Beadnell, who had been the great [lo]ve of his youth and who had recently, with disastrous results, [bu]rst back into his life. Flora's idiolect is rooted in the standard dialect and is coloured by touches of the genteel register (though she is far too *un*pompous to go the whole hog) and many aspects the sentimental one as borrowed from cheap novelettes. H major individualising feature is her never-ending garrulity – th longer torrents are overwhelming and often have to be read mar times before one can even begin to understand them. However, will be established that she does, in her round-about way, actual say all she wants to, torn continually between what might ha been and what is; as the author himself so amusingly puts it: 's left about half of herself at eighteen years of age behind, ar grafted the rest on to the relict of the late Mr F; thus making moral mermaid of herself' (155).

A great deal of what she pours out falls upon the ears of Arth Clennam, the love of her youth, and for him she has a variab speech tag: variations on his name. The manner in which he addressed or referred to ranges from a simple 'Arthur' throug 'Mr Arthur', 'Doyce and Clennam' (his firm), 'our mutual frien (to Amy), to 'Mr Clennam', which is frequently embellished wi 'far more proper'. Almost everything, in fact, is a play on the former relationship, with many intervening references to h dead husband, 'Mr F', these reminiscences allowing her to w comically eloquent in her very own delightful version of t sentimental-poetic mode: 'ere we had yet fully detected t housemaid in selling the feathers out of the spare bed Gout flyi upwards soared with Mr F to another sphere' (285).

Not letting up for a second, Flora indulges in mock attacks her former love in the manner of those famous Dickensian 'asid usually found in the narrative voice. Typically, she does not w for an answer but supplies her own, speaking continually in derogatory way of herself and throwing out a whole succession quaint, even zany, observations which, more than anything e she says, show the vivid vitality of her unconquerable imagir tion: 'I only hope she's not a Pagodian dissenter' (152), she sa about Clennam's supposed Chinese wife; and about the sar 'Little Dorrit': 'like a place down in the country with a turnpi. or a favourite pony or a puppy or a bird or something from seed-shop to be put in a garden or a flower-pot and come speckled' (270).

There is, however, a certain underlying pattern in all h apparently disjointed verbal wanderings, and Dickens achie this in two ways: by endowing the speech with a specific rhythn symmetry, and also (as indicated above) by supplying a definite thread of logic to her meanderings. In the former case, the rhythms are either the natural ones of the delicious sentimental-poetic mode or, and these are far more effective in the sense under discussion, syntactic groupings in three or multiples of three – compound time, so to speak – and are frequently rounded off with some kind of coda or other: 'I am a mere fright, I know he'll find me fearfully changed, I am actually an old woman, it's shocking to be so found out, it's really shocking' (150).

Over and above the rhythmic patterns and the 'thread of logic', Flora – who is in a weird way as much a prisoner of society as everybody else – succeeds, through her idiolectal flights into her own special kind of fantasy, in partially freeing herself from her bondage; more precisely, she manages to a high degree to preserve her essential self in a world which is trying to destroy it. As with the Micawbers before her, language acts as a liberating instrument, and no other character in the novel stands out in this way as she does. She is the one bright light in the general gloom; all the brighter, perhaps, because of the contrast.

In their reactions towards Arthur Clennam – and he seems to obsess both of them – it is possible to view Flora and Mr F's Aunt as two sides of the same coin. In that case, in contrast to the kind, tender, cheerful half of Flora's nature, an aggressively unpleasant side finds expression through Mr F's Aunt with the sudden ferocious broadsides she directs at poor Arthur: his punishment for not marrying her (Flora). These broadsides are startlingly colloquial with a touch of non-standard detail, and in which the brutal, peremptory directness is self-evident: 'Bring him for'ard, and I'll chuck him out o' winder!' (820) or 'You can't make a head and brains out of a brass knob with nothing in it' (273). Poor Arthur, indeed. It is difficult in the end to know whether to laugh or not, for, funny though her violent ejaculations can be, there is also a real warning in them – something stemming from the evil influences in life. More, her verbal violence springs from a complete rejection of Arthur Clennam, which in turn springs from a complete inability to understand his true motives in respect to Flora. In other words, Mr F's Aunt, like almost everyone else in the book, is unable to communicate, is a prisoner within the grotesque world of her own imaginings, thus fulfilling a very real, though minor, function in the novel as a whole.

JOHN CHIVERY: OBSEQUIAL ELOQUENCE AND BACKWARD SYNTAX

This character – Amy Dorrit's weak-headed, unrequited, gentle lover, and on his own confession 'Never anything worth mentioning' (220) – carves out in a unique manner his own immortal niche, a little private one, in the overall structure, by mentally supplying an inscription for his future gravestone every time he receives a setback in love. One of the most effective is that composed in bed by an extremely sorrowful John who, his soft, sentimental heart getting the better of him, has just previously helped his arch-rival, Arthur Clennam, to settle in at Marshalsea (734). The effect is all the more amusing by their being presented in the book in gravestone form. But they are more than just the amusing fancies of a weak-minded boy; in Dickens' hands they become expressive, double-edged, verbal conceits, supremely comic yet darkly so, for they also illuminate the underlying death-wish the turnkey's son shares with so many characters in this sombre novel.[12]

'For . . . do not be so base as to deny that dodge you do, and thrown me back upon myself you have!' (726); thus an indignant John to Mr Clennam. Reference has already been made to this curious syntactic feature and its possible structural role in the backward moving world of *Little Dorrit*. Specifically, in John, the feature can be viewed as a verbal emblematisation of the utter confusion reigning within the basically kind heart of this simple-minded person. In respect of his arch but unknowing rival Mr Clennam, for instance, John is torn between going backwards or forwards, between giving in to the baser emotion of jealousy or behaving honourably. To the inner confusion is added his complete inability to articulate his position publicly to others, but only to himself, melodramatically, in the form of epitaphs. He is in a direct line with Mr Toots, but far more subtly drawn and more effectively integrated into the general structure; and technical progress has brought melancholy.

MR PANCKS: ESCAPE THROUGH THE INDEFINITE

That 'panting little steam-tug' (276) who is the impetuous nail-biting rent-collector of the grasping hypocrite, Casby, has a deal of the old Dickens in his idiolect, in spirit at least. Pancks is basically a kind man whose better nature is imprisoned almost against its will in a foul, cheating world. Small wonder that he is constantly to be found 'cropping [his] scanty pasturage of nails' (160); all the more reason for his also taking refuge in a flood of words. However, unlike Flora and many others in the novel, he does so through rigidly straightforward syntax, this hitting the eye at once: short, functional sentences, simply constructed and almost invariably imperative or interrogative. Thus he wards off in advance any intrusion upon his inner life, the one predication following the other in a breathless hurry. Yet another impersonal speech feature forced upon him by the heartless world in which he is so helplessly embroiled is the use of the indefinite, 'you', 'a person' and 'a man' occurring with obsessive frequency. This aggressive, self-justifying mode comes out very clearly when he feels he is being criticised:

> As to being a reference ... *you* know in a general way, what being a reference means. It's all *your* eye, that is! Look at *your* tenants down the Yard here. They'd all be references for one another, if *you*'d let 'em. ... *A person* who can't pay, gets *another person* who can't pay, to guarantee that *he* can't pay ... [Four wooden legs] don't make either of them able to do a walking-match. And four wooden legs are more troublesome to *you* than two, when *you* don't want any. (*LD*, 273; my italics.)

The brisk, non-standard, colloquial manner is, then, deceptive, and in his desperate attempts to justify what he knows deep down is a dishonourable business, Pancks hits in such indefinites upon a mode of expression which somehow seems – temporarily, at least – to take the guilt from his shoulders. He can generalise it as unavoidable, and at the same time provide himself with his own personal philosophy, distorted though this is. His habit of inserting an often picturesque but apologetic comparison can be placed under the same heading. These features speak volumes against the society which forces him to adopt them; are, indeed, a telling indictment of the whole system. Moreover, Dickens has handled the gradual unfolding of Pancks' true character with considerable artistry, the essential decency gleaming repeatedly and increasingly through the 'indefinite manner' until finally the reader feels he is standing, if not before a new man, at least before one who has become more significantly realised.

FANNY DORRIT: BETWEEN PUBLIC GENTILITY AND PRIVATE INSTABILITY

Like Mrs Skewton, Mr Dorrit's elder daughter is a character with two distinct idiolects: one that is brought out only in private, primarily before her younger sister, Amy (with others of her family circle the genteel touch does begin to creep in); the other reflecting her public face – the face she puts on for Society. This latter idiom is, naturally, of the genteel register rooted in the standard dialect and perfectly acquired from her arch-enemy, Mrs General, a woman she openly rejects yet who holds her in the bondage of the 'rules' of Society. Within the freely-chosen constraints of such a world, Fanny – compared by George Gissing to the type of London shop girl![13] – is at once alertly and pugnaciously witty, dogmatic, domineering, fitfully plaintive, petulantly aggressive and (true daughter of the father) inordinately sensitive about her social standing. This last is, of course, revealed in that cloak of genteel utterance she has been trained to don as the occasion demands. Needless to say, it is a genteel idiom of high individuality – full of peremptory phrases, moral protestations, angry expletives, sarcastic witticisms, rhetorical questions and statements forever signalled by the tag 'I do declare once for all'.

Towards her sister she can also be domineering, but will follow this in rapid succession with attitudes that are in turn patronising, impatient and (very occasionally) loving. These attitudes help to mould her other, private idiolect, one in which the extreme modal vacillations are a perfect mirror of her natural, unstable self, and in which her actual choice of vocabulary and syntax is completely *un*pretentious. Acutely relevant to this 'uncertainty manner' is her conspicuous habit of attaching some sobriquet or sundry epithet to her sister, not all of which are complimentary. She appears to have an unlimited amount at her disposal, varying them according to the mood of the moment and displaying an intriguing range of animal imagery: 'little Mole', 'Miss Bat', 'my Anchor', 'Angel', 'my Pet', 'little owl', 'little Tortoise', 'silly puss', 'little mouse', 'little Marplot' and, about Mrs General, 'cat in gloves'. These are some examples from just one scene (588–93), adding weight to the assertion that probably no other character in Dickens carries this trait to quite such an extreme.

Fanny's schizophrenic outlook on life, of which her two speech idioms are an accurate reflection, is clearly a direct result of the desperate but futile struggle she carries on with herself. It is an outlook that has been forced upon her by the operation of the appalling circumstances of her young life on a selfish, snobbish nature inherited to a large degree from her father. More, perhaps, than any other character in the novel, she has chosen her prison, for, as her private utterances show, she is intermittantly aware of the baleful significance of the steps she is taking. But she takes these steps notwithstanding, and turns her back finally on Amy's example, erecting walls to shut out the voice of common-sense and decency. She is the image of perverting states of imprisonment.

The depth of achievement which is *Little Dorrit* owes its overwhelming force above all to the even greater progress Dickens had made in mastering the tools of his trade when facing the complicated demands raised by the goals he had set himself. In none of his previous novels has the fictional speech been so thoroughly and artistically subordinated to the thematic needs, and in no other of his novels, before or after, has the author so successfully struck a compromise between the eloquent – though now more subtle – variations on single idiolectal ground themes and the necessities of the overall structure. His genius, dramatic in every sense, is everywhere, pervading every line, his whole artistic personality taking the reader/listener by the throat and convincing him through the sheer intensity of his incomparable writing techniques. To come were new triumphs of a different nature: the stylistic triumphs of the 'oral style', with the unique possibilities of its grand unifying web of interrelated rhetorical modalities, the artistic results of which are to be discussed in the next chapter.

11 *Great Expectations* to *Edwin Drood*

Great Expectations,[1] basically a tragi-comic Victorian morality oscillating between the realistic and the fantastic and including, typically, fairy-tale elements, is above all a masterpiece of construction. Neatly divided into three parts, it depicts the innocent childhood, fall and regeneration of a person subject to the corrupting influence of money. The blossoming of the author's personal style – his 'new' style – is taken a whole stage further from the startlingly vivid developments revealed in the descriptive passages of *A Tale of Two Cities*.[2] Now there is a perfect ease, grace and restraint in what Graham Greene has called 'Dickens's secret prose'[3] with its 'delicate and exact poetic cadences, the music of memory, that so influenced Proust'.[4]

All this comes out beautifully in the varying modes employed by Dickens to put over the story as told in the first person by the now middle-aged Mr Pirrip. These variations were necessary if the reader were to differentiate clearly between the two 'I's ('now' and 'then') and the two sets of thoughts and feelings. Just how successful the author was can be seen in an early episode, the one in which Pip the child, hastening through the early morning mist with stolen provisions for the escaped convict, Magwitch, has to run the gauntlet of cows grazing on the marsh (14). Despite the basic narrative being in fully mature, adult language, Dickens still manages to capture the uncontrolled flights of imagination, the curiosity, the fears and the naivety so typical of children. All this is dramatically enhanced by the simplicity and ingenuousness of the 'real' speech of a child as directly blubbered out by the boy.

Of crucial interest in regard to the fictional speech, and a fact which makes a study of its role imperative if one is to achieve a full understanding of the complex web of modal relationships in *Great Expectations*, is the manner in which it has been made to serve three functions: that of bringing out the subtleties of individual relationships through idiolectal interaction, that of defining the steps taken in Pip's *Lernprozess*, and that of acting out its part within the overall structure. All this has been executed with immense skill and artistry, pointing up the comedy and tragedy with equal effect, and simultaneously giving the reader a microcosm of society with all its pressures and constraints.

As pointed out above, each individual speech idiom plays its part in illuminating Pip's progress towards maturity. In this respect, it is possible, with one exception, to divide these speech idioms into two groups: those that reflect hostility towards Pip and his fortunes, and those reflecting goodwill and succour. The exception is supplied by the idiolect of Mr Jaggers, the apparently all-powerful, amoral laywer, whose utterances, in manner and content, would seem to bespeak a god-like omniscience and ability to control at will all those who come within his sphere of influence – and this includes practically everyone in the novel; even the redoubtable Miss Havisham is 'afraid of him' (227).

MISS HAVISHAM: SPEECH IN THE SERVICE OF HATE AND REVENGE

This key character – a 'rich and grim lady ... who led a life of seclusion' (xv) – belongs, for all her later regrets, to the negative group mentioned above. Her idiolect is rooted in the standard dialect. Its salient feature – at least until the change of heart she experiences in her last scene – is a vehemently imperative manner towards those who are unfortunate enough to come into contact with her. The resulting syntax is short, simple and functional to the extreme (53–4), and this is how Pip gets to know her. Thus, her speech manner at once sets not only her perverted nature, but also her role in the general structure: the sowing of hate through the ugly manipulation of children at a formative age. There is, for example, a world of meaning in the brutally abrupt 'Beggar him' (55) order to Estella when Pip admits that the only card game he can play is 'beggar my neighbour'. The significance of her imperative mode becomes even greater if taken together with a key phrase she had thrown out immediately before: 'You can break his heart' (55).

Miss Havisham's variations on this key locution are drummingly, morosely insistent – corresponding in form to the chief stylistic feature of this period in Dickens' creative life – and possess at times a [dramatic poetic quality] as in the outburst in which she tries to push Pip deeper into his fateful feelings for Estella: 'Love her, love her, love her! ... Love her, love her, love her! If she favours you, love her. If she wounds you, love her. If she tears your heart to pieces – and as it gets older and stronger it will tear deeper – love her, love her!' (226). Note, too, how Dickens' fondness for three-fold syntactic rhythms breaks through. Such groupings can be framed, as in the same scene, by Miss Havisham's mannered imperatives: 'Hear me, Pip!' and 'Love her!' (226). There is also very obvious irony in this particular passage, as Pip himself comments – 'more like a curse' (227) – for this is a mockery of the word 'love', driven home, so to speak, by the very repetition. Later, however, in the dramatically charged scene in which Estella repudiates her, Miss Havisham becomes passionately bitter, and her syntax falls into the less elegant but more poignantly direct four-square structure of double time: 'O, look at her, look at her!'; 'Let her call me mad, let her call me mad!'; 'So proud, so proud!'; 'So hard, so hard!'; etc. (290–1).

For Miss Havisham and her idiolect, this moment – Estella's repudiation – is the turning point. What follows is a triumphant confirmation of Dickens' now more thoughtful, more artistic, techniques. Gone are the days when the reader was subjected to a clumsy reversal of idiolectal purpose; now there is a gradual unfolding of a subtly modified speech idiom corresponding perfectly to the severe psychological shock undergone by a character who has seen the whole *raison d'être* of her existence collapse into ruins. In the next episode in which she appears, she is already moving towards a less positive, more drawn-out, genteelly petulant idiom (341–2). By the time she reaches her last climacteric scene, the alteration is complete. The sentences have become yet longer and, although lexically just as simple and straightforward, there is now a poetical aura about her reiterated appeals to Pip and her comments on the sincerity and dignity of his new-found honesty. Sometimes the choice of phrase can be just a shade too artificial, archaic even: "'Tis noble' (376), for instance. Of particular interest is the subsequent semantic softening of her deep-rooted propensity for using the imperative form, as in her desperate plea to justify her manipulation of Estella and its appalling consequences: 'My dear! Believe this: when she first came to me, I meant to save her from misery like my own' (378). It is fitting that her last words – 'said innumerable times' (381) after she has been burnt like an evil witch at the stake – should be: 'What have I done! ... I forgive her!' (382).

Composed as it is of the domineering language of hate and rancour born of her obsessive desire for revenge, Miss Havisham's idiolect in its original form fulfils consummately all its functions within the general structure. Like a witch, she is the death of life, and as she decays, so the perversions and aggressions of her speech idiom also decay until they are finally cauterised, to be followed by a painful rebirth of a new speech idiom corresponding to her new awareness of self and what she has perpetrated. More, it is in the interaction with Pip as a boy and man that this gradual modification of her idiolect can be seen as running parallel to certain changes undergone in his speech, each development throwing the other into greater relief. In both cases, the changes stem from increased self-awareness, but, whereas in Pip's speech they mirror groping steps in his growth towards maturity, in that of Miss Havisham they simply stem from static feelings of guilt, resignation, despair even. Similar, though less glaring, contrasts are to be observed in her idiolectal reactions to other characters, above all to her protégée, Estella.

ESTELLA: THE RHETORIC OF ROBOT FUNCTIONALISM

We eventually learn that this character is the daughter of Magwitch, Pip's convict benefactor, and Molly, Jaggers' servant and a suspected murderess. She has been adopted and brought up by Miss Havisham as an instrument of revenge on all men. A knowledge of her origins and subsequent fate are of crucial importance in attaining a full understanding of the complexities of this novel. Like Miss Havisham's, her idiolect also undergoes a change, two in fact, both in keeping with personal circumstances: firstly, there is the move from the speech idiom of Estella the hard-bitten, spiteful child to that of the poised, sophisticated (though still cold and hard) young woman she later becomes; secondly, there is the further alteration arising in the final chapter (both versions), which will be discussed presently.

Typical of Dickens' new psychological subtlety is his endowment of the child's speech idiom with, as would be only natural in real life, many of the features also to be found in that of Miss Havisham, her guardian, above all the same sharp imperative manner and lexical simplicity. To this Estella adds robot-like, coldly vituperative reactions typical, we may assume, of children brought up in the same way. On their first meeting, the unfortunate young Pip has to put up with a great deal of this aggressive speech: 'don't loiter, boy', 'Don't be ridiculous, boy', 'He calls the knaves, Jacks, this boy!' (51–5); and a little later: 'You little coarse monster', 'you little wretch' (76).

In Estella's first episode in the second part of the novel, there is, logically, a change, but it is a surprising one. She is now, of course, older and has been to a finishing school abroad, with all that this entails. Yet, for all that, her new idiom does not convince. She is found speaking in a rather more elaborate, certainly more polite mode, hovering between the genteel register and plain, straightforward English: 'I must have been a singular little creature ... I remember I entertained a great objection to your adversary' (223). The choice of this mode, colourless as it is, could be reckoned a slip-up, for, in her next appearance, Estella moves over to a speech manner far more in keeping with a creature who, although covered with a thin veneer of refined civilisation, is still clearly the unfeeling, robot-like creation of Miss Havisham's perverse methods of upbringing. The mechanical instructions she gives to Pip – functional to the extreme – are the verbal reflexes of the fully manipulated puppet she has so shockingly become: 'We have no choice, you and I, but to obey our instructions. We are not free to follow our own devices, you and I' (251). The influence of Carlyle's obsession with determinism is as evident here as in the previous novel,[5] and through it all there is a shimmering irony lending a double perspective to everything Estella says. In the great quarrel she has with Miss Havisham, the functional plainness and directness of her grown-up idiom is an obvious manifestation to her guardian of the enormous rift now between them (289–92). However, despite her cruel, self-possessed indifference, Estella is to some degree aroused, this coming out in the rising intensity of the rhythms, in the two- or three-fold anaphoric structures of her devastatingly cutting utterances (291).

Perhaps no stronger argument could be brought forward in defence of the original, cancelled conclusion written for this novel than the single utterance Estella makes. In contrast to the falsely genteel rhetoric of the revised version inserted upon Lord Lytton's advice (457–60), it is sensible, direct and without any elaboration (cf. *GE* Appendix). Be that as it may, Estella's essential (grown-up) idiolect is one supremely adapted to the hard, clear ruthlessness of her attitude to men in general and to Pip in particular. Its functional bareness lays waste to his heart, sits continually in harsh judgement on him and, more intensely, on Estella's perverting guardian, Miss Havisham. Estella's idiolect, in the logic of its origins and development and in its thematic validity, is admirably woven into the complex patterns of the novel.

JOE GARGERY: NON-STANDARD IDIOM AND SIMPLE INTEGRITY

Of those characters basically friendly towards Pip, Joe Gargery – that soul of purity radiating a child-like unaffectedness and artlessness – occupies a key position in the novel, embodying the moral norm against which Pip's progress through life can be measured. Much of the essential goodness of his nature shows itself in his choice of words; Magwitch, for example, is a 'poor miserable fellow-creatur' (36), and his own father, who had never done anything but beat his wife and Joe, 'were that good in his hart' (42). But this quality comes out most of all in his advice to Pip after the latter has admitted telling lies – it is perhaps a key sentence in the whole book: 'If you can't get to be oncommon through going straight, you'll never get to do it through going crooked. So don't tell no more on 'em, Pip, and live well and die happy' (66). He possesses, moreover, an evident inborn vitality – not neurotically forced like that of his wife – which, together with the qualities already mentioned, renders his idiolect both arresting in itself and of considerable structural importance.

Joe's idiolect is well and truly rooted in the non-standard dialect, being adorned with a larger variety of such detail than any other working-class character – except for the special case of

Stephen Blackpool's Lancashire dialect – since Jo (*BH*). Some indication of the density involved can be deduced from the following, found on one page alone: 'onmerciful', 'a'most', "xcepting', 'wigour', 'anwil', 'a-listening', 'hart', 'abear', 'tremenjous', 'we was', 'doo', 'a-biling', 'tolerable hard', 'kep', 'Whatsume'er', etc. (42). His uncertain lexical command leads to word construction of marked ingenuity, such as his 'purple leptic' (apoplectic) from the same page referred to above. Later, equally exotic examples are 'outdacious' (66), 'architectooralooral' (210), 'coddleshell' (codicil) and 'Mrs Camels' (Camilla) (441). Despite this non-standard complexity, Joe's idiolect is not difficult to follow.[6] Moreover, there do not seem to be any inconsistencies in its presentation – a considerable achievement amidst the demands of weekly serial-writing.

Joe has two speech tags, both reserved for Pip: 'old chap', often preceded by 'I say, you know! Pip', and, mirroring the innocent naivety of his soul, 'what larks' – this latter being the first thing Pip hears when he comes to himself after his long illness (439). His most conspicuous rhetorical feature, however, is the habit of emphasising certain words, phrases, even whole sentences. Dickens indicates this with capitals, italics or unorthodox use of hyphens: 'Ram-paged', 'Mog-ul', 'How AIR you', 'GOD', 'as-TON-ishing'; Mrs Joe is 'a-fine-figure-of-a-woman' (43).

Joe's integrity is so strong that it finally makes him a verbal match – pointedly, the only one in the whole novel, despite the touch of incoherence involved – for even the redoubtable Mr Jaggers who, in his bullying manner, does not believe that the simple blacksmith will not accept money for losing Pip: 'Which I meantersay ... that if you come into my place bull-baiting and badgering me, come out! Which I meantersay as sech if you're a man, come on! Which I meantersay that what I say, I meantersay and stand or fall by!' (134). The strongly marked and for Dickens now very characteristic use of the anaphoric mode is immediately obvious and extremely effective.

Simple and full of unspoilt goodness though Joe may be – the warmth of his nature being symbolised by the hearth and forge which dominate so much of his life – he is fully and sadly aware of the world's social divisions. This is extremely marked in the opening lines of his parting words to Pip, now the snobbish young gentleman in London embarrassed by Joe's presence: 'Pip, dear old chap, life is made of ever so many partings welded together, as

I may say, and one man's a blacksmith, [and] one's a coppersmith. Diwisions among such must come, and must be met as they come' (212). The passage as a whole is Joe's only really extended speech in the novel, and the one most free of non-standard detail – usually a sure sign that Dickens has something more noble in store. And this proves to be the case, for it is used to sum up Joe's homely, fundamentally Christian approach to life, thus realising a typification role in the personal sense. More, it also draws out the representational function served by his idiolect in the overall structure, expressing in a nutshell the very essence of Dickens' own answer to Pip's moral dilemma, one pervading the book from beginning to end. The tone of regret, reinforced by the short, direct, repetitive naivety of Joe's syntax, suffuses the entire statement with a trace of that melancholy sadness which pervades this, in many respects, most unusual of Dickens' novels.

With Joe, the author was faced with the problem of creating an idiolect that expressed simultaneously the blacksmith's essential simplicity of heart and the complexity of his vital role in the novel. A solution was found by using straightforward syntax to underscore Joe's simplicity and incorruptible honesty, and, to a fluctuating degree, complicated rhetorical and lexical features to represent his structural significance as a whole. He, more than any other character in the book, is the yardstick against which Pip's progress towards maturity can be measured. Further, he is the only one to retain fully his purity and integrity, no matter with whom he comes into contact. His idiolect reflects this by remaining basically unaltered throughout, the only changes being the slight fluctuations indicated above and which occur when he is deeply moved. Hence, his speech is fully realised and deeply convincing at both a personal and general level, displaying the theatricality of Dickens' stylised idiolectal mode at its best.

ABEL MAGWITCH: THE RHETORIC OF EMPHASIS

Abel Magwitch, alias 'Provis', is a convict transported to Australia and forbidden to return to the 'old country' under pain of death. He turns out to be not only Pip's benefactor, but a person who in every respect, material and spiritual, plays a decisive role in the narrator's development. His clearly defined idiolect contains a fair sprinkling of non-standard detail, making clear the lack of formal education without disturbing the general flow. However, it is primarily through its rhetorical features and rhythmic patterns that the speech is truly individualised.

The most eye-catching feature of this idiolect is the scrupulous indication of emphatic tone, a feature obviously springing from the same creative forces which produced the obsessive reiteration of Dickens' later style. Magwitch's speech is punctuated throughout by italics, capital letters and exclamation marks. But even more suggestive is the constant stressing of the first person singular pronoun 'I', despite the character's completely unegoistical nature. A glance at a speech he makes to Pip, after the latter, to his snobbish horror, has established that the convict and not Miss Havisham is the source of his income, will dramatically reveal just how emphatic his delivery can be: it is literally riddled with the features referred to above, plus a certain obsessive use of the word 'gentleman' – used no less than five times here and, significantly, not once presented in non-standard orthography (313). Also very distinctive is Magwitch's marked predilection for affixing various appellations to the people with whom he talks. Those used towards Pip are of particular interest, for they show the gradual alteration in Magwitch's feelings towards him: at first 'little devil', 'young dog', then, on his illegal return from Australia, 'Master', 'Noble Pip', 'dear boy' (this very frequently) and 'my gentleman ... the real genuine One'. With deliberate derogation, he refers to himself as 'warmint', 'heavy grubber', 'a old bird' and 'dunghill dog'.

Knowing the kicks and rebuttals of his whole tragic life (his is perhaps the deepest tragedy of the book), the very decided tone of his idiolect is clearly representative of his determination to fight back, to achieve something in a world interested only in keeping him down. There is, indeed, a note of desperation in it all, underlined, for instance, in Magwitch's very first words in the novel, to Pip in the churchyard: 'Hold your noise! ... Keep still, you little devil, or I'll cut your throat!' (1–2). His insistent use of 'I' can also be viewed as a humble searching for his own identity, sublimated in the desire to make a 'gentleman' out of the only person – Pip as a boy – who had ever shown him true kindness. In one short passage alone, he resorts to 'I' no less than nine times (304). Besides serving to reflect his personal tragedy and trigger off Pip's development towards maturity, Magwitch's idiolect is also an embodiment of one of the book's major themes: the pitiless workings of society on individuals, especially on those from the lower classes. The nobility and courage that finally emerge in the convict's idiolect are further proof of the considerable sympathy, insight and artistry Dickens was now bringing to his presentation of psychological development through standard or non-standard fictional speech.

JOHN WEMMICK: DICHOTOMY IN SPEECH

If any one character through his speech and life actually personifies the dichotomic existence forced upon all members of the society depicted in the novel, it is Jaggers' clerk. In his official state, he is 'dry', 'square' and 'wooden' with a 'post-office of a mouth' and 'mechanical smile'. At home, however, in his preposterous but lovingly built 'castle' in Walworth where he tenderly looks after his old father, the 'Aged', he is warmer, more natural and kind, smiling 'with relish not mechanically'. As is to be expected, his office idiom is completely functional: the syntax, for instance, really is 'square' and 'wooden', the choice of phrase 'dry', short, to-the-point, and the verbal reactions almost as mechanical as his 'post-office smile'. Both office and private idioms are sparingly decorated with non-standard usage, in particular slang and other colloquialisms: "'em', 'made ... express', 'it don't', 'thankee', 'ain't', 'rum', 'bit of game', 'deuce a bit of a lady', 'blade', 'cove', 'Yah', 'Stinger', 'Ecod devilish', etc.[7] It would seem that he has gathered some of this from contact with the upper-class register. There are just enough traces of the legal register to typify Wemmick unmistakeably.

Both at work and at home, Wemmick's idiolect displays two extremely characteristic rhetorical features. His speech tag 'portable property', which occurs far more at the office, places his professional philosophy in a manner at once succinct and wrily amusing, despite its frightening amorality. It is an approach which is drily underlined in his answer when Pip comments that people are only cheated, robbed, and murdered, If there is bad blood':

'Oh! I don't know about bad blood. ... There's not much bad blood about. They'll do it, if there's anything to be got by it.'
  'That makes it worse.'

'You think so?' returned Mr Wemmick. 'Much about the same, I should say.' (161)

Thus Wemmick, too, begins to play a part in Pip's development, a further step being when the clerk defends himself for accepting gifts from clients (190). However, in a novel in which many characters stress their words to an unusual degree, Wemmick brings the idiosyncrasy to a high art, it being without a doubt the chief rhetorical feature of both aspects of his idiom. Dickens uses four methods to indicate this emphasis: italics, predominating, especially in respect to pronouns and auxiliaries; repetition, either of his own words or those of others; hyphens, as in 'Ca-pi-tal' (188); and capital letters. They are not crowded one upon the other in single episodes, but are spread with a fair amount of consistency right through Wemmick's every appearance. The resort to such emphasis could be put down to his determination to infuse careful precision into each utterance. Be that as it may, the habit certainly sits so deep that it also pervades the speech of his private sphere.

The remarkable dichotomy of Wemmick's nature comes strikingly to the fore when Pip, bent on giving Herbert a financial start in life, asks the clerk for his advice at the office. In his function here, Wemmick informs Pip that a person should never 'Invest portable property in a friend. ... Unless he wants to get rid of the friend – and then it becomes a question how much portable property it may be worth to get rid of him' (277). When Pip presses him for a more positive response, his reply contains the essence of his split nature: 'Walworth is one place, and this office is another. Much as the Aged is one person, and Mr Jaggers is another. They must not be confounded together. My Walworth sentiments must be taken at Walworth; none but my official sentiments can be taken in this office' (277). Needless to say, he gives Pip helpful, constructive advice – at Walworth. When he walked from his home back to the office, 'Wemmick got dryer and harder... and his mouth tightened into a post-office again' (198). It seems he feels continually obliged to stress the gulf between the worlds: 'the office is one thing, and private life is another' (197). With this statement, Wemmick pinpoints the split role assigned to him within the overall structure, by which he is a living indictment of the society he trades on yet, privately, ignores. More, the same dichotomy can also be taken as a parody of Pip's schizophrenic scale of values, of his vacillation between the world that attracts him (its false values blinding him – temporarily, at least) and that simpler world he has left behind him. In place of verbal fireworks, Wemmick's idiolect displays a fine range of artistic subtlety, both in its gradation of psychological penetration and in its crucial interaction with the speech of others, above all with that of Pip.

MR JAGGERS: BULLYING IN THE INTERROGATIVE MODE

The wily, domineering, seemingly omniscient legal adviser to both the recluse Miss Havisham and the convict Magwitch, is connected in some way or other with nearly every person in the book. In fact, his position in relation to the two sets of characters converging round Pip is a rather ambiguous one. In the power given him by his knowledge of all those he has dealings with, in his authoritarian, amoral approach to his profession and bullying manner of dispensing justice, he creates an impression of almost god-like omnipotence. His idiolect, though, is real enough, with its very strong element of the legal register. This is evident less in its actual phraseology and more in the manner of delivery, which is aggressively interrogative.

Jaggers is always cross-examining, even in private life, never admitting anything, his idiolect being, as a result, syntactically and lexically plain to the extreme. It comes as a surprise, therefore, to find in his speech an extended example of the syntactic reiteration otherwise typical of this period. This crops up when he characteristically warns Pip that if his benefactor chooses to reveal himself, he (Jaggers) will have nothing to do with it. The three-fold repetition of the subsidiary clause is anaphoric, and the whole completely symmetrical. However, his cross-examining mode remains far more typical: 'Understand,' he says to Pip, 'that I express no opinion, one way or other' (134). He makes 'no admissions' (392), tolerates 'no feelings' (394), and rejects such a concept as 'Recommendation'. This last comes up in a scene when Pip learns that he is 'a young fellow of great expectations' (130). After abruptly mentioning Matthew Pocket as a possible tutor for Pip, Jaggers shrewdly realises that Pip knows the name. He finally bullies him into discarding the word in question and substituting 'mention'. By being presented in indirect speech, Pip's responses are kept as neutral as possible. This draws out the pugnacity of the lawyer's idiom in such a manner that it stands there in stark relief, overwhelming and unanswerable (132). Small wonder that even the most hardened criminals are afraid of him.

Jaggers' speech idiom is more completely functional than that of any other character in Dickens. Yet it is saved from becoming dry by the tremendous vitality of the aggressive interrogative mode he almost invariably adopts, and also, of course, by the fact that the idiom as a whole is unusual, despite its simplicity of structure; for who, indeed, speaks thus, even in fiction? The meaning of Jaggers goes beyond that of being the novel's puppet-master; it reaches out into the future, into our time, with its cultivation of pseudo-personalities, of an amoral form of leadership based on ruthless manipulation of those who come under its sway.

The virtues of *Great Expectations* are plain for all to see: its structure is well-nigh perfect, and the psychological insight and modal flexibility of the language, particularly as manifested in the fictional speech, are nothing less than masterly. If any criticism can be made, it is that this work presents merely in rationed form, so to speak, some of the author's more characteristic and rewarding qualities – I refer especially to his wonderful gift for humourous locutions and his peculiar flair for theatrical stylisation. Still, the compensations are considerable, not least the 'oral quality' of the prose style; for this novel – like those to follow – is one to be read aloud and listened to with enjoyment. With this in mind, it is no surprise to learn that Dickens actually did prepare a version for public reading; that he did not, in fact, make use of it, was probably due to a length excessive for such a purpose.

Our Mutual Friend[8] is the last and most viciously satirical of Dickens' panoramic views of the Victorian world. The striking stylistic developments of the years immediately preceding now add up to an ideal technique for exposing the illusory vacuity of a world nurturing itself on an ever-increasing greed for money, a commodity clearly symbolised by the filth of the Harmon rubbish heaps. It was this obsessive cupidity, one consuming the prosperous and powerful England of the 1860s, that inevitably led to the 'Waste Land' society dominated by the 'Hollow Men' so pungently depicted by the author in this, his last completed novel.

But, despite a certain erratic application of this or that character's speech, it is above all the ironic detachment, poetic expressiveness and elliptical brevity of the author's style in this 'truly mimetic'[9] work that prove to be nothing less than masterly. Every aspect of the society under observation is reflected as objectively – and devastatingly – as in a mirror. The mirror metaphor crops up in the novel again and again, directly or indirectly, Dickens presenting the reader with a world turned upside down. It is a world, then, of inverted relationships, in which the role of the one character is reflected in that of the other, and in which the 'pathetic fallacy' (or its opposite, the 'thinging' of human beings) is a salient factor, the effect being continually reinforced by the application of that finely tuned, beautifully balanced rhetorical tool, the author's 'oral style' now, in this novel, reaching full flower. The long, often pedantic, rambling narrative prose of immediate – and not so immediate – tradition, heavy with Latinisms, sidetracking clauses and choked phraseology, had now been completely thrown out of the window, Dickens having fully arrived at a mode of writing more subtly and economically responsive to the demands he was making on it. We now have a style that is, in Norman Page's words, 'so much more flexible and astringently individual ... [seeking] to imitate the emphatic rhythms and repetitions of speech – not ... spontaneous or informal speech, but a heightened and often emotional rhetoric'.[10]

Unfortunately, the speech of some of the characters – key ones at that – reveals at times a certain haziness of direction, as a result of which each of those concerned tends unexpectedly to adopt a mode of speech utterly out of keeping with the one usually employed. We have, for example, Gaffer Hexam, first as he talks to Rogue Riderhood (4–5), then in his manner to Mortimer Lightwood (22); Betty Higden when she meets Mrs Boffin for the first time (198), and later her unbelievable rhetoric regarding the Poor Law (383); further, the convincingly deceptive ridiculousness of Alfred Lammle's speech when turning on the charm to Georgiana Podsnap (258–9), against the preposterously clumsy wit of his answers to Fledgeby (273–4). Worst of all is Mr Boffin, who displays far-reaching inconsistency between his initial scenes, particularly with Wegg (51), and those that follow, such as his confrontation with the fortune-hunting Lammles (644): on the one hand, speech that is keenly redolent of Cockney cheek, wit and quick-thinking; on the other, obviously slower in delivery, dry to the point of colourlessness, and with a touch of pomposity. Nameless, they would never be identified as the same person. Such idiolectal fluctuations – the book's chief weakness, in fact – cannot simply be put down to structural needs, nor are they by any means typical. They indicate, perhaps, a Dickens sporadically succumbing to an uncharacteristic but not surprising tiredness.[11]

MR BOFFIN: FROM COCKNEY SPARKLE TO POMPOUS GENTILITY

We have drawn attention above to the marked inconsistencies apparent in Mr Boffin's speech, and must underline what a pity this is, for the Boffin of his first appearance – and in occasional flashes later – is the possessor of a real language gem, one sparkling with especial brilliance in his lively sallies with Silas Wegg, his 'court poet'. Complete with delicious malapropisms, in which Dickens reverts to his early mastery of the form, and sundry other comic distortions, the whole also reveals a picturesque turn of phrase plus a habit of rising in intensity when its owner gets a bee in his bonnet. Moreover, following Dickens' tendency in these later works to more frequent indication of strong emphasis, Boffin's speech at all times contains a large number of capitals ('Fashion', 'Sociability', 'Comfort', etc.) and much lexical repetition: 'Morning, sir! Morning! Morning!'

How shattering, then, to move to the later idiom, dry, pompous, stiffly genteel, with the non-standard colouring unbelievably reduced. The tedium is slightly relieved in his aggressive – vituperative even – manner towards his secretary, Rokesmith, in which, so typically for the author though here somewhat unconvincingly, the rise in temper is delineated by anaphoric repetition (590). The about-turns of Boffin's speech seem to suggest that Dickens either found it impossible to settle on a fixed concept for this character's idiolectal role in the novel or, for a variety of reasons, fell into periodic bouts of mental tiredness in this or that instalment. The fluctuations are too frequent that a definite structural purpose can be discerned behind them.

MR WEGG AND MR VENUS: POETIC AND SENTIMENTAL GENTILITY IN DUO

To a greater extent, perhaps, than in any of the previous novels, the idiolects of the various characters come more truly into their own when played off against each other in dialogue: Fledgeby's against that of Mr Riah, the worthy Jew, for instance, or those of the members of Society one against the other, to mention just a few. It is in his interchanges with Mr Boffin and Mr Venus, then, that Silas Wegg can be most appreciated.

For a man referred to by the author as 'dull and overreaching' and full of 'wooden conceit', Wegg is of a surprisingly imaginative and adroit turn of phrase, this being strengthened by sudden interpolations of doggerel as well as by his uproarious version of the poetically genteel manner. Using this mode, he takes the hand of Mr Venus in 'friendship' the moment he discovers he might get something by it: 'I scorn all lowlier ties betwixt myself and the man walking with his face erect that alone I call my Twin' (301). Mr Wegg is constantly and deliciously striving after a speech manner way beyond the limits of his normal Cockney idiom, this being brought out facetiously when Mr Boffin asks him if he 'know'd' the 'Decline-and-Fall-Off-The-Rooshan-Empire': 'I haven't been not to say right slap through him, very lately. ... But know him? Old familiar declining and falling off the Rooshan? Rather, sir!' (52). His is unquestionably a rewarding language collage, in both its external detail and intrinsic qualities. The parodic nature of its non-standard gentility lays bare the obsessive greed of Wegg's grasping, parasitic nature and the tawdry values of a society that has brought him to such a state.

Mr Venus, the taxidermist and articulator, is a melancholy soul, forever bemoaning his lot in a singular blend of the genteel, sentimental and professional registers rooted in the non-standard dialect, though less obviously so than is the case with Wegg's idiolect. He can be sparked off by, in particular, any thought connected with the love of his life, Pleasant Riderhood, Rogue's equally squint-eyed daughter, who, unfortunately for Mr Venus, objects to his profession: 'I sit here of a night surrounded by the lovely trophies of my art, and what have they done for me? Ruined me. Brought me to the pass of being informed that "she does not wish to regard herself, nor yet be regarded, in that bony light!"' (84). Later, gazing at the stars, his sentimental mode takes on a distinctly morbid note (306), only to be rudely and unromantically cut short by an impatient Wegg. There is, too, a rhythmic symmetry in his melancholy whimpering brought out when he is irritated. In one quavering outburst, directed against an impudent boy whom he has just served with a tooth by mistake, the first two sentences are not only anaphoric in form but are themselves repeated *in toto* on the same page (81).

Mr Venus' sentimental effusions and the reasons Pleasant gives for declining marriage with him bring love down to the level of comic nonsense, turning upside down the subtle interplay of the dramatic, highly-charged relationship that develops between Lizzie and Eugene. More, the very trade which Pleasant so suggestively rejects can be seen as an image of a society that is, to all intents and purposes, equally dead – emotionally so to all true values of the spirit. Finally, the genteel aspirations that he shares with Wegg, like the latter's overriding greed, are significant reflections of the same driving forces which govern the higher reaches of Society.

ALFRED AND SOPHRONIA LAMMLE: FROM PUBLIC GLITTER TO PRIVATE FUNCTIONALISM

Alfred 'the captivating' and Sophronia 'the mature young lady' – that fortune-hunting couple in the jungle of Society – are each, in the way Mrs Skewton also is, the possessors of two clearly defined idiolects: the one full of seductive, easy glitter, the shiny veneer covering the cheap product and reserved for public entrances; the other functional and to-the-point, with no frills, and automatically assumed for their private moments of truth together, when they are more like cat and dog than lovebirds.

Like so many with long training in Society, they are both consummate actors in their public role, their utterances complementing one the other ideally. Only seldom are they at a loss for words – words which, moreover, are never to be taken at their face value. Knowing as we do their true attitude towards each other, it almost hurts to hear 'my own', 'my soul', 'my life', 'Mr Inquisitive Pet', 'my Ownest', being tossed backwards and forwards between them. It is well-nigh incredible how they are continually able to perform their public role although receiving no encouragement from the objects of their brilliant (in form, not content) chatter. One superbly executed scene in this vein is that involving the procuring of those mute young 'lovers', the cruel, emotionally retarded Fledgeby and the simple-minded Georgiana Podsnap (262–7). Here, the idiolectal ease and surface glitter of the Lammles in duo as they try to feed the necessary words into the dumb mouths of their two hopeless protégés, vividly points up the whole tragi-farcical situation.

The two confidence tricksters perform with similar contrapuntal glitter – keeping up their virtually non-stop patter for three pages (641–3) – when taking breakfast with the painfully silent Boffins. Never at a loss for a word, the two arch-swindlers run on endlessly and effortlessly, each catching the tail-end of the other's remark and developing it further. It is like a never-ending game of tennis with language as the ball; a game played elegantly, genteelly, but between equally-matched partners neither of whom intends to defeat the other, for the performance is the thing – the spectators must be impressed:

'My Sophronia ... your too partial estimate of your poor husband's character –'
'No! Not too partial, Alfred ... never say that.'
'My child, your favourable opinion, then, of your husband – you don't object to that phrase, darling?'
'How can I, Alfred?'
'Your favourable opinion, then, my Precious, does less than justice to Mr Boffin, and more than justice to me.'
'To the first charge, Alfred, I plead guilty. But to the second, oh no, no!'
'Less than justice to Mr Boffin, Sophronia ... because it represents Mr Boffin as on my lower level; more than justice to me, Sophronia, because it represents me as on Mr Boffin's higher level. Mr Boffin bears and forbears far more than I could.'
'Far more than you could for yourself, Alfred?'
'My love, that is not the question.'
'Not the question, Lawyer?' (*OMF*, 641)

It is a shock to be brought down to earth in their private moments, especially when they are speaking to each other. Now there is no glamour, no sparkle; only a directness of diction, rude even, mixed on both sides with terms of abuse, this coming out particularly in the altercation concerning Fledgeby (267). Moreover, it will be observed that in contrast to their public idiolects, which differ almost not at all, their private speech idioms reveal distinct differences. In the altercation referred to, although each is sarcastic to the other, Sophronia's choice of word is distinctly milder, more feminine ('Booby'), whereas that of Alfred is harder, more masculine ('dolt', 'Devil'). Her sentences, too, are shorter, more under control; his longer, taking the sarcasm to greater lengths by repeating her words, and bringing out the latent brutality in his nature ('Get to bed').

The dichotomy between the Lammles' public and private speech forms, the one the reverse of the other, lays bare the whole sham that is the world of Society and is part and parcel of the topsy-turvy landscape of this bitingly satirical novel. The partnership this scheming couple has cynically agreed upon is rooted in greed and opportunism, not love, and it is just such an unscrupulous partnership that, at the other end of the social scale, Gaffer Hexam, although also living as a scavenger, has honour enough to reject (4–5). The differences that become apparent between their private, hence truly individual, idiolects are an eloquent commentary both on the appalling extent of the façade put up for Society and on the spiritual wretchedness of their own lives. No matter how or where he allows them to speak, Dickens makes his symbolic intentions devastatingly clear, realising this fully within the complex socio-parodic structure of the overwhelming stylistic achievement that is *Our Mutual Friend*.

EUGENE WRAYBURN AND MORTIMER LIGHTWOOD: THE AIMLESS SOPHISTICATION OF INDOLENT ABSURDITY

Bearing some formal similarities with the public voices of the Lammles, though very differently motivated, is the speech form shared, for the most part, by these two briefless (virtually) 'bastions' of the law. The intentional self-mockery of their diverting exchanges – also all surface glitter – not only serves a vital function in the novel's parodic-satiric structure, but also provides a striking prefiguration of the language of Oscar Wilde's brilliant social comedies written thirty years or more later – a remarkable instance of the depths of Dickens' sensitivity to the society around him, a society which had already (to most people, imperceptibly) begun to decay and disintegrate.

Eugene, particularly, exudes an irresponsible verbal charm, an amoral attitude which ridicules everything, above all that which takes life seriously and gives it a purpose. The absurd philosophising and airy witticisms of an indolent man utterly bored with the prospects before him could have been taken straight from the mouth of Algernon Moncrieff, as when Eugene admonishes Mortimer to do precisely what he himself does not do: 'I very much wish,' he says, 'that my example might induce *you* to cultivate habits of punctuality and method; and by means of the moral influences with which I have surrounded you, to encourage the formation of the domestic virtues' (284). Mortimer's subsequent request for 'an earnest word' with him – they have a new kitchen with no money to pay for it – only provides more fuel for the fire of his wit: 'In this desire for earnestness ... I trace the happy influences of the little flour-barrel and the coffee-mill. Gratifying' (285). As well as prefiguring the speech form of such as Moncrieff, that of Eugene also hints back in time to the 'Drone philosophy' (*BH*, 93) of Dickens' own Skimpole, especially in the sally provoked by Mr Boffin's unfortunate admonition to work like a bee if he wishes to get on (94). It must be remembered, however, that whereas the idiolect of Skimpole is a faithful reflection of his shallow, parasitic nature, that of Eugene, for all its ease and self-possession, conceals an otherwise very different, far more serious-minded person. The same verbal self-possession is more than a match for the barely controlled passion of the socially ill-at-ease Headstone, all the latter's remarks being turned back on him in the form of taunts until he is beside himself with rage (288–93).

Mortimer's 'flippant' manner is very similar, being, in fact, as the author himself tells us, directly 'founded on Eugene' (816). It is seen to its best advantage in his 'professional' talks with Mr Boffin (88–90). As is the case with the Lammles, the differences between the two friends come out when they drop the artificiality of their 'flippant' manner and shift over to a more direct idiom, one aimed, no matter how rarely, at a serious expression of their views. With Mortimer, though, there is an uninspired move into the stereotyped genteel register reserved by Dickens for so many members of the educated classes. On the other hand, even when serious, Eugene retains much of his covering – one could say, defensive – manner. More than anything else, it is this idiolectal difference between the two which, paradoxically enough, makes it clear that Eugene is fundamentally the deeper, more sensitive character, the one who is more convincingly depicted. The shallow pose he adopts towards life – accurately mirrored in his idiolect – is presented with such artistic conviction that we never lose sight of the basic earnestness of the man and his desire to find an object worthy of his serious dedication.

In Dickens' satirical depiction of Society, it is clear that for an intelligent, basically sincere character, a mask of aimless sophistication, with its indolent tossing off of one absurdity after the other, remains the easiest way to conceal – and thus protect from ridicule – the quest for something more worthy of its attention. What other subterfuge, anyway, is left to such a person in a world so emotionally deadened to the spiritual longings of others? Lizzie, brought up in a radically different social sphere, becomes Eugene's salvation and, as he moves into rhetorical reverse towards her, gradually shedding his flippant manner for one at once more functional, expressive and subtle, so she moves towards him, shedding equally gradually what lower-class idiom she had previously possessed until, linguistically, the class barriers are crossed. The reversals that their speech idioms undergo, correspond at a personal level to the changes in their fortunes, and at a general level to the symbolic purposes of the book's overall structure. At both levels, the achievement is one of considerable artistic address.

MR JOHN PODSNAP: THE RHETORIC OF DOGMATIC INSULARITY

Still within Society but at the other end of the rhetorical scale is this character's pompous, formulaic speech idiom, one thoroughly permeated by unfeeling, impatient didacticism. It would seem that the manner as a whole was founded on that of the author's by then middle-aged friend John Forster, who – obviously refusing to recognise himself – makes reference to the 'vulgar canting Podsnap'.[12] Be that as it may, Dickens makes use of this unpleasantly overbearing 'man of the City' to show up English insularity at its worst: 'Podsnap always talks Britain,' he writes, 'as if he were a sort of Private Watchman employed, in the British interests, against the rest of the world' (816). He gives this narrow-minded attitude the delicious title of 'Podsnappery', a mode consisting of a series of short, dogmatically emphatic declarations which, although rooted in the genteel register, exhibit no lexical complications – it is the tone which is everything. This is rendered with splendid comic insight in the banquet episode in which he questions (and, typically, lectures) a bewildered Frenchman who ends up having difficulties with the language: 'Our Language,' says Mr Podsnap, 'is Difficult. Ours is a Copious Language, and Trying to Strangers' (133). He has a sweeping answer for everything; one can almost hear the voice booming into and through the unfortunate foreigner: 'Our Constitution, Sir. We Englishmen are Very Proud of our Constitution, Sir. It Was Bestowed Upon Us By Providence. No Other Country is so Favoured as This Country' (133).

Although allowing Podsnap relatively few appearances in the book as a whole, Dickens has drawn in sharp relief, for all the world to see (or rather, hear), the deadening inanities of the ruling classes in his own land. Indeed, through the glaring insensitivities of his fulminating manner of delivery, Podsnap actually personifies the spiritual and emotional poverty of the nineteenth century English ruling classes that Dickens had fought for so long and which, in this his final completed novel, had become one of the major structural elements. As with all Dickens' most successful characters, Podsnap *is* his speech. Through it he fulfils a key satirical role, providing a brief yet eloquent indictment not only of his own mean-spirited character, but also of the very social order he stands for. In passing, it is worth observing that Podsnap – like Lady Tippins, the Veneerings, Mr Twemlow and, too, the four 'stuffed Buffers' – has almost as much written about him as is actually put into his mouth, and all in that marvel of economy and ironic detachment: Dickens' 'oral style'.

BELLA WILFER: A MATTER OF WILFUL PETULANCE

In respect of the small band of more convincingly drawn Dickens heroines, this character is a further progression in the line Dora–Estella, her strongly-delineated idiolect showing only traces of that conventional hero–heroine register which the author did not consciously begin to discard until he reached the figure of Amy Dorrit. The reader is presented with a clear and gradual development from the speech of a spoilt, petulant girl in her late teens towards that of a young woman standing at the gates of maturity.

Initially, the speech of this impetuous, unpredictable, mercenary young lady – cheated of her fortune and with 'widowhood' thrust upon her – swings dramatically from explosions of scorn towards her sister ('nasty', 'chit', 'And did I say I did, miss'), back to moments of self-pity ('It's a shame'), and out again in inconsequent bursts of affection for her father ('dearest', 'silly', 'kindest'), who in her own peculiar way she truly loves. Linguistically, she just cannot keep still for a minute, and very much part and parcel of these erratically sudden changes is an inordinate fondness for the superlative mode in all its forms, as well as for streams of adjectives of a virulent nature.

Not surprisingly, this fickle 'double spoilt' young lady has a formidable temper, one which brings strongly marked rhythms of a stabbing nature to her idiolect (36–7) plus a habit of reiterating words until she can do so no more; she comments on her unusual position, for instance, by repeating the adjective 'ridiculous' no less than eight times in one short passage (37). The major change in her later speech is the much lower frequency of the sudden, petulent about-turns. It is a change brought about in a gradual, almost imperceptible process manifesting great artistry and subtlety in its execution. There is now a touch of gentility, too, though with such a personality the effect can be somewhat unreal, this coming out clearly in the contemptuous manner she adopts when pulling the secretary, Rokesmith, down a peg (374–8). Moreover, the rhythms are less staccato-like and of a longer nature, usually involving symmetrical anaphoric structures, as when she openly admits her mercenariness (321) or angrily puts Mr Boffin in his place: 'I shall never be sorry for it ... and I should always be sorry, and should every minute of my life despise myself, if I remained here after what has happened' (600). One wonders how much of this was Ellen Ternan![13]

If ever a Dickens heroine comes to life – whether attractively or not is beside the point – it is this wilful creature, one whose complicated, fiery nature can shake off all gentility and lead her into roundly attacking the very person she likes, simultaneously preserving a perversely critical honesty. Poor, well-intentioned Mr Boffin comes in for some of this: 'I hate you! ... You're a scolding, unjust, abusive, aggravating, bad old creature! ... I am angry with my ungrateful self for calling you names; but you are, you are: you know you are! ... you're – you're a Monster!' (597). The nicely caught variety which is her idiolect gives the reader all sides of her spirited, capricious nature, of her impetuous switches from the saucily flirtatious to the disdainfully proud, from the self-seeking to the self-denying; she is offensive, irritating, appealing by turns; she will turn the world upside down and immediately set it to rights again – in short, she is *alive*, and makes this dramatically clear in every word she says, a factor of no mean thematic import in a world governed by so much deadening, meaningless rhetoric. Bella Wilfer is, then, one of the novel's positive characters – perhaps the most positive – and a person who, before she leaves the reader, finally succeeds in taming her wayward self, plumping for what is good, sincere and generous.

FANNY CLEAVER ('JENNY WREN'): THE STRUCTURAL IMPLICATIONS OF 'QUEER' SPEECH

The dolls' dressmaker – 'a little quaint shrew; of the world, worldly; of the earth, earthy' (243) – is the most singular character in the whole work. Her extremely varied idiolect, with its enigmatic mixture of sharp, pert dignity and ambiguous precocity, and her significant role as 'queer' daughter turned mother to her weak, helpless, drunken father, together furnish the most prominent illustration of the upside-down values of the world depicted by Dickens in this novel.

Although she is obviously of the lower classes, her speech – albeit colloquial to a high degree – is notably free of non-standard detail, the colour being provided by the rhetorical and rhythmic features. Despite the fact, too, that she is a cripple, the author has resisted the temptation to sentimentalise her through typification. Her speech, for instance, with the peremptoriness of its swift aggressive darts and the sharpness of its irrepressibly direct predications, is anything but halting in manner. For all that, she is perversely determined to draw attention to her physical disability, doing so with words which appear so frequently that one can refer to them as speech tags: 'I can't get up ... because my back's bad and my legs are queer' or 'But I'm the person of the house'. This is only too true, she *is* just that person and her father 'the bad child', her abrupt, domineering manner towards him reaching a disquieting extreme in the merciless diatribe to which he is subjected when once more coming home drunk (and late): 'Go along with you! Go along into your corner! Get into your corner directly!' (240) – and after he has done so: 'Oh-h-h! ... You bad old boy! Oh-h-h you naughty, wicked creature! *What* do you mean by it!' (241) – then, on receiving grovelling tears: '*I* know your tricks and your manners ... *I* know where you've been to! ... you disgraceful old chap!' (241). And so this incredible tirade continues until, after forcing him to empty his pockets of all the money he has, she sends him to bed without any supper.

A very typical feature of her speech is supplied by her constant readiness to attach some suitable epithet – often ironic, even sarcastic – to those with whom she comes into contact: 'bad child', 'noodle', 'conjuror', 'Lizzie-Mizzie-Wizzie', 'money godmother', 'Wolf in the Forest', 'wicked Wolf', 'Little Eyes', 'fox', are just some. There is something very redolent of the true Cockney in the speed and readiness of these flashes as well as of other asides: 'Don't look like anybody's master' (280), she whips out when hearing that Fledgeby is Riah's master. In all this can be detected a certain weird sense of humour – if humour it is – a quality taken to perverse lengths in the punishments Jenny Wren delights to think up for those who annoy her. They form a grotesque part of the perpetual war she wages on so much of mankind, in particular on men, whom she sees as the root of all evil, and on children, towards whom this 'old child' seems at times to bear something amounting to hate. These conceits – for they are nothing less – exhibit considerable imagination, and necessitate continuous resort to the conditional, a form often found in Jenny's speech, underlining as it does the uncertainty dominating her life. Consider, for instance, what she would do to 'Him' (the man bold enough to marry her) if he came home late: 'When he was asleep, I'd make a spoon red hot, and I'd have some boiling liquor bubbling in a saucepan, and I'd take it out hissing, and I'd open his mouth with the other hand – or perhaps he'd sleep with his mouth ready open – and I'd pour it down his throat, and blister it and choke him' (243).

Rhythmic patterns of two kinds can be determined: firstly, the very personal incremental rhythms arising from the multiplication of certain words or grammatical forms. These create a kind of incantatory effect, confirming the witch-like impression she sometimes makes: 'Him, him, him', she cries when hearing Sloppy's name mentioned; and on the roof with Lizzie she bursts out with 'Crying, working, calling'. Others that occur are 'work, work, working here' and 'skip-skip-skipping' – the hyphenation in the last example is puzzling, but is, perhaps, meant to indicate an accelerating effect. Secondly, she occasionally slips in what appear to be improvised rhymes, not in itself so original, but hers are odd in their content, stabbing metre and underlying suggestiveness. Sitting with Lizzie and seeing Eugene (whom she distrusts) approaching, she comes out with: 'Who comes here? /A Grenadier./ What does he want?/ A pot of beer' (234). Another arises when she tells Lizzie, Bradley and Charley Hexam to carry on talking: 'You one two three, /My com-pa-nie,/ And don't mind me' (225). Their oddness corresponds very aptly to the oddity of Jenny Wren's own somewhat warped, certainly eccentric, nature – a nature reminding one, to a degree, of the initial Miss Mowcher, the dwarf.

Great structural importance is attached to Jenny's profession – the dolls *are* Society, as her way of talking about them directly indicates (436). Indeed, she goes to rich houses to watch Society coming and going, a fact poignantly drawn out by Marcus Stone's illustration (417). The dolls are also cleverly utilised when Jenny takes one, calls it 'Mrs Truth' – Mrs T – and makes it serve as a kind of judge in her questioning ('grilling' might be a better word) of Bradley Headstone as to his motives regarding Lizzie (342–3); the whole procedure unnerves the agitated teacher completely. But the doll metaphor is put to its most compelling use, subtle and significant, in the Eugene/Lizzie sub-plot. When Eugene informs Jenny he is thinking 'of setting up a doll', she tells him he 'had better not' for he is 'sure to break it. All you children do' (238). The 'doll' is, of course, Lizzie who, be it noted, is still in the room, though there is no indication that she understands the implications of the exchange. Be that as it may, the dialogue between Eugene and Jenny works on several levels at once, shedding light on the individuals involved, on both their personal problems and general attitudes, as well as on the clash between two opposing moralities, a clash that forms the very basis of the author's artistic conception and over which he retains a convincing hold from beginning to end of the novel. As a piece of writing, the passage is as profound as it is revealing.

A mode very much Jenny's own is that one best described as 'exalted' and occurring when she is lifted out of and above her normal manner, turning her into a symbolic figure. In a sense, the mode is of a prophetic nature, pointing up in heart-rending ambiguity the underlying moral intention of the work as a whole, as well as revealing Jenny's dreams of a better world. At such moments, the rhythms of her speech move from the brief four-square directness of the previously mentioned patterns into a more measured rhetorical tread suffused with poetic overtones. Following on the exchange resulting from Eugene's flippant remark about 'setting up a doll', for instance, she describes how she smells flowers while working, and develops this like an incantation until she has worked herself up into something approaching a state of ecstasy while continuing to recount her spellbinding vision (238–40). Shorter, but equally pregnant, is the double-edged 'Come back, and be dead!' which she calls out to Riah when sitting on the roof with Lizzie, and which is reiterated again and again (281–2). In a similar vein are her words when looking into the fire (once again she is with Lizzie), wrung out of her by her pity for Lizzie's position in respect to Eugene (349).

Robert Morse – who cogently points out the expressive binding principle of 'doubleness' that permeates the novel under discussion – sees Jenny as 'all doubleness, with her double life of visions, her crippled legs and vigorous hair, her precocious insight'.[14] To this could well be added her grotesque double role of mother-daughter to the same dissolute man, and, further, that of vicious enemy or intensely loyal friend to those in the hostile, alienated world around her. Not for her the arbitrary parasitic machinations of such as the Lammles, but only utter, unselfish devotion to the chosen few such as Lizzie and, later, Eugene, whom she significantly calls back to life. Small wonder that in her baleful circumstances, she lives on dreams of diabolical punishments and resorts so often to the use of the conditional. Hers is, indeed, a complex soul, one acutely suited to stand at the heart of the novel's conflicting values, and one which is, moreover, perfectly mirrored in the extraordinary intricacy and subtlety of her wide-ranging, many-levelled speech idiom. Of the *dramatis personae* in this profound satirical panorama of Victorian life, she is far and away the most striking creation.

Without a doubt, one of this work's most considerable achievements is the extent to which each character, through his or her speech, has been moulded into the novel's general structure, each in turn becoming an inevitable and indivisible part of the author's total thematic concept, the one reinforcing the other and vice versa. Never before had Dickens displayed such delicacy of touch, such nuances of colour, such suggestiveness of tone in such a variety of idiolects, and simultaneously such artistry of integration. In all this he was aided by the immense flexibility of the authorial modalities – his 'new' style, one which could absorb, it would seem, any fictional speech without any sense of incongruity or abrupt change-over. Whatever else, then, may be charged against *Our Mutual Friend*, its prose is, with minor exceptions, on a level of its own, one above anything Dickens had produced up to this time. If *Little Dorrit* is a triumph of personal expression, albeit beautifully written, *Our Mutual Friend* is first and foremost a signal triumph of style. It is, as Jack Lindsay puts it, 'one of the greatest works of prose ever written. A work which finally vindicates Dickens's right to stand, as no other English writer can stand, at the side of Shakespeare'.[15]

In relation to the novelist's previous fictional achievements, *The Mystery of Edwin Drood*[16] – his last, half-finished novel – occupies, both stylistically and psychologically, a position similar to that occupied by *Parsifal*, Wagner's final opera; for, in his unflagging search for new worlds to conquer – or in his, as Barbara Hardy puts it, 'attempt to push beyond the frontiers of his genius'[17] – with its demand for improved, more responsive techniques, Dickens arrived at a unique richness of expressive power in his writing. The strikingly suggestive qualities of the previous novel's prose have now been heightened by the addition of a peculiar kind of nervous energy, entirely new in his output and which may have been stimulated by the histrionic excitation brought upon by the public readings.[18] The presence of this quality seems to add an extra dimension of perception to everything the author puts before us, a depth of insight into the ambiguities of life that he had never achieved before.

All this is, of course, as true of the truncated book's fully realised idiolects as it is of its authorial modalities, and even though the fictional speech is in a few cases rhetorically conventional, there is nowhere that uncertainty of purpose that occasionally marred *Our Mutual Friend*. With immense artistry and wide-ranging flexibility, Dickens has succeeded in creating speech that explores and reflects the deep-rooted divisions and de-personalisation of the decaying microcosm of society that is the cathedral town of Cloisterham. In no other of his novels is there such a complete and subtle marriage of character trait, rhetoric and structural intention, and in no other have the narrative voice and fictional speech been so perfectly integrated, the one merging so naturally and effectively into the other.

JOHN JASPER: THE SPEECH OF DISSOCIATION

This character plays a vital role in the half-completed novel, his sinister, obviously split, personality dominating in some way or other almost every page, even when he is not actually present.[19] The peculiarities of his dissociative personality are strikingly reflected in the dramatic swings he makes between three different modes: standard English with a touch of the genteel, an intensely original form of the melodramatic register, and the odd, disjointed speech he falls into when under the influence of opium. The resulting contrasts are considerably heightened by the deliberate neutrality of tone and absence of colour in the dominant mode, Jasper's form of standard English.

It is clear, such contrasts will be all the more effective if they occur suddenly. In the middle of bidding a courteous goodnight to the stonemason Durdles, for instance, after their midnight tour of the Cathedral, he is interrupted by a hail of stones from that 'hideous small boy', the Deputy, whose unexpected appearance acts on Jasper's already guilty conscience and arouses him into a blazing fury: 'What! Is that baby-devil on the watch there! ... I will shed the blood of that impish wretch! I know I shall do it!' (140). It is undeniably melodramatic language, but melodramatic in the most positive, most electric sense of the word and a long way from the unreal reflexes of (say) Ralph or Nicholas Nickleby. In this relatively early outburst, Jasper is unwittingly indicating the presence of that other side of his nature, one normally hidden and over which he has no real control – he can only try to conceal it. There is, too, a world of dramatic irony in 'shed the blood', particularly when one remembers that the words are being spoken outside the cathedral, the very place he has planned to desecrate with his dastardly deed.

It is above all the overpowering rhythms of Jasper's melodramatic mode that make it so utterly convincing, terrifying even. They bring a highly-charged, 'live' quality to the general tenseness of this otherwise purely theatrical language. It is at its most electric in his wild declaration of love to the terrified Rosa, an intensely-felt flood of words which rises to an irresistible climax. The following excerpt shows how an unrelenting impulse is achieved by a symmetrical sequence of four temporal-conditional clauses, succeeded at once by a catalogue of his tortured feelings in which the gradual disintegration of the rhetorical symmetry signals the break-through of the now unbridled emotions in all their chaos. The whole is intensified to an unbearable degree by the agonised epistrophic reiteration of 'I loved you madly':

Rosa, even when my dear boy was affianced to you, I loved you madly; even when I thought his happiness in having you for his wife was certain, I loved you madly; even when I strove to make him more ardently devoted to you, I loved you madly; even when he gave me the picture of your lovely face so carelessly traduced by him, which I feigned to hang always in my sight for his sake, but worshiped in torment for years, I loved you madly; in the distasteful work of the day, in the wakeful misery of the night, girded by sordid realities, or wandering through Paradises and Hells of visions into which I rushed, carrying your image in my arms, I loved you madly. (219–20).

Jasper's addiction to opium, on the other hand, gives rise in his speech to the above-mentioned disjointed effect (13), an effect that is magnified to an exotic and significant extreme by the bizarre collection of visions he experiences when coming out of a stupor. It is the book's opening scene (1–3). Here Dickens takes upon himself the immensely complicated task of presenting the reader simultaneously with two cultures, those of the East and West, and over and above this with the confused ramblings of a schizophrenic drug addict. It is important to remember that all these factors form the very basis of this novel's thematic structure as the author obviously conceived it. Jasper, while slowly coming to himself again, sees the rusty iron spike of the opium den's bedstead hovering before his eyes and, rising in the background, a vision of Cloisterham Cathedral – Rochester Cathedral transferred to fiction and symbolising here Western culture. At first he cannot imagine what it all means and where he is; a riot of fantasy overcomes him (1). Apart from the symmetry of the metrically balanced rhythms in which archaic usage ('thrice', 'Stay!') falls naturally into place, there is a lowering, sinister foreboding in much of the phraseology: 'impaling', 'clash', 'scimitars' and 'still no writhing figure is on the grim spike' – a phrase hinting horrifically at the crime Jasper intends to carry out on his nephew, Edwin Drood, a crime around which the whole book revolves. Suggesting as it so artfully does the divisions of Jasper's tortured nature as well as the fusion of two utterly opposed cultures, this is structural use of language at its best, revealing consummate skill in the creation of an uncannily weird atmosphere that cogently sets the scene for the rest of the book.

All the divisions of Jasper's idiolect mirror directly the divisions within his own nature. Through his deep-rooted dissociation, he can be seen as a creature from the lower depths of Dickens' vision of society *and* as a model of Victorian respectability from a surface made unstable by the decaying influences of a moral code that has lost its meaning. But he is more: with his built-in divisions he is simultaneously a reflection and a horrifying reproof of a society alienated from itself, a society in which words have become automatic, unthinking responses totally unrelated to what the speakers actually think or do. More than any other character, Jasper, with his rhetoric of dissociation, fulfils a structural role as significant as it is all-pervading.

EDWIN DROOD AND ROSA BUDD: PARODIC VACILLATION AND REPRESENTATIONAL ABSURDITY

It is the artificial engagement forced upon these two characters in childhood that is to have such fateful repercussions for all concerned. Edwin's capricious idiolect, however, contains no doom-laden overtones, no baleful hints of what is to come. On the contrary, what strikes the eye most immediately is his breezy, colloquial manner, one full of youthful high spirits and studded with baby-talk ('moddley-coddley', 'Pussy') and rhymes as well as with teenage emphasis (notably the pronouns 'I' and 'you') and idiom ('jolly old', 'queer old', 'kind of'). This is, of course, only to be expected from one so young and inexperienced. But a closer look reveals abrupt changes of mood and tempo that spring from weakness of character rather than from immaturity. This inability to concentrate for more than a moment on any one theme indicates a lack of depth and conviction of which he himself is only too well aware: 'I am but a shallow, surface kind of fellow' (15), he says. Indeed, his rhetorical waywardness leads him as much into flashes of honesty and impulsive acts of affection (161) as into thoughtless selfishness (12).

A general feature stemming directly from Edwin's immature vacillations and lack of confidence is his decidedly varied manner of delivery towards those with whom he is talking: towards Jasper, his uncle, free and easy; towards Rosa, uncertain and querulously selfish, his grumbling tone expressing how sorry he feels for himself; towards Neville, downright arrogant and provocative, his language full of contemptuous phrases; towards the shrewd but fundamentally kind Mr Grewgious, who, as Edwin is painfully made to realise, is disappointed by his thoughtlessness, he is embarrassed and insecure – this leading to 'PRosa' (117), that delightful blending of 'Pussy' and 'Rosa'. These idiolectal fluctuations can be viewed as an ironic parody of Jasper's own rhetorical dissociation; but not only that: they actually draw out and heighten the warring aspects of his uncle's dual personality. Certainly, Edwin's varying speech manner serves to highlight the character of each person he comes into contact with, and his disappearance must have caused some structural problems for the author.

Rosa Budd – or 'Rosebud' as she is called – is the orphan girl promised in marriage to Edwin. She is, perhaps, even more spoilt than he is, but less conceited and more aware of the serious implications of the unusual relationship forced upon them. Her speech is equally immature and full, if anything, of even more verve. Rosa, however, is rhetorically more consistent, passing only from the speech of a childish – though sometimes amusing – schoolgirl to that of a young woman on the threshold of life and conscious of its seriousness.

Towards Edwin, initially her chief partner in conversation, she adopts a tone which is a mixture of childish petulance and the peremptory – she is clearly the dominating partner! Dickens has caught not only the light, lexically somewhat limited, idiom of a lively young schoolgirl ('ridiculous', 'absurd', 'tiresome', 'Ugh',

'Eh', etc.), but also the 'whimsically wicked' (27) mixture of contempt and affection she feels for Edwin: 'I *like* him' (88), she declares. She even invents another fiancée for him, plus a preposterously illogical reason why this 'person' '*must* hate the Pyramids', continuing

> Ah! you should hear Miss Twinkleton . . . bore about them, and then you wouldn't ask. Tiresome old burying-grounds! Isises, and Ibises, and Cheopses, and Pharaohses; who cares about them? And then there was Belzoni, or somebody, dragged out by the legs, half-choked with bats and dust. All the girls say: Serve him right, and hope it hurt him, and wish he had been quite choked. (27–8)

Part and parcel of this schoolgirl idiom is her constant recourse to exaggerated emphasis, shown through italics, repetition, capital letters, hyphens and an almost inordinate use of 'so' as an adverb.

Through Rosa's idiolect – as through those of Dora Spenlow and Bella Wilfer – the author has presented the kind of heroine who, even if she can be foolishly irritating, is at least thoroughly alive and individual. The absurdity of her position in relation to Edwin finds its structural counterpart in the absurd flights and reiterations of her airy, delightfully realised schoolgirl idiom. For all her immaturity, she stands on the positive side of Dickens' vision. Nowhere can it be said that she has succcumbed to the moral decay otherwise pervading so much of the work. Nor can the division between Rosa and Edwin – present before and after they part – be put down to her: his position and the necessary break between them sadden and mature her until she becomes one of the author's most rounded heroines. As George Gissing writes about her, 'Change of times, growth of experience, widening of artistic consciousness and power – all are evident in this study.'[20]

THE REV. SEPTIMUS CRISPARKLE: BETWEEN GOOD HUMOUR AND HARSH JUDGEMENT

This character arouses interest with respect to both his profession and his idiolect. The novelist's writings make it clear that in general he had little sympathy for organised religion, whether

Roman Catholic, Church of England or one of the nonconformist sects. The Rev. Frank Milvey (*OMF*), although a minor character, had been the first Anglican minister depicted with sympathetic understanding. Now, with Mr Crisparkle, the author goes one stage further and gives such a character an important function in his fiction, presenting him, too, with speech that clearly defines and reflects his generally likeable yet, on occasion, somewhat equivocal nature.

'Mr Crisparkle, Minor Canon, fair and rosy ... musical, classical, cheerful, kind, good-natured, social, contented, and boy-like' (7) – thus the author's succinct description to which the cleric's light, uncomplicated speech manner corresponds utterly. His high spirits and good humour bubble over almost everywhere, as in his half-sung response when Jasper tells him he cannot appear at a musical evening, an example which also shows the success with which Dickens tackled phonological difficulties: 'we shall miss you, Jasper, at the "Alternate Musical Wednesdays" tonight; but no doubt you are best at home. Goodnight. God bless you! "Tell me, shep-herds, te-e-ell me; tell me-e-e, have you seen (have you seen, have you seen, have you seen) my-y-y Flo-o-ora-a pass this way!"' (8–9). Crisparkle's speech, and hence his good nature, is also shown to good effect against the gentility of his mother's feminine stubbornness (96–8), and in the polite, controlled humour of his initial brushes with the overbearing oratory of Mr Honeythunder (56). There is, however, something unreal in his last encounter with this unbelievable 'philanthropist'. The canon's final, very extended answer (194–5) is the kind of reply many of us would like to give under similar circumstances if we had the time and ability; Dickens has fallen into the temptation and taken the time. A trifle more convincing and certainly more amusing is Crisparkle's later remark to Neville about Honeythunder, with its neat play on prefixes: 'it signifies nothing ... whether he is *ad*verse or *per*verse, or the *re*verse' (198).

If anything mars this portrait, it is the feeling – aroused above all by the authoritarian tone of some of his admonitions to Neville – that in his own purity of soul he sometimes comes down rather hard on others; that he is, indeed, a 'goody-goody', a 'creeper' even. There are three specific occasions when such doubts arise: firstly, his unnecessary and insensitive correction of the English of Mr Tope, the not over-educated verger. This is, moreover, Crisparkle's very first appearance in the book, creating at once, unfortunately, a rather negative impression. Then, secondly, there is his exceedingly overbearing reaction towards Neville after the latter has confessed his deep feelings for Rosa, albeit feelings kept fully under control and secret from the recipient. Such expressions as 'outrageously misplaced', 'monstrous', 'irrational and culpable fancy', 'sullen, angry and wild', 'blind and envious wrath' (104–5) barely merit the hand-kiss Crisparkle then receives from Neville's twin sister Helena. Finally, the reader is left with the canon's speedy, ignominious submission to the Dean's hypocritical, un-Christian demand that Neville (suspected, unjustly, of murder) must leave Cloisterham – although here it must be admitted that his whole existence and that of his mother very probably depended on the decision.

These blotches, minor though they may be, are clearly the result of the inroads made by a morally decaying society into even such a sincere man as this otherwise fearlessly upright minister of the church. They are faint signals of that de-personalisation that could – who knows – go further even here. On the other hand, these blotches apart, Crisparkle's idiolect, with its irrepressible energy, is a relentless force for good, this being brought out to its best advantage in his exchanges with Jasper, exchanges that take a vital place – thematically and morally – in the general structural development.

MR GREWGIOUS: DROLL, STIFF AND PRECISE

This key character is Rosa's guardian and legal adviser, 'an arid sandy man' of 'incorruptible integrity' (84), 'awkward [and] agreeable' (85), and with a voice 'hard and dry' (87). His singular idiolect is as much a mirror of his direct honesty as of his basically affectionate (though reserved) nature and quaintly whimsical, almost zany, humour. This last-named trait emerges when, leaving his professional register behind, he decides to try and lighten the situation a little. In an interview with his young ward, for instance, he tries to make strict use of a 'guiding memorandum' (86) to remind himself of what he is to say – the results are hilarious: '"Well and happy" ... "Pounds, shillings and pence" ... "Marriage" ... "Will" ... "Wishes" ... "Leave"' (86–91) – the last word is a reminder, and nothing else, that he must take his leave! Forgetting where he is, he often goes even further, slipping inadvertently into the most droll, nonsensical observations. Rosa, in fact, comes in for a great number of these affectionate, well-meant quips: 'My visits ... are, like those of the angels – not that I compare myself to an angel. ... I merely refer to my visits, which are few and far between. The angels are, we know very well, upstairs' (85). Small wonder that 'Miss Twinkleton looked round with a kind of stiff stare'. When his feelings are aroused, he has a typically Dickensian predilection for piling up words, sometimes in an agreeably ridiculous fashion: 'Untenable, unreasonable, inconclusive, and preposterous!' (91). He also continually resorts to such exclamations as 'Just so', 'In short', 'Dear me', 'Lord bless me' and 'Ah me!'

When acting seriously in his professional character, especially if his suspicions are aroused. Mr Grewgious makes use of the legal register with an ironic precision that is nothing less than devastating. We see this in action when, for the benefit of a highly embarrassed Edwin, he attempts – and very successfully, too – to 'draw a picture of a true lover's state of mind'. The whole passage is quietly relentless in its search for the truth (121–3). But it is with Jasper that Mr Grewgious is at his most precise. Indeed, his entire verbal manner towards this sinister figure is coloured by a sharpness otherwise missing from his speech. He obviously neither likes him nor trusts him, calling him on one occasion a 'slinking individual' (201), and on another going to the lengths of saying 'Damn him!' (228), following this with an unexpected burst of vicious rhyme. His words with and about Jasper have, it is clear, considerable bearing on the thematic development. An instance is their conversation immediately after Edwin's disappearance when Mr Grewgious rebukes Jasper for having made up his mind that Neville is the suspect (175–6). Clever structural use is also made of the very slight difference between his and Jasper's final words together about Edwin and Rosa:

> 'God bless them both!'
> 'God save them both!' cried Jasper.
> 'I said, bless them,' remarked the former ...
> 'I said, save them,' returned the latter. 'Is there any difference?' (95).

The difference, in fact, not only illuminates the personal nature of each, but also carries a hint of the catastrophe to come, being yet a further indication of the extent to which speech has become a multi-functional tool in Dickens' efforts to achieve greater structural unity.

The idiolect of Mr Grewgious, oscillating as it does between the awkward comedy of unhappily chosen words, the stiffly reserved listing of duties he has to discharge, and precise, well-directed observations, shows up, even in this loveable, essentially honest character, the divisions that pervade the society depicted in this half-finished novel. Yet, in this case, the divisions do not run deep – they are but cracks on the surface caused by the moral decay around him. He *is* sure of himself and of what he feels is right or wrong. He has perforce a built-in suspicion of the ways of the world, an attitude which he tries to combat in the case of those he feels affection for: and it is this conflict that accounts for the oscillations of his speech idiom. However, this suspicion, allied with his ironic precision, comes into its own in certain exchanges with others, especially those with his arch antagonist Jasper. Every remark he then makes is loaded with wide-ranging implications, all having an immediate bearing on the plot. In this dry man of the law, therefore, the marriage of personal rhetoric and structural intention has been achieved with no loss of individual interest; the reader never loses the feeling that the person before him is truly alive. As a study in psychological penetration and functional validity, the character of Mr Grewgious belongs firmly on the new paths Dickens was now taking.

DURDLES AND 'DEPUTY': DE-PERSONALISED SPEECH AND 'STONE 'EM' PHILOSOPHY

Of all the idiolects in this book, Durdles' – or rather, that of the combination Durdles and the 'Deputy' – is the oddest; the one, too, which is obviously meant to serve a deeper, more universal purpose than those of its fellows. Both these characters – like Mrs Billickin in the same novel – are brilliant throwbacks to the early Dickens, with respect to both eccentric behaviour and non-standard detail. That cheeky, irrepressible urchin, the 'Deputy' is, in particular, far more a product of the London streets than of those of the provincial town Cloisterham. Only, both offer far more than mere eccentricity of speech and personality.

Stony Durdles is the Cathedral stonemason and a 'wonderful

sot'. The most immediately noticeable feature of his idiolect is the habit of referring to himself in the third person, a habit to which the author himself draws attention (37). Durdles' aggressive response when Jasper comments on the coldness in the tombs not only highlights this speech habit as such, but also shows itself, despite its brevity, as rich in implications for the plot as a whole: 'And if its bitter cold for you, up in the chancel, with a lot of live breath smoking out about you, what the bitterness is to Durdles, down in the crypt among the earthy damps there, and the dead breath of the old 'uns ... Durdles leaves you to judge' (39). Quite apart from the ironic overtones of 'live breath smoking out about you', this snippet underlines that Durdles is constantly among the dead and decaying – the state of the society Dickens is depicting – and can be taken as symbolising this, his use of the third person de-personalising him for the purpose. Further, he also serves the direct purpose of unknowingly supplying the means by which Jasper gains the key to Mrs Sapsea's tomb, for of so much in the unresolved plot we are certain.

Although frequently – and with reason, perhaps – surly, Durdles is always simply and directly honest. There is no false respect or servility about him, his speech exuding something 'earthy', a kind of folk wisdom. This is very evident in a further reaction to Jasper who has just called the stonemason's ability to establish the thickness of vault walls 'a gift': 'I wouldn't have it at a gift. ... I worked it out for myself. Durdles comes by *his* knowledge through grubbing deep for it, and having it up by the roots when it don't want to come' (47). He is nothing if not bluntly articulate. His rude honesty comes into its own in his interchanges with Sapsea, for whom he has the greatest of contempt (130) and over whom he always, in his way, triumphs – the triumph of personal integrity over the blindness of moral corruption: 'I never was brought afore him', he says when told he must call Mr Sapsea, now the Mayor, 'His Honour', 'and it'll be time enough for me to Honour him when I am' (214). Durdles follows this by making Sapsea the subject of a sarcastic ditty, such rhymes being an additional feature of his idiolect, although the level of inspiration is not always high.

The 'Deputy' is that 'hideous small boy' (42) hired by Durdles to throw stones at him. However, the relations between them are, as the author himself points out, 'of a capricious kind' (44). The stonemason's own comment (to Jasper, again) on the 'Deputy' –

whom he calls 'own brother to Peter the Wild Boy' – not only tells us a great deal about the character of each, but also represents a bitingly sarcastic appraisal of the laws of capitalism at work. The description reveals a Durdles beginning, rhetorically, with an anaphoric structure, moving then into the 'catalogue' technique so typical of the author during the last period of his creative life:

'I took him in hand an gave him an object. What was he before? A destroyer. What work did he do? Nothing but destruction. What did he earn by it? Short terms in Cloisterham Jail. Not a person, not a piece of property, not a winder, not a horse, nor a dog, nor a cat, nor a bird, nor a fowl, nor a pig, but what he stoned, for want of an enlightened object. I put that enlightened object before him, and now he can turn his honest halfpenny by the three penn'orth a week.'

'I wonder he has no competitors.'

'He has plenty, Mr Jasper, but he stones'em all away.' (44)[21]

Although the 'Deputy' is not given much to say in the book as a whole, what he does say is non-standard to an almost unintelligible degree, as in the furious rage he feels for Jasper whom he (significantly) mistrusts: 'I'll blind yer, s'elp me! I'll stone yer eyes out, s'elp me! If I don't have yer eyesight, bellows me!' (141). His passion is certainly as violent as that of his adversary, but there is a pointed difference between the threat 'I'll blind yer' and Jasper's menacing 'I will shed the blood of that impish wretch!' (140). Some of the Deputy's non-standard detail is exotic, to say the least. His 'Kinfreederel' (Cathedral), for instance, which on one occasion is written with an '-al' at the end (208), and on another rendered thus: 'KIN-FREE-DER-EL' (276), offers, as G. L. Brook has pointed out, 'enough material to keep a philologist happy for a long time'.[22] The 'Deputy' has, too, a speech tag 'Yer lie' which, although short, is a pregnant comment on society as a whole. He also makes use of an extended motif that is a transformation of a children's rhyme of the time, and which he 'chants like a little savage' (42) when going through his ritual of stoning Durdles:

Widdy widdy wen!
I – ket – ches – Im – out – ar – ter – ten,
Widdy, widdy wy!
Then – E – don't – go – then – I – shy –
Widdy Widdy Wake-cock warning! (42 ff.)

As indicated above, the chief structural importance of the 'Deputy' lies in his relationship with Durdles and Jasper, although [it] seems clear enough that the author intended to build up a further relationship: that with the mysterious stranger Datchery. Indeed, the 'Deputy' becomes so friendly with this 'investigator' that he even tells him his real name: 'Winks' (274). Again, the subsequent comment of the 'Deputy' carries a world of meaning in the simplest of language: 'But, I say . . . don't yer go a-making my name public. I never means to plead to no name, mind yer. When they says to me in the Lock-up, a-going to put me down in the book, "What's your name?" I says to them, "Find out." Likewise when they says, "What's your religion?" I says, "Find out"' (274–5). This is, to some extent, reminiscent of Jo's evidence at the inquest on Captain Hawdon (*BH*, 148), but the characterisation of the 'Deputy' goes much further in its inferences: Jo, bewildered, accepts his appalling lot; the 'Deputy', equally bewildered, stones it. He and Durdles together, in their aggressive rejection of the decaying world around them, are its most telling indictment, the one inarticulate, the other articulate. The impact they make is of both immediate import and universal significance.

With the exceptions of those of Neville and Helena Landless and, partly, of Mr Honeythunder, the speech idioms of all the half-completed book's characters, even those in the most minor roles, have been drawn to such idiolectal perfection that the only fair investigation – which space precludes – would be one involving them all. Mr Sapsea, for instance, the preposterously pompous Mayor of Cloisterham spouting meaningless phrases and repetitions in the genteel manner; his overbearing attitude to others, sweeping aside all contradictions and brooking no criticism, reminds one only too well of a lower-class Podsnap. Then we have Mrs Billickin – 'The Billickin' – with a miniature idiolect which is a gem in its own right as well as being, in some respects, a throwback to Dickens' earlier days. Against a very non-standard background, her vain attempts at the genteel add a glorious touch of the zany (250). The verbal tussles with Miss Twinkleton, which the boarding-house keeper wins hands down, are nothing less than sheer delight, the author playing with great artistry on the contrast between the educated and uneducated forms of the genteel register (255–9).

In the language of this book, Dickens displays to the full a unity of conception and achievement without equal in his previous work. This is reflected above all in the complete and unobtrusive integration of the fictional speech into the general flow of the narrative, an integration aided by the oral qualities of the 'new' style as well as the thematic implications of the speech itself. There is hardly a passage of dialogue that has not been charged with both a restless, forward-driving energy and a wide spectrum of meaning ranging from the immediately functional to the universally significant. Each idiolect has been made to mirror divisions that exist either within the characters themselves or in the world beyond, a world of decaying moral values and hence divided against itself. Thus, to a far more comprehensive degree the fictional speech has been endowed with an extra dimension of perception, a quality enhanced by the nervous energy pervading the writing as a whole. It is this quality that gives the prose of *The Mystery of Edwin Drood* its richly expressive power and depth of psychological penetration. The book, half-finished or not, remains the most convincing witness to the novelist's consummate powers in this his mature period.[23]

2 Dickens' Achievement

The idiolects of Charles Dickens are the highest and most extreme extensions of his unique, highly-stylised theatrical storytelling manner, and the artistry revealed in their development and utilisation makes decisively clear the author's gradual progress towards a bettering of his fictional art. A glance at the available literature will indicate that the present investigation is the first attempt at a systematic study of Dickens' chief idiolects on a comprehensive scale, one aiming to approach them both individually, the idiolect as a separate entity, and structurally, the extent to which this or that idiolect has, if at all, been integrated into the work to which it belongs.

In the foregoing investigation, it was possible to outline three brief periods of idiolectal development separated by two of a transitional nature. The individual brilliance of the great improvised idiolects of the first four novels helps to demonstrate, too, that whereas initially the authorial prose modalities – 'idiolects in the authorial mode', if one will – were not flexibly related aspects of a single unified style but a conglomeration of styles absorbed from virtually every influence coming in on the would-be novelist, the fictional speech was, in a great many cases – particularly that containing the non-standard features of London – already so strikingly original that it stood out entirely on its own. Thus, our study shows that right from the beginning it is possible, to a greater or lesser degree, to speak of *idiolects*, of 'private languages', and not merely attempts to reproduce as closely as possible the speech of living persons. Nor, further, were such speech idioms directly modelled on those of other fictional characters that ha[ve] gone before; however, there are clearly many significa[nt] influences, especially from Smollett and the world of the stag[e,] whether serious or variety. At their best, though, Dickens' idi[o]lects are quite simply triumphs of literary collage.

In these lines, the word collage has been very deliberate[ly] chosen, for in any such systematic analysis of the idiolects it soo[n] becomes manifest that they are entirely synthetic in characte[r.] For the sake of convenience (there are cases of overlapping), th[e] various features have been roughly classified under four heading[s:] linguistic individualising features; those of a rhetorical natur[e;] typifying manners of general delivery; and, finally, rhythm[ic] patterns. It was found that in many idiolects, all four could b[e] present to some extent or other. Further, that within eac[h] category any number of features with varying degrees of intensi[ty] and exaggeration were utilised, the pronounced individualisatio[n] and/or typification of a character's speech idiom springing fro[m] the drumming insistence with which any one feature has been p[ut] over. In this respect, it also becomes apparent that the idiolects [of] the earlier novels reveal a definite trend towards an increasin[g] density of linguistic and rhetorical features, non-standard typif[y]ing features being on the whole fairly sparingly applie[d] (especially after the character's first appearance). This tren[d] reaches its peak in *Martin Chuzzlewit*, in the idiolects of those tw[o] incomparable characters Mrs Gamp and Seth Pecksniff. Th[e] subsequent progress from *Dombey & Son* onwards is one in whic[h] an ever-growing artistic subtlety makes itself apparent, this goin[g] hand in hand with the author's determination to bend th[e] artificial speech modes to the exigencies of the thematic structur[e.]

The techniques so rapidly evolved to make each idiole[ct] uniquely interesting in itself had their roots to a high degree in th[e] influence of both the serious and variety stages. The necessity [to] apply some kind of easily recognisable language features ha[s] been thrust upon Dickens by the need in complex serialised fictio[n] – a form new at the time – to identify a character quickly an[d] readily. Of these, the best-known borrowings from variety, fo[r] instance, are the speech tags and the famous Wellerian compar[i]sons and, as far as typification is concerned, the 'staccato' an[d] 'never-ending' modes.

From the beginning, Dickens was also greatly assisted by h[is] knowledge of the speech forms of lower-class Londoners. It wa[s] this knowledge that led to the development of those *typifying qualities* rooted in and so characteristic of that wonderfully varied pastiche which in Dickens' works is the non-standard dialect of London. This is coloured with extreme effectiveness by, as the case may be, the cant, occupational, oratorical and – to a much slighter extent – the melodramatic registers. It was a fusion springing from the author's chief working method, a mimetic one involving selection, concentration and exaggeration of certain speech habits. In other words, far from being an attempt to present an exact phonetical transcription of the dialect concerned with all its diverse elements, it was much more a deliberate and in the main fairly consistent artistic synthesis of certain arbitrarily chosen non-standard features, common or otherwise, through which a very convincing *impression* is given of the actual speech upon which it is modelled. As suggested, its chief success is due – and this is a point which up to the time of writing had not been drawn out clearly by any of the critics – to Dickens' uncanny ability to catch and then stylise both the rhythms of the prototype as well as its actual idiomatic features. The significance of these two aspects outweighs by far that of any phonological, lexical or grammatical borrowings.

Parallel to the evolution of the above, but with more variable success, *typifying speech* rooted in the standard dialect was also being presented to the reader. Here the professional and genteel registers led the way, being often highly original. However, the upper-class, oratorical and melodramatic forms – particularly the first- and last-named – approached, initially, caricature. In the first of these cases, the author's lack of first-hand knowledge (plus the somewhat juvenile sarcasm he sometimes indulged in), and in the last his weakness for artificial diction and stilted melodrama, are underlined. These latter defects come out very clearly in the speech of the serious heroes and heroines and even some villains in Dickens' works, right up to and including *Hard Times*. It is an unbelievably artificial mode, oscillating between a stiff, colourless form of the genteel and the preposterously melodramatic. From *Little Dorrit* onwards, the speech of such characters, although at times still rather colourless, is imbued with more natural, flowing rhythms and less portentous phraseology, the author exercising increasing flexibility, diversity and artistry. Almost from the very beginning and increasingly, Dickens took his use of stylised typification a stage further by making the fictional speech actually mirror either the moral or physical qualities of the character concerned (*personal typification*) or the dramatic situation he or she happened to be in (*situational typification*). It was a technical development of considerable artistic significance, and one that was put to subtle structural effect in the novels that followed.

Again right from the outset, all of Dickens' best idiolects manifest without exception those distinctive *rhythmic patterns* so characteristic of his stylised storytelling world. These can be divided into two chief categories: *metrical patterns* from the world of poetry and *schematic patterns* from the world of rhetoric. The former category ranges from the simple though often adroitly satirical insertion of (mis-)quotations from poetry or popular ditties and rhymes, through the application of blank verse – this being particularly cleverly done in Mrs Gamp's idiolect, in which standard and non-standard forms are resorted to according to the needs of the rhythmic moment – to highly elaborate metrical patterns which often come close to the stylised rhythmic structures of music. The schematic category, one usually involving 'doubling' or 'tripling' patterns (or compound versions of such), ranges from lengthy syntagmatic progressions, through such rhetorical figures as anaphora, epistrophe, symploce and anadiplosis, down to a mere piling up of the simplest parts of the sentence, 'cataloguing' as it has been called. From about the middle of the 1850s, the relentless rhythms of these cumulative structures became all-pervasive. It was observed that the rhythmic patterns invariably help to provide a firm framework to what at first might seem chaotic verbal rambling or – as in the case of the interaction of two or more idiolects (i.e. dialogue) – they supply what are, in effect, 'vocal tableaux', ideally suited to Dickens' stylised stage.

The most decisive and far-reaching step taken in connection with the evolution and employment of the idiolects, and one which embraced all the ingredients that went to make up these language collages, was that leading to their structural use in the fiction in which they appeared. It is a technique coming under the general heading of what Randolph Quirk has called '*structural representation*'. As a result of this, the now multi-purpose fictional speech forms serve in single cases not only to individualise and typify, but also to reflect, parody, symbolise, support or underscore general or particular elements of the thematic structure, including even the speech of other characters. This metonymical mode was one that simultaneously succeeded in incorporating all the previous idiolect techniques, furthering the plot, illuminating the character and his role, and – especially through the parodic contrasts – heightening the drama. It is a mode that Dickens gradually learned to employ with masterly assurance and flexible, pointed artistry.

A technical achievement that was undeniably promoted to a high degree by the influence of the fictional speech in general and some of the chief idiolects in particular was that final prose amalgam sometimes called the *oral style*. The influences referred to to made their decisive effect through the public readings, and were also aided by the key-word technique. This particular stylistic development reached fruition by the late 1850s. As a result, Dickens' whole authorial style moved progressively nearer in tone and rhythms to that of the spoken language, albeit in stylised form. This in turn brought it much nearer in the same works to the fictional speech, transitions, therefore, being made smoother or even eradicated altogether. The ensuing all-pervasive, multi-functional, highly-expressive rhetorical mode proved to be of exceeding flexibility, subtlety and dramatic expressiveness. It now conveyed with far greater precision and concentration biting satire, gentle irony or finer shades of feeling. For the fictional speech and the author's storytelling voice, this 'oralisation' proved of reciprocal artistic value.

Both the development of the idiolects themselves from the very earliest days and the evolution of the stylistic unification just pointed out can be traced in a most illuminating manner if one follows Dickens' utilisation of *free indirect speech* ('erlebte Rede') over his whole creative life, from *Sketches by Boz* (in which there are already a few examples) right up to the half-finished *Edwin Drood*. The value of this literary device lies both in the subtle incorporation into a fast-flowing narrative of the character's individual speech idiom (with all the dramatic colouring of the prose style which it brings), and in the ironic transmission of the character's unspoken reflection delivered with the typical features of his or her speech idiom, thus avoiding the necessity for a longwinded explanation of something which is better left equivocal. We saw that Dickens made fairly consistent (though rarely very extensive) use of free indirect speech right from the beginning of his career as a writer of fiction, until finally, in the last decade in particular, it helped to blur the boundaries between the modalities even more. By this period, indeed, one can almost speak of a singular, all-pervading Dickensian *oratio obliqua,* with the actor-novelist's various storytelling voices speaking through everything – narrating, commenting, describing, mimicking – in one all-embracing web of stylistic unity.

A further factor observed to be bound up with the evolution of the idiolects is that many characters possess either a public and private idiolect, each quite distinct from the other, or a series of sub-idiolects adjusted to the listener of the moment and not always related to the speaker's chief idiom. In the former category, it was established that the public speech idiom of the characters concerned almost invariably belonged, logically enough, to the genteel register; these people must, of their very nature, put on a show for Society. In private, before people whose knowledge of them makes pretence worthless – even a hindrance – they usually present a basic, shorn-down idiom remarkable for its mixture of petulance, directness and truth. In the latter category, the flexibility of idiom is either the direct product of professional needs or the reflection of a hypocritical nature, the object being in both these cases to weedle something out of whoever the recipient happens to be. There are, in addition, cases of characters who end up with two very distinct speech idioms as a result of a change in concept on the part of the author. This differs from the above in that they do not alternate right through the novel concerned, but are divided by the two halves of the book; we have, in effect, two separate characters. This kind of doubling was a typical product of his earlier writing, arising when, conscious of the necessity to plan, he lacked the experience to do so effectively. From *Bleak House* onwards, there are in his works no more such illogical transformations, Dickens having learnt enough to steer clear of them from the very beginning. Of a very different nature are the gradual changes indicating either the growth towards maturity or some deep psychological disturbance or other. The process here is a considerably more artistic one, and sometimes the differences are so slight that it takes a keen eye to find them. Examples of this minor tendency – for it is not strongly developed – do not begin to make their appearance until the works of the author's maturity.

Connected in some measure with the aspect of 'double' or 'sub'-idiolects are the speech idioms of certain character pairs, two persons who are closely related structurally and whose idiolects seem to complement each other to such an extent that an investigation of the one involves of necessity an investigation of the other. In some cases, the feeling can arise that we are viewing two radically opposing sides of the same person. This is, arguably, an unconscious extension of the *Doppelgänger* theme occurring in the works of many nineteenth century writers. Above all in *Our Mutual Friend* and the half-finished *Edwin Drood* – the works marking the end of Dickens' career as a novelist – many of the idiolects are deliberately contrasted one with the other. This is in stark contrast to the early novels, especially, in which the possessors of the most pronounced idiolects dominate the stage as if they were performing a solo act. In a sense, the later practice was forced upon Dickens by his own technical maturity, for in the works of the final period it was no longer a question of a group of leading figures with very pronounced idiolects being supported by a cast of typified 'also-rans', but one of a world in which each separate character is the possessor of a sharply-delineated speech idiom which cannot be ignored. Indeed, the mode is all gain, for the contours of the contrasted idiolects are drawn out yet more sharply, enhancing the general effect.

In the first four novels – *Pickwick Papers*, the very first one, being the most pronounced example – the majority of the characters are typified more than they are individualised, despite a fairly liberal use of speech tags. The latter in themselves were not enough, useful though they often proved, and Dickens was to increase the density of other features to a considerable degree. *Jingle* in the first novel is, with his staccato manner, a triumph (albeit a short-lived one) of personal typification. But in the idiolects of *Sam Weller* and his misogynous coachman father, *Tony Weller*, for the first time a large and varied assortment of individualising features – linguistic, rhetorical and rhythmic – are moulded together into two very persuasive comic wholes. In *Oliver Twist*, the subsequent novel, typification still rules the day but in the defiantly inventive idiolect of the '*Artful Dodger*' are first revealed distinct glimmerings of the kind of structural integration later consciously aimed at and, in most cases, successfully achieved. To a somewhat slighter degree, the same can be maintained of the parodic pomposities of Mr Bumble's highly imaginative idiolect.

The dominance of the typifying technique still continues in *Nicholas Nickleby*. The heavy emphasis on the melodramatic register in particular underlines very clearly where some of the young author's major strengths and weaknesses lay. When the register is used seriously by characters whose speech is rooted in the standard dialect, the results can be atrocious. On the other hand, the theatrical idioms of the Crummles company can be sheer delight, because Dickens never leaves us in doubt that they are truly acting, whether on or off the stage. Two characters in this novel – *Mrs Nickleby* and *Mr Mantalini*, especially the former – have been not only typified but also individualised to a high degree. The far fetched pretentiousness of Mantalini's idiolect is, it is true, on a rather lower level of inspiration – his speech features being more sparse and somewhat too repetitious – but for all that his idiom is living proof that the young writer's techniques are infinitely more impressive when mocking the upper-class register than when attempting to represent it accurately. The patterned garrulity of Mrs Nickleby's disconnected but class-bound irrelevancies – she is the first of Dickens' great female ramblers – is a striking instance of personal typification. Her idiolect is a direct reflection of her congenital lack of reasoning power, her incurably snobbish attitude to life, and the appalling superficiality of her nature. She is more than simply funny; her idiolect is that of one frighteningly out of touch with the world around her – a person forced to supply her own questions and answers.

With the completion of *The Old Curiosity Shop*, improvisation – though it cropped up on and off in the years to come – ceased to play so dominating a role in Dickens' fictional writing. *Dick Swiveller*'s complex, violently-contrasted idiolect provides a classic illustration of the lack of real forethought which went hand in hand with the improvisation. This idiolect's role perceptibly changes from the purely comic one of the first half of the novel to a significant parodic comment in the second half. The structural change is actually (and with a fair amount of subtlety) indicated through the idiolect features. Their basis is the *contrast manner*, as a result of which he switches abruptly from one to another of a large variety of styles. It enables him to throw himself into that play-acting so characteristic of his nature, and which was the only way to shed a glow on an otherwise barren life. The increasingly self-questioning tone of the second half is shown above all by his moments of self-parody. The idiolect gives us an image of the irrepressible Cockney, Dick being a kind of middle-class Sam Weller. In stark contrast is the savage bluntness and simplicity of

Quilp's idiolect. This is of considerable interest in that it is the first clear-cut case in Dickens of one in which individualisation is achieved by foregoing rhetorical and (seemingly illogically) non-standard features well-nigh completely, and relying almost entirely on a form of personal typification. It employs ruthlessly direct syntax plus brutally sarcastic standard vocabulary and parodic imagery. Thus, although the force of its impact is immediate and obvious, it is perhaps difficult to put one's finger on the reason.

When turning to *Barnaby Rudge* and *Martin Chuzzlewit* – those two novels which, particularly in respect of the idiolects, mark the first transitional phase in the progress made by Dickens in his art – it will be observed that the number of cases in which the speech idioms of the characters are strongly etched and hence more strikingly individual, is steadily increasing. This increase marks the beginning of the trend from which developed the all-embracing network in the later works of strongly contrasted idiolects. In this first transitional phase, it must also be remembered that parallel to the initial development of the trend in question, there is in the main a gradual growth in density of the idiolect features themselves. By the early 1840s, then, we have greater diversity within and without the speech idioms of the characters; but not only this – there is also more artistry and subtlety in the presentation of the various language characteristics themselves, their realisation being less erratic. It is unfortunate that the author's serious heroes and heroines still use an incredibly artificial mode, moving between a stiff, colourless form of the genteel and the preposterously melodramatic. However, through the coquettish speech idiosyncrasies of *Dolly Varden* (*BR*) we have the first unsentimentally-drawn heroine in Dickens. In the same novel, *Miss Miggs*' idiolect can be singled out for the multifariousness of its lexical, rhetorical and rhythmic features. The uneven application of some of them reveals, though, that the author was still conceiving part of the idiolect during the progress of the novel's weekly numbers. Many of the features are highly imaginative and obsessive, manifesting, too, distinct marks of structural significance in a novel so bound up with the theme of imprisonment, riots and general lawlessness.

In *Martin Chuzzlewit*, the extremely complex idiolects of *Mrs Gamp* and *Mr Pecksniff* form the very summit of the initial individual development in Dickens' stylised collage techniques, as well as a distinct turning point. From *Dombey & Son* onwards, none of the idiolects – with the exception perhaps of those of Mr Micawber and Flora Finching – ever reaches the same brilliant heights of language invention, the succeeding emphasis being chiefly on structural integration. There are still a few inconsistencies to be detected in the idiolects resulting, probably, from the haste forced upon Dickens by serialised writing. Especially in the ornate zaniness, rich imagery and abrupt contrasts of Pecksniff's exotic idiolect, there is a definite discrepancy between the author's original conception and a subsequent development which seems at times to be a parody of the same, the conflict between the various categories leading to a certain lack of general balance. Further, Mrs Gamp's speech shows a gradual increase in the density of certain features – though not the non-standard ones – as Dickens discovered that the belatedly introduced character was becoming popular. The speech of both is, of course, stylised to an extreme and each also supports (to a degree) the novel's basic theme of selfishness, although this particular structural aspect achieves less significant proportions than perhaps Dickens aimed at. On the other hand, Sairey Gamp *is* her speech, more completely than any other character in Dickens. Her idiolect is unique not only in the originality of so many of the individual idiosyncrasies, but also in the very range it covers. From the enormous flexibility and diversity of the non-standard features, whose richness underscores her startlingly vivid imagination, through her general typifying manners, of which she has no less than three, to both the mass of rhetorical devices (above all the religious phraseology and the incomparable invention of 'Mrs Harris') and the very distinctive rhythmic patterns, whether staccato or that blank verse which makes such original and telling use of the unusual effects achieved when the stress is laid on the non-standard usage.

Dombey & Son, the next novel, presents the first concentrated attempt to integrate the fictional speech structurally, an attempt which proved only partially successful, and also led, in most cases, to a considerable loss in originality, verve and brilliance. However, the darker thematic structure provides an admirable framework for *Major Bagstock*'s obscenely brutal idiolect, with its harsh, explosive syntax, apostrophising incriminations, hypocritical sycophancies and vituperative epithets. The zany patterns of *Mrs Skewton*'s preposterously-mannered public idiolect have also been effectively integrated into this structure, providing a striking image of a decaying aristocratic order fighting a losing battle against the already-dominating mercantile class, refusing to accept time and change. Further, the contours of this public idiom are sharpened by contrast with the aggressive, down-to-earth darts of her private idiom, and the later aphasic idiom is a savagely ironic comment on the flimsiness of her tawdry values. Taken against these two, *Captain Cuttle*'s idiolect, original though it so often is in content, is more conventional in the rhetorical and typifying forms it assumes. Together with the weird, cryptical nonsense uttered by his companion figure, *Bunsby*, Cuttle is, through his speech, part of the other world found in this book, helping to counteract the verbal obscenities of such as Bagstock.

In contrast to those of the preceding novel, the idiolects in *David Copperfield* are a truly happy blend of old and new techniques, the *Bildungsroman* form of the novel enabling Dickens in considerable measure to leave the structure to itself, so to speak. This has resulted in a lush flowering of the idiolects which he was never to repeat in this intensity. The speech of almost each and every figure is so clearly delineated and personalised in itself, as well as being perfectly merged into the general narrative, that an ideal balance is struck between structural needs and brilliance of individual realisation. Although the speech of some 'serious' characters still relies on stilted techniques, the new approach is particularly apparent in the speech of such as *Dora*, *Steerforth* and *Traddles*. The elaborate idiolects of that resilient, epistle-loving duo *Mr and Mrs Micawber* – he with the bizarre complexities and contrasting rhythms of his genteel circumlocutory style, she with the irrelevant asides, logical progressions and more regular rhythms of her prim, precise gentility – are, structurally, part of Dickens' parodic criticism of society, of the dehumanising influence it exerts on its members. Their language parodies this society, transmuting their 'downs' into a world of delight, complete in itself. Furthermore, like all the author's twosomes, they attain their greatest value together.

The impudent imperatives, vulgar sarcasm and derogatory euphemy which form the basis of the idiolect of the initial *Miss Mowcher* lead to an impact out of all proportion to the little space she takes up. If developed, she could, structurally, have provided the 'other', worldly, side with invaluable idiolectal support. In the straightforward, emphatic ejaculations of *Betsey Trotwood*'s idiolect, Dickens dispenses with linguistic or rhetorical fireworks, yet succeeds in presenting a convincing picture of a woman outwardly grim, austere and uncompromising but inwardly warm-hearted, generous and loving to those who win her affection. Despite the insolent sliminess of *Uriah Heep*'s 'smooth' mode, his whole idiolect simmers at times with genuine passion. Structurally, he is yet another who shows up David's character in many unlooked-for lights, not all favourable, thus revealing the subtlety of Dickens' portrait of the narrator as well as of the other characters in the book.

The deliberate subjection of flamboyance to structural and thematic requirements is immediately evident in the prolific but controlled inventive genius of the next novel, *Bleak House*. This is a devastating and topical satire of Victorian society on a panoramic scale in which the untrammelled, impetuous inspiration of the younger Dickens is now conspicuously absent. In the, by this time, firmly-established parodic-echoic structure, each speech idiom is so moulded as to fulfil to a greater or lesser degree the multifunctional roles previously discussed, roles among which that of *structural representation* now takes pride of place. The development towards constant metonymical employment of fictional language is, in this impressive novel, virtually complete. The characters, for example, now exist far less for their own sake than for their ability to personify and/or parody at least a part of the world within which they find themselves. In other words, these speech forms are often just as complex as those in previous novels, but the complexity is differently, more subtly based, being on a structural plane and not a surface one. For instance, the wide variety of speech registers between which that irrepressible social-climber *William Guppy* continually switches, or which he simply mixes at will, is a comic parody of *Inspector Bucket*'s wide-ranging, formidable flexibility and amoral adjustability of idiom. Thus it is an idiolectal mode that is shown to particularly good advantage in Guppy's investigations into Esther Summerson's past. Further, *Chadband*'s unctious verbal posturing contrasts with *Jo*'s non-standard inarticulations, drawing out dramatically the sins of society towards the ignorant crossing-sweeper. *Skimpole*'s superficial charm and lightness of idiom, with its airy springs from one short, simple predication to another, is highly individualised as well as being a parody of the speech of similar social parasites.

Structurally, it shows him to be as much a systemised prisoner of society as those he would fain despise.

If the fictional speech of the two subsequent novels, *Hard Times* and *Little Dorrit*, evinces anything in stronger measure than all that had gone before, it is a darker, more poetic tinge combined with an even greater subtlety and flexibility of technique – this being particularly true of the latter novel. In addition, there is a distinct move towards greater psychological penetration. In *Hard Times*, for example, the speech of *Mr Gradgrind* is already occasionally hinting at the new approach. The speech idiom of that languid, idle gentleman, *Mr James Harthouse*, with its half-finished sentences and tiredly polite ejaculations in the upper-class register, does so even more – the new mastery in this social group being continued in the related figures of *Henry Gowan* and all the members of the *Barnacle* clan (*LD*). A deeper, more significant aspect of the new psychological insight is exhibited in the masterfully delineated idiolect of that poor, weak, pompous snob *William Dorrit* (*LD*) with its ritualistic rhythms, nervous interjections and groping search for the right – in this case the least embarrassing – word against the pathologically affected use of the genteel register, the whole ironically underlined by a periodic move into free indirect speech. This interesting psychological development is continued in the speech of such later characters as *Miss Havisham*, *Estella* and *Pip* himself (*GE*), *Wrayburn* and *Headstone* (*OMF*), and *John Jasper* (*ED*). Further, the artificial register used for heroes and heroines has, in *Little Dorrit* – through the figures of *Arthur Clennam* and *Amy Dorrit* – been imbued with more natural, flowing rhythms and less portentous vocabulary. Amy's speech, in particular, is very rarely melodramatic and not at all sentimental. When it is seen or heard within its thematic context, rather than terming it colourless one can only feel the subtle strength radiating from the plain directness of vocabulary and syntax. The variegated, rambling idiolect of *Flora Finching* (*LD*) – together with that of her alter ego, *Mr F's Aunt* – can hold its own away from its context in a way that the great idiolects of the early period can. In addition, the combined speech idioms of these two characters are just as effective within the general structure of *Little Dorrit*, into which they are thoroughly integrated, for although a prisoner in and of society like all the other characters in this profoundly disturbing novel, Flora is able, through her wild, meandering flights of fantasy, to escape into another world, thus preserving at least a part of her essential self in a world which is out to destroy it. Mr F's Aunt is the other – aggressively unpleasant – half of her split personality, and it was surely a stroke of genius to present them together as a pair. Flora's sprawling, seemingly unconnected sentences and clauses are, moreover, part of a general syntactic disorder which crops up in the mouths of a variety of characters in this novel, a disorder symbolising its reversals of ordinary expectations.

In *Great Expectations*, the speech of the characters supplies the pattern which is the organising principle of the novel. Even the language of the narrator, *Pip*, is not only subtly adjusted from the various points in time, but is also far more oral in character than the two previous first-person narrators, *David Copperfield* (*DC*) and *Esther Summerson* (*BH*). *Great Expectations* reveals, too, a Dickens moving away from that mode which reached its zenith in *Bleak House* and began to be replaced in *Hard Times* and *Little Dorrit*. Now the speech idioms of the various characters are no longer so completely a series of variations on basic, unchanging linguistic or rhetorical ground themes, but receive subtle modifications in accordance with the changes they undergo, those of *Miss Havisham* and *Estella* being pointed examples. In which respect, it is of interest that from Estella's grown-up idiom alone one can argue in favour of the novel's original ending. In this she continues the plain, functional manner previously given to her adult self, one in stark contrast to her idiom in the revised final chapter, which is stiffly genteel with a touch of the melodramatic. Worthy of note in this novel is the extent to which the dichotomy between the hard, ruthless, workaday world and the intimate, private life (or what there is of it) is reflected in the two aspects of *Wemmick*'s idiolect; further, the increasing lengths to which Dickens now goes to indicate *emphasis* by visual means – a tendency kept until he died – doing so primarily through italics, capitals, hyphens and exclamation marks. The speech of *Joe Gargery*, *Magwitch* and *Wemmick* is full of such indications. One could argue that it is a sidekick of the emphasis resulting from the obsessively reiterated rhetorical patterns characteristic of this period.

Some of the speech idioms in *Our Mutual Friend* reveal certain inconsistencies, a factor detracting a little from the otherwise general excellence of this last of Dickens' panoramic satires of Victorian society and a novel exhibiting otherwise a tight economy of language means. The poetic manner which had tinged so much of the speech in *Little Dorrit* and, to a slighter degree, in *Great Expectations*, is now often parodied by the sudden addition to this or that idiolect of a ditty or poetic rhythms, pseudo-romantic or sarcastically scathing – *Mr Venus* and *Silas Wegg* are addicted, for instance, to the habit. It is also found in *Edwin Drood*, in the mouths of, among others, two such widely diverse characters as *Durdles* and *Mr Grewgious*. To the language of society in *Our Mutual Friend*, Dickens has brought an assured brilliance of manner, especially in the light, empty variations of the *Lammles*, and in the deliberate absurdities of *Wrayburn*. It is either the shiny veneer covering the cheap, tawdry object or just simply the product of aimless boredom. In the latter case, Dickens – continuing the development of this upper-class register begun in the speech of Steerforth (*DC*) and carried on in that of Harthouse (*HT*), Gowan and the Barnacles (*LD*) – now captures with supreme conviction the off-hand manner of the register concerned with its careless, deceptively disinterested ease. In the early exchanges between Wrayburn and Lightwood, Dickens is, in fact, prefiguring by almost three decades a similar mode from the mouths of many of Oscar Wilde's characters. *Podsnap* is another who, with his pompous, formulaic language, is a triumph of concise, structurally-aware, idiolectal writing. The successes are not merely confined to the puppets of Society: each and every idiolect in this wide-ranging novel has its own individual niche in the thematic structure, from the deep, complex significance of the speech of the crippled dollmaker, *Jenny Wren*, to the halting, repetitive syntax of *Headstone*'s passionate utterances; from the petulant rhetoric of the wilful *Bella Wilfer* – a heroine who at last breaks away completely from the stereotyped gentility or stodginess of the heroines who have held the stage in the novels up to and including *Hard Times* – to the fretful, 'romantic' effusions of *Mr Venus*. These and many others underline just how far Dickens had travelled in the three decades which had elapsed since the publication of his first novel.

In the half-finished *Edwin Drood* – a novel presenting, on the small scale of a provincial town, society in decay – Dickens moves on in his collage and integrating techniques towards both a new intensity and a mellowed, finished mastery, there being, if anything, even greater economy and structural cogency. The new expressive flexibility is apparent in the speech of many of the characters: *Edwin Drood*'s speech fluctuations, to take just one case, are an unconsciously sinister parody of the speech divergencies springing from his uncle's split mind. Dickens also demonstrates how, with a seeming return to older techniques – the zany non-standard speech of *Durdles*, *Deputy* and *Mrs Billickin*, particularly the first two – he can still triumphantly mould them so that they serve both particular and general purposes: the particular purpose of furthering the novel's plot, and a universal one in which what they say is a piercingly ironic commentary on the world at large.

It would be fruitless to speculate how far the mature idiolect techniques would have taken Dickens had he lived longer; what we have from the last period, for instance, is – with the exception previously pointed out – almost above criticism within the stylised world for which it was created. The triumphs of literary collage, many originally composed merely for amusement or to keep the story going along somehow, were gradually developed, changed, moulded and adapted, moving from the initial individualising and typifying qualities – which in themselves moved toward greater complexity and subtlety – to embrace representational characteristics as well, thus beginning to take their rightful place in the general structure concerned. All this was later accompanied by a stylistic transformation which took in Dickens' fictional writing as a whole, one which finally succeeded in merging all the elements involved – including the idiolects – into a finely balanced whole in which nothing (unless the author nods) jars, in which everything, great or small, has some significance or other, even down to single words. It is an artistic achievement in which the finished idiolects provide complete vindication of the author's singular mode of presenting fictional speech, a mode which forms so important a part of and merges so convincingly into what we have come to accept as the 'Dickens world', that world so vast in panoramic scale and complexity, so unique in the range, diversity and felicity of its language and humour, and so overwhelming in rhythmic energy, moral vehemence and sheer cogency. To put it another way: it was within such a world that, through a piercing intensity of feeling and vision, a wide-ranging order of sympathy, plus what can only be called a certain unspoiled naivety in the workings of his creative faculty, all acted upon by the exceptional natural gifts he brought to his craft, Dickens' composite language figures became as living creatures, but larger than life – at least life as our conditioned eyes usually apprehend it. To Dickens suredly, they *were* life, were as real people, and within the stylisation of his theatrical storytelling world he attained a very high degree of success in conveying this 'aliveness' to the reader/listener.

NOTES

INTRODUCTION

1. Cf. Dorothy Van Ghent, *The English Novel: Form and Function* (New York 1953) p. 125. Further references in this vein are to be found in V. Pritchett's *The Living Novel* (London, 1946) esp. pp. xi, 77, 78, and Edwin Muir's *The Structure of the Novel* (London, 1928; 2nd edn 1946) esp. pp. 14, 146.
2. Charles F. Hockett, *A Course in Modern Linguistics* (New York, 1958) p. 321. In the *OED*, Supplement, vol. II, H–N (1976) the earliest written usage of the word is pinpointed as *1948* with B. Bloch, in *Language*, xxiv, 7, writing 'The totality of the possible utterances of one speaker at one time in using language to interact with one other speaker is an *idiolect*', and R. A. Hall J in *Studies in Linguistics*, vi, ii, p. 31, 'Language exists in individuals, as a set habits which each individual possesses (*idiolect*)'. Similar definitions, though from writers referring chiefly to the artificial idiolects of fiction, are to be found in, among others, G. L. Brook's *The Language of Dickens* (London 1970) p. 138, and Norman Page's *Speech in the English Novel* (London, 197 pp. 90–1.
3. Hockett, *A Course in Modern Linguistics*, p. 322. Interesting, in this respect, the following much more recent observation: 'the term "dialect" as it presently employed is inadequate in that it fails to account for the extensive patterned variations which occur both within the speech of an individual and within that of a language community. Dialect as a concept must be expanded to include the patterned variations a speaker produces and the even wider range of such variations which he accepts as part of the same dialect.' (Lyn Kypriotaki, 'A Study in Dialect: Individual Variation and Dialect Rules', in *New Ways of Analyzing Variation in English*, ed. Charles James N. Bailey and Roger W. Shuy (Georgetown University, 1973) pp. 208–9.)
4. Norman Page, 'Eccentric Speech in Dickens', *Critical Survey*, 4, II (1969) p. 96. Further references to this point have been made by Ian Gordon in *T.*

Movement of English Prose (London, 1966) pp. 9, 162, and G. L. Brook in *The Language of Dickens*, p. 138.
5. Norman Page, 'Eccentric Speech in Dickens', p. 97.
6. Angus Wilson, 'Charles Dickens: a Haunting', in *DCr*, p. 379.
7. Ibid.
8. *Peregrine Pickle* (OUP, 1964) pp. 36–7, 140, 359–60 ff.
9. *Humphry Clinker* (OUP, 1949) pp. 434–5, for example.
10. Walter Allen, *The English Novel* (London, 1954) p. 75.
11. John Forster, *The Life of Charles Dickens* (London, 1874) p. 41.
12. Mamie Dickens, *My Father as I Recall Him* (London, 1897) pp. 47–8.
13. It was during his activity here that he began his reading at the British Museum, applied for – and withdrew from – an audition as a performer along Mathews' lines, and fell hopelessly in love with Maria Beadnell, all significant milestones in his early life.
14. Illustrative of the acuteness of his aural sensitivity, as well as of the sarcasm aroused by the extent to which the exaggeration of the frequently heard artificial intonation grated on his nerves, is an attempt in an article appearing later in *Household Words* to make a rather rough and ready use of a musical stave to notate the excruciating modulation of such insincere voices (*MP*, 336–7).
15. F. R. Leavis, *Dickens the Novelist* (London, 1970) pp. 206–7. It is important to remember in this case that Dr Leavis took these words, unaltered, from his book *The Great Tradition* written nearly a generation previously (London, 1948) and in which he was otherwise far more limited in his praise of Dickens.
16. In Dickens' idiolects, the three aspects indicated under 1(b) – these being almost invariably, though not entirely rooted in the non-standard form of English peculiar to the London lower classes – are marked by a highly personal use of the linguistic traits here generally referred to, and are simply extreme exaggerations of selected usages common to most people sharing the same dialectal background.
17. Cf. K. J. Fielding, '*David Copperfield* and Dialect', *TLS*, 30 April 1949.
18. Cf. Louise Pound, 'The American Dialect of Charles Dickens', *American Speech*, XXII (1947) pp. 124–30.

CHAPTER 1: LINGUISTIC IDENTIFIERS

1. It is no surprise to learn from the 'mems' (his working sheets) that a great deal – perhaps all, we can only guess – of what Dickens' characters say is actually conceived as speech (this is also true of incident), being then incorporated either with slight alterations or none at all. Betsey Trotwood's tag 'Janet! Donkeys!' is a case in point. (Cf. John Butt and Kathleen Tillotson, *Dickens at Work* (London, 1957) p. 129.)
2. This receives marked confirmation in the following excerpt from a letter he wrote during this period: 'Invention seems the easiest thing in the world; and I seem to have such a preposterous sense of the ridiculous ... as to be constantly requiring to restrain myself from launching into extravagances in the height of my enjoyment.' (*Nonesuch*, vol. II, p. 352.)

3. The same letter also refers to the fact that Dickens once even applied for an audition as a performer on the same lines as Mathews, and that his application was taken seriously. At the last minute, however, he cried off. (Cf. Forster, *The Life of Charles Dickens* (London, 1874) p. 53.)
4. In Mathews' defence, though, it should be emphasised that a great deal of his success must have clearly been due to the immediate impact of his stage personality. However, as Mathews did not publish his scripts, the various accounts, available in the library of the British Museum, are pirated editions, having been written down by stenographers in the audience. The illustrations of the badly printed booklets were, incidentally, drawn by George Cruikshank. It will be seen that Mathews on paper is no match, regarding originality of content, development and continuity, plus the actual context against which the various speech devices and mannerisms are set, for the genius brought by Dickens to the borrowed techniques after he realised their need and value in his serialised novels.
5. Sylvère Monod, *Dickens the Novelist* (Norman, Okla, 1968) p. 112.
6. The following are some of this character's efforts in the same line: '"I am down upon you", as the extinguisher said to the rushlight'; '"Come on", as the man said to the tight boot'; '"Why, here we are all mustered", as the roast beef said to the welsh rabbit'. (Cf. Percy Fitzgerald, *The History of Pickwick* (London, 1891) p. 136.)
7. Especially in Low German, cf. Horst Kunze, *Dunkel war's der Mond schien helle* (Munich, 1940), and called by the author *Beispielsprichwörter* (pp. 126–7); he also refers to Sam Weller's use of the same (p. 143). Further references are to be found in Edmund Hoeffer, *Wie das Volk spricht* (Stuttgart, 1876) and Seiler, *Deutsche Sprichwortkunde* (Munich, 1922).
8. Holcroft, *The Road to Ruin* (1792) Act II, Scene 1.
9. Jane Austen, *Emma* (OUP, 1971); on pp. 139–40 there is an excellent illustration in which Miss Bates, delighted to have visitors, gabbles on at great length which 'spoken extremely fast obliged Miss Bates to stop for breath'.
10. Cf. John Forster, *The Life of Charles Dickens* (London, 1874) p. 101.
11. Letter to John Forster, 27 September 1842. (Cf. *The Letters of Charles Dickens*, ed. House, Storey and Tillotson, vol. III, *1842–1843*, p. 333.)

CHAPTER 2: ROOT DIALECTS AND REGISTERS

1. Readers are referred to the explanatory diagram at the end of the Introduction (p. 10–11).
2. Norman Page, 'A Language Fit for Heroes: Speech in *Oliver Twist* and *Our Mutual Friend*', *Dickensian*, 65 (1969) p. 100.
3. Ibid. p. 100. Typical examples are the speech idioms of such as Oliver Twist, Fagin (to a degree), Smike (*NN*), Amy Dorrit (*LD*) and Pip as a boy (*GE*).
4. Steven Marcus, *Dickens: from Pickwick to Dombey* (London, 1965) p. 359.
5. John Butt and Kathleen Tillotson, *Dickens at Work* (London, 1957) pp. 230–1.
6. A further point illustrated in detail by Professor Page in 'A Language Fit for Heroes', p. 100.

7. G. L. Brook, *The Language of Dickens*, ch. 6 (heading), pp. 168–207.
8. From Mrs Nickleby and Mrs Wititterly (*NN*), through Pecksniff (*MC*), Mrs Skewton (*DS*), the Micawbers (*DC*), Skimpole (*BH*), Mrs Sparsit (*HT*), Mr William Dorrit and Mrs General (*LD*), Mrs Pocket (*GE*), Mr Podsnap and Mrs Wilfer (*OMF*), up to Mr Sapsea (*ED*), to name only the most prominent.
9. *PP* alone provides such words and expressions as '*cognovit*', 'prayed a tales', 'the proecipe book', 'The ca-sa' (i.e. *capias ad satisfaciendum*), '*amicus curiae*', '*ad captandum*' etc.
10. Cf. Philip Collins, *Dickens and Education* (London, 1963) for a thorough and revealing study of Dickens' attitude to education.
11. Humphry House has made some interesting observations on this point (cf. *The Dickens World* (London, 1941) p. 106).
12. It is difficult at this distance of time to judge its true effect and value on the stage, but Macready obviously possessed a quality peculiar to only the greatest of actors, the ability to rivet the attention of an audience through the sheer power of his personality, regardless of the methods being used.
13. Ernest Weekley, 'Mrs. Gamp and the King's English', in *Adjectives and Other Words* (London, 1930) p. 140.
14. Although it is true that such characters, as P. J. Keating points out, 'may be classified under the general heading "lower class" [they] often possess vague, undifferentiated social backgrounds'. (P. J. Keating, *The Working Classes in Victorian Fiction* (London, 1971) p. 15.)
15. Professor Brook, in his book *The Language of Dickens*, devotes one chapter to 'Class Dialects', another to 'Regional Dialects', and between them is one entitled 'Substandard Speech', this being in effect the speech of the London Cockney! In this respect, it is interesting to compare Dickens' Sam Weller (*PP*) with Thackeray's Charles Yellowplush (*The Yellowplush Papers*, in *The Oxford Thackeray*, London, 1908), both of whom appear in books written more or less around the same time (1836–8).
16. For general treatments of this or that linguistic feature of the Cockney dialect, the reader is referred in particular to the following: Stanley Gerson, *Sound and Symbol in the Dialogue of the Works of Charles Dickens* (Stockholm, 1967), plus the same writer's 'Dickens' Use of Malapropisms', *Dickensian* (January 1965) pp. 40–5, and 'I spells it with a "V"', *Dickensian* (September 1965) pp. 138–46; the discussion in the *OED* (vol. XII, s.W.) on the V/W confusion; Tadao Yamamoto, *Growth and System of the Language of Dickens* (Osaka, 1950); Robert Bruce Glenn, *Linguistic Class-indicators in the Speech of Dickens' Characters*, PhD thesis (University of Michigan, 1960); William Matthews, *Cockney Past and Present* (London, 1938); Julian Franklyn, *The Cockney* (London, 1955); G. L. Brook, *The Language of Dickens* (London, 1976); Norman Page, 'Convention and Consistency in Dickens's Cockney Dialect', *English Studies*, 51 (1970) pp. 339–44 and 'Eccentric Speech in Dickens', pp. 96–100; Ernest Weekley, 'Mrs. Gamp and the King's English', pp. 138–61. Tadao Yamamoto's book is basically a collection of 'idioms' and nothing more; Professor Brook goes over Dickens' use of language from the philologist's standpoint and Stanley Gerson from that of the phonetician. Both Brook and Gerson make here and there a telling remark, but then stop short where significant critical insights seem called for.

17. Ernest Weekley, 'Mrs. Gamp and the King's English', pp. 146–7.
18. It is possible – as in the case of Lizzie Hexam (*OMF*) or Oliver Twist – that Dickens may have been aiming at a linguistic indication of inner purity.
19. P. J. Keating, *The Working Classes in Victorian Fiction*, p. 253. However, when referring a few lines later to the scene (*BH*, 628–35) in which Jo returns to Tom-all-Alone's and meets there both Allan Woodcourt and Jenny, the brickmaker's wife, Mr Keating is not quite accurate to maintain that the latter 'speaks Standard English throughout'; her usage in this scene of 'It don't', 'It do', 'One as I calls mine' etc. proves otherwise. The difference between Jenny's speech idiom and Jo's lies far more in the actual phonetic presentation: in her speech, Dickens relies on *lower-class idiom* presented in the standard orthographical manner – thus a cursory glance could well create the impression that this character is speaking standard English. If the same words were read aloud with the appropriate intonation, there would be no doubt as to the class origins. Together, the two speech idioms in question form a classical illustration of Dickens' varying methods in the presentation of lower-class dialect.
20. Possessing, as it does, several more or less related meanings, the term is somewhat ambiguous. Within these lines, it is applied only to that particular kind of speech in Dickens peculiar to the closed group of London underworld characters depicted in *OT*, and which the criminals themselves would have called 'flash' (*OT*, 53). As in Dickens it is confined to *OT* alone, only the page numbers of this novel will be indicated after quotations.
21. George Gissing, *Charles Dickens: A Critical Study* (London, 1898) pp. 74–5. However, in his own novels, Gissing clearly drew the line at a direct transcription of what he called 'that vituperative vernacular of the nether world' (*The Nether World* (London, 1899; 2nd edn 1937) p. 158). Also of interest in this respect is an observation contained in an article written in 1876 about the underworld characters in *OT*: 'That he should have portrayed such characters in their hideous reality, and still have denied to them their favourite outlets of expression in ribaldry and blasphemy, proves both his skill in characterization, and his instinctive perception of the verbal proprieties demanded by modern taste.' (Cf. Stanley Gerson, *Sound and Symbol*, p. 370, footnote 2.) Dickens himself interpolates an authorial comment on why Sikes' use of cant is kept down (*OT*, 87).
22. This reduction of people 'to thing-like characteristics' (Dorothy Van Ghent, *The English Novel*, p. 130) is the converse, of course, of the *pathetic fallacy*, and both techniques were continually and increasingly put to grotesque but effective structural use by Dickens. In this subregister, it is seen at its most humorous and convincing in the distinctive idiolect of Christopher, a headwaiter in 'Somebody's Luggage' (cf. *CS*, 317–30).
23. The external descriptions of Inspector Bucket (*BH*, 308) and a certain Inspector Wield (*UT/RP*, 486) alone confirm that the latter served as the original of the former. In addition, any comparison of the speech of the two also makes it plain how closely the one follows the other in basic qualities, although the fiction on the whole contains somewhat more of the professional register than the interviews. Among those also interviewed by Dickens, incidentally, was a Sergeant Witchem, a bare disguise of the famous Sergeant Witcher who in turn served as the model of the admirably characterised Sergeant Cuff in Wilkie Collins' *The Moonstone*.

CHAPTER 3: RHYTHMIC PATTERNS

1. Graham Greene, *The Honorary Consul* (London, 1973) p. 194.
2. Cf. Park Honan, 'Metrical Prose in Dickens', *VNL*, 28 (Autumn, 1965) pp. 1–3, for a discussion of the historical development involved.
3. When Dickens started his writing career, this particular tradition was already being ardently followed by such of his contemporaries, for instance, as Bulwer Lytton and Disraeli, with some appalling results, one might add. (Cf. Benjamin Disraeli, *The Young Duke* (London, 1831) and Bulwer Lytton, *Eugene Aram* (London, 1832).) Small wonder, then, that the young author – awake to all influences – just absorbed this one as he did so many others at the time.
4. Cf. W. J. B. Owen, 'Mrs. Gamp's Poetic Diction', *Dickensian* (May, 1971) pp. 81–96, for a detailed discussion of this aspect of Mrs Gamp's speech.
5. John Gross, *Dickens and the 20th Century* (London, 1962) p. xv.
6. Both Angus Wilson ('prefiguration of Joycean linguistic experiments', *Dickens Critics*, pp. 378–9) and Earle Davis ('a foreshadowing of Joyce's Molly Bloom ... Stream-of-consciousness is just around the corner', *The Flint and the Flame* (London, 1964) p. 48) rightly refer to Dickens' significant anticipation of the stream-of-consciousness technique in the language of such characters. In view of the pronounced dramatic qualities exhibited by Mrs Lirriper's idiolect – exemplified in the first place, as we have seen, in that rhythmic patterning which, especially when read aloud, gives coherent shape to her unending verbal outbursts – it is a source of wonder that Dickens did not work up either or both of these Christmas tales into public readings, the more so when one considers the strong vein of sentiment (always popular with his audiences) running through both.
7. Despite their lack of a concrete narrative, it is certainly no coincidence that Chopin's four 'Ballades' are all in either $\frac{6}{4}$ or $\frac{6}{8}$ time in which they all unfold their tale [giving] an easy movement, a flowing and sometimes deceptively gentle persuasiveness to the strange events which present themselves' (Alan Rawsthorne, 'Ballades, Fantasy and Scherzos' from *The Chopin Companion*, ed. Alan Walker (New York: W. W. Norton, 1966) p. 43). The same words could surely also be applied to the Dickens passage.
8. W. A. Ward, 'Language and Charles Dickens', *Listener*, 23 May 1963, p. 874.
9. Norman Page, *Speech in the English Novel*, p. 142.
10. John Lucas, *The Melancholy Man* (London, 1970) p. 150.
11. Cf. Amy Cruse, *The Victorians and Their Books* (London, 1935) ch. VIII.

CHAPTER 4: REPRESENTATIONAL SPEECH

1. Descriptive prose – of which there are many beautiful passages (cf. *BH*, 663) – still, however, held its own, exhibiting on the whole, indeed, more precision and purpose.
2. It is interesting to compare Snagsby's speech idiom with the speech forms of this character type in Wells' social comedies written in the first decade of the

twentieth century (especially Artie Kipps and Mr Polly), and in those of certain characters, above all James Thurber's Little Man figure, in American humoristic literature of the 1920s and 1930s.
3. Robert Garis, *The Dickens Theatre* (London, 1965) p. 114.

CHAPTER 5: RHETORICAL EXTENSION

1. This technique can be made to cover a great deal more, of course; as Professor Ullmann has underlined, 'Most inquiries concerned with keywords are statistically orientated, but the concept can also be defined in qualitative terms. [G. Matoré] has described them as "lexicilogical units expressing a society ... denoting person, a feeling, an idea which is alive in so far as society recognizes in them its ideal." This approach can also be applied to individual authors.' (*Stephan Ullmann*, 'Style and Personality', *REL*, 6 (1965) p. 27.)
2. David Lodge, *Language of Fiction* (London, 1966) p. 152.
3. Twenty-one readings in all were, to our knowledge, prepared, and sixteen (to a degree varying according to popularity) actually put to use. Of these, nine were taken from the tales for Christmas (*CB* and *CS*), and seven were continuous episodes extracted from the novels written up to and including *DC*, i.e. from the first half of Dickens' creative career. This is revealing, for it helps to stress in the earlier extended works (especially those preceding *DS*) that looseness of construction which has so often been commented upon, a factor which, on the other hand, made it easier to extract isolated episodes for purposes of oral narration. The later works (in particular *GE*, *OMF* and *ED*) are, generally speaking, too complicated and closely knit to allow for such treatment, each individual section depending on another (or others) for full comprehension. This by no means signifies that they are 'unoral' in quality, but the only alternative (a reading taking in the *whole* of the novel concerned) would, for obvious reasons, have been utterly out of the question, unless put over in the form of instalments. Dickens actually did draw up readings from *TTC* ('The Bastille Prisoner') and from *GE* (of which little is known), but never performed them. Of the later works, then, Dickens only resorted to some of the occasional works written for Christmas which, being shorter, more compact and more uniform in tone, possessed obvious advantages in respect of a public reading.
4. Cf. Sylvère Monod, 'Some Stylistic Devices in *A Tale of Two Cities*', in *DtC*, pp. 165–86, for a discussion of Dickens' stylistic developments in this novel.
5. Norman Page, *Speech in the English Novel*, pp. 142–3 (my italics).
6. Steven Marcus, *Dickens: From Pickwick to Dombey*, p. 40.
7. The literature on the subject makes it clear that it has proved difficult to agree on an all-embracing, generally acceptable phrase for such a fictional technique. In English criticism, the term 'free indirect speech' seems to have ousted that of 'erlebte Rede'; besides these two, five others at least are also occasionally in use: Bally's 'le style indirect libre' (cf. 'Le style indirect libre en français moderne', *Germanisch-Romanische Monatsschrift*, vol. IV (1972) pp. 549–56, 597–606); Otto Jesperson's 'represented speech' or 'vorgestellte

Rede' (*The Philosophy of Grammar* (London, 1924) pp. 291–2); Curme's 'independent form of direct discourse' (ibid.); Kalepsky's 'verschleierte Rede' or 'veiled speech' (ibid.); and Tobler's 'mingling of direct and indirect discourse' (ibid.) – however, the last three can, for all practical purposes, be ignored). A related form of speech representation, *free direct speech*, has also been categorised (cf. Harmer, *The French Language Today* (London, 1954) pp. 300 ff.), it being one in which the direct speech is not introduced by a verb of saying or indicated in any way by conventional graphological signs. Occasional examples of this technique are also to be found in Dickens.
8. Randolph Quirk, *The Use of English* (London, 1962), p. 247. The technique of free indirect speech is one which has cropped up in the literature of many languages, Flaubert's artistic application in *Madame Bovary* (1856) being particularly well-known (cf. Stephan Ullmann, *Style in the French Novel* (Cambridge, 1957) esp. ch. II). In English literature, Jane Austen was the first writer – and probably still remains the most successful – to turn the technique to extensive and effective use, the impression made being both extraordinarily subtle and gently (though on occasion bitingly) ironic (cf. Norman Page, *The Language of Jane Austen* (Oxford, 1972) pp. 123–36, and K. C. Phillipps, *Jane Austen's English* (London, 1970) pp. 204–6). Since her time, many other writers of English fiction – notably Thackeray – have also made use, sometimes considerable, of the technique under discussion (cf. Lisa Glauser, 'Die erlebte Rede im englischen Roman des 19. Jahrhunderts', *Schweizer Anglistische Arbeiten* (Bern, 1948); Günter Steinberg, '*Erlebte Rede*'. *Ihre Eigenart und ihre Formen in neuer deutscher, französischer und englischer Erzählliteratur* (Göppingen, 1971); Willi Bühler, 'Die "Erlebte Rede" im englischen Roman', *Schweizer Anglistische Arbeiten* (Bern, 1937); George L. Dillon and Red Kirchoff, 'On the Form and Function of Free Indirect Style', *Poetics & Theory of Literature* 1, 3 (1976) pp. 431–40; and Fritz Karpf, 'Die Erlebte Rede im Englischen', *Anglia*, 57 (1933)).
9. Cf. Humphry House, *The Dickens World*, pp. 32–3 (including footnote), where the reader will find first a report – colourless, factual – of the questioning to which an alderman submitted a poor, ignorant fourteen year old boy who is a witness in an action for assault, this being followed by the above-mentioned transposition of Jo's evidence (*BH*, 148).
10. Cf. Michael Gregory, 'Old Bailey Speech in *A Tale of Two Cities*', *REL*, VI, 2 (April, 1965) pp. 42–55, for a thorough and illuminating analysis of all the categories of fictional speech used in this court scene.

CHAPTER 6: FICTIONAL APPRENTICESHIP

1. At this time, Lytton and Ainsworth were following the fashion for the so-called 'Newgate Novel' (cf. Keith Hollingsworth, *The Newgate Novel: 1830–1847* (Detroit, 1963)). Two of Dickens' early novels (*OT* and *BR*) were more or less in this tradition.
2. Cf. Philip Collins, *Dickens and Crime* (London, 1962). Dickens' peculiarly intense interest in crime (or rather, in the criminal) was, of course, not only confined to the lower classes but stretched over the whole social scale. His

first work, *Sketches by Boz*, already reveals both this interest and that in the theatre. Indeed, Dickens remained very much the journalist, but one whose creative imagination turned to and transformed virtually everything going on in the world around him, especially those matters of topical interest. (Cf. Humphry House, *The Dickens World*, and Philip Collins, *Dickens and Education*.)

3. The 'First Series' of *Sketches by Boz* was published in February 1836, a month before the appearance of the first number of *Pickwick Papers*. The first of these *Sketches* had been published in 1833, and most of the others in the intervening time. There is an extremely rewarding treatment of the *Sketches* in *Dickens at Work* (Butt and Tillotson) ch. II, '*Sketches by Boz*: Collection and Revision', pp. 35–61). In the subsequent references to this book, page numbers will be indicated without prefix.

CHAPTER 7: *PICKWICK PAPERS* TO *THE OLD CURIOSITY SHOP*

1. This work was written in 20 monthly numbers, of which the first appeared in March 1836 and the last two in September 1837, by which time Dickens had already begun *Oliver Twist*!
2. Sylvère Monod, *Dickens the Novelist*, p. 113.
3. *Oliver Twist* was published, with several interruptions, between 1837 and 1839, in monthly numbers which were only half as long as those that became the norm, and of which the opening ones overlapped the tail-end of *Pickwick Papers* and the final ones the beginning of *Nicholas Nickleby*. It was the author's chief contribution to the succession of so-called 'Newgate Novels' (in some respects *Barnaby Rudge* also belongs to this genre) appearing in the 1830s and early 1840s, and in which vein the novels of Bulwer Lytton and Harrison Ainsworth especially enjoyed at the time considerable popularity. For all that, Dickens' efforts in this genre, uneven though they are, remain the only ones which have truly stood the test of time. Moreover, the original full-length title, 'Oliver Twist, or the Parish Boy's Progress', with its recollection of 'The Rake's Progress' by Hogarth, an artist whom Dickens greatly admired, is surely an indication of the differing direction of the writer's thoughts, feelings and intentions concerning the themes and background of this 'Newgate' vogue. Indeed, despite the conventions and evasions pursued in the writing of *Oliver Twist*, Dickens succeeded in creating a work of art which, in addition to the other qualities pointed out above, possesses 'great vitality' (Keith Hollingsworth, *The Newgate Novel*, p. 121).
4. *Nicholas Nickleby* was published in 20 monthly numbers between April 1838 and October 1839.
5. John Lucas, *The Melancholy Man*, p. 55.
6. G. L. Brook, *The Language of Dickens*, p. 56.
7. George Gissing, *The Immortal Dickens* (London, 1925) pp. 109–10.
8. *The Old Curiosity Shop* appeared as a weekly serial between April 1840 and January 1841, bolstering up that ill-fated periodical *Master Humphrey's Clock*.

9. It is this enchantingly varied manner of delivering his thoughts to others (and to himself!) that lifts Dick's idiolect as a whole above those of such as Mrs Skewton (*DS*) and Inspector Bucket (*BH*), who, although they possess sub-idiolects, keep the one mode very separate from the other, tuning in according to the occasion and recipient. Dick's approach resembles far more that of Mr Micawber (*DC*), and he even resorts to the same transfer technique 'in short' (376).
10. Gabriel Pearson, '*The Old Curiosity Shop*', in *DTC*, p. 87.

CHAPTER 8: *BARNABY RUDGE* AND *MARTIN CHUZZLEWIT*

1. *Barnaby Rudge* was published in weekly instalments from February to November 1841, as a part of *Master Humphrey's Clock*.
2. A case based on an actual historical incident and which the author refers to in his preface (xxv). The woman in question was executed for stealing linen; she needed money to buy food for her starving children.
3. In all the five scenes (pp. 72, 170, 312, 537, 616) offering Miggs the chance of extended speech, this sister is mentioned, each reference being identical in detail (three in free indirect speech).
4. Angus Wilson, *The World of Charles Dickens* (London, 1970) p. 148.
5. James Kincaid, *Dickens and the Rhetoric of Laughter* (Oxford, 1971) p. 126.
6. For *Martin Chuzzlewit*, the author returned to the rather less pressing process of monthly instalments, the novel appearing in 20 numbers between January 1843 and July 1844.
7. A. H. Gomme, *Dickens* (London, 1971) pp. 33–4.
8. Steven Marcus, *Dickens: From Pickwick to Dombey*, p. 216.
9. Mrs Gamp does not make her first appearance (ch. 19, p. 312) until the end of the eighth number. She was such an immediate success, however, and a favourite of Dickens himself, that she appears from this point onwards in no less than sixteen scenes, although by no means an essential character in the plot. Her particular version of the Cockney dialect is so extraordinarily complex that, with the exceptions which will be indicated, Mrs Gamp's deviations from the standard language can be taken in their totality as the typical ingredients from which the author formed his unique, stylised version of this dialect. As we have already seen, the number of non-standard features actually chosen for the speech of any one character and the intensity of application thereof can vary considerably from character to character as well as within the actual speech idiom of this or that person. But Mrs Gamp's idiolect provides far and away the most striking illustration of Dickens' art in this respect.
10. This is a 'form of ANACOLUTHON in which a sentence is begun with what appears to be the subject, but before the verb is reached something else is substituted in word or in thought, and the supposed subject is left in the air' (H. W. Fowler, *A Dictionary of Modern English Usage* (London, 1968) p. 393).
11. Ibid.

12. Sylvère Monod, *Dickens the Novelist*, p. 219.
13. W. J. B. Owen, 'Mrs Gamp's Poetic Diction', p. 96.
14. Angus Wilson, *The World of Charles Dickens*, p. 177.
15. Amy Cruse, *The Victorians and Their Books* (London, 1935) ch. VIII.
16. George Gissing, *Charles Dickens: a Critical Study*, p. 121.
17. James Kincaid, *Dickens and the Rhetoric of Laughter*, p. 151.
18. *The Letters of Charles Dickens*, vol. III, *1842–1843*, p. 441.
19. Cf. William Golding, *The Spire* (London, 1964), concerning – as far as I can make out – the same cathedral.
20. Sylvère Monod, *Dickens the Novelist*, p. 236.
21. Edgar Johnson, *Charles Dickens: His Tragedy and Triumph* (London, 1953) p. 481.
22. G. K. Chesterton, *Charles Dickens* (London, 1906; reissued New York, 1965) pp. 113–14.
23. John Lucas, *The Melancholy Man*, p. 113.

CHAPTER 9: *DOMBEY & SON* TO *BLEAK HOUSE*

1. *Dombey & Son* was written in the now usual 20 numbers, appearing between October 1846 and April 1848.
2. Dorothy Van Ghent, *The English Novel*, p. 130.
3. This is a mode somewhat reminiscent of the kind of technique George Eliot uses in similar circumstances, especially in *Middlemarch* (published a generation later than *Dombey & Son*), for the development of the inner life of Dorothea Brooke or Lydgate (cf. Riverside Edition, ed. Gordon S. Haight (Cambridge, 1956) chs 20 and 73, for instance).
4. J. Hillis Miller, *Charles Dickens: The World of His Novels* (Cambridge, Mass., 1958) pp. 145–6.
5. With respect to Florence, the emptiness of these flowery situations is tellingly shown up in Mrs Skewton's verbal reaction when told Florence is out with Edith. Now the trappings have all disappeared; all is violent directness – no adjectives at all (529).
6. Of interest in her last speech to these two characters is Mrs Skewton's use of the auxiliary in the past tense: 'did' (575). It is a reminder of Dickens' complete identification with the character through the speech, right down to the smallest detail. Although Mrs Skewton will not openly admit it, she realises deep down that her days are numbered – hence the past tense. Previous to her stroke, she had expressed her forgetfulness in the present; from that point onwards, her use of the past in respect to herself is consistent.
7. In a discussion of the restraints put on Victorian writers by the conventions of the time, Steven Marcus draws attention to the ingenuity exhibited by Dickens in his depiction of Bagstock 'without having recourse to open sexual language ... from his very name, which conceals a sexual pun, to the descriptions of him swilling hot spiced drinks and then swelling apoplectically and turning red and blue, to his frequent reference to the old "Bagstock breed"' (*The Other Victorians* (New York, 1964) p. 110).

8. *David Copperfield* was written in 20 monthly numbers between May 1849 and November 1850.
9. Sylvère Monod, *Dickens the Novelist*, p. 354.
10. In his book *Tolstoy or Dostoevsky* (London, 1960) p. 190, George Steiner refers to the 'borrowings from the figure of Steerforth' for Stavrogin in *The Possessed*. Dostoevsky's interest in certain aspects of Dickens' art – particularly in his presentation of the warped mind – is not, perhaps, generally realised. In his book *Dostoevsky and Dickens: A Study of Literary Influence* (London, 1973), N. M. Lary traces the effect of this interest above all in *The Idiot* and *The Devils (The Possessed)*; he, too, points out Stavrogin's origins in Steerforth (pp. 119–23), a theory first propounded by G. Katkov in his 'Steerforth and Stavrogin: On the Sources of *The Possessed*', *Slavonic and East European Review*, 27 (1949) 469–88, and also followed up by Loralee MacPike in her *Dostoevsky's Dickens* (London, 1981).
11. Cf. *The Letters of Charles Dickens*, ed. House, Storey and Tillotson, vol. v, *1847–1849*, pp. 674–5, 676, 676–7, for details of the subsequent complications, which even involved threats of legal action.
12. In a novel that is as full of name-calling as perhaps no other by Dickens, Uriah is forced to endure a great many derogatory appellations, most of which stem appropriately enough from the animal world (it will be observed that the book as a whole is full of animal imagery): 'red fox' (518), 'serpent' (711), 'red-headed animal' (381), 'Ape' (516), 'eel' (517), 'malevolent baboon' (573). In addition, we are told that 'his hand felt like a fish' (236), that when reading his finger 'made clammy tracks along the page ... like a snail' (234), and of his 'snaky undulation' (378).
13. Feodor Dostoevsky, *The Brothers Karamazov*, bks 5 (6), 11 (6, 7, 8).
14. K. J. Fielding, *Charles Dickens: a Critical Introduction* (London, 1958) p. 130.
15. *Bleak House* appeared in 20 monthly numbers between March 1852 and September 1853.
16. Leonard W. Deen, 'Style and Unity in *Bleak House*', in *TCI/BH*, p. 56.
17. A brilliant illustration of the growing multi-functional flexibility of Dickens' fictional speech is provided in the dramatic scene that forces Jo, the poor, ignorant crossing-sweeper, and Lady Dedlock into oral communication at the grave of Captain Hawdon, Lady Dedlock's former lover and father of their child, Esther (223–5). The two barely understand each other; indeed, at times not at all – a daunting example of just how widely diverse two dialects of the same root language can be. The mutual incomprehension underlines the basic message of this great novel of society: that, despite the yawning gulf existing socially (and hence linguistically) between the classes, no level of society in London can remain free of the taint projected from the depth of this and similarly repulsive slums. In the face of such consummate structural use of fictional speech, it is impossible to call any of these characters 'frozen' or 'flat'.
18. In Dickens, there are other characters like Mr Snagsby, but none, perhaps, is more reminiscent of the 'Little Man' figure recurring in Wells' social novels of the early 1900s and in much American humorous literature of the 1920s and 1930s (Cf. Chapter 4, footnote 2).
19. Although Chadband appears in only three scenes (chs XIX, XXV, LIV), he manages to pour out a great deal, dominating, indeed, the first two of the

three episodes. During his final entrance he is rather less verbose, his unmasking as a mercenary schemer somewhat cramping his style, particularly with the sceptically voluble Inspector Bucket in full command of the situation.
20. A fact underscored by both Humphry House (*The Dickens World*, ch. v) and Mrs Leavis in a book she completed together with her husband, Dr Leavis (*Dickens the Novelist*, p. 137).
21. As in the example beginning 'from whence ...' (263–4); note how the syntactic divisions gradually get smaller until in the end there is little more than a list of nouns each preceded by the same preposition. Directly after this passage Dickens himself inserts a sarcastic comment, one which also reveals a little of the author's repudiative attitude to this type of person (264).
22. George Gissing, *Charles Dickens: a Critical Study*, p. 117.

CHAPTER 10: *HARD TIMES* AND *LITTLE DORRIT*

1. After a gap of 13 years, Dickens had been forced to return to weekly serialisation, *Hard Times* appearing in 21 numbers from April to August 1854. For all his aversion to the procedure, of the four novels written between 1854 and 1861, three were produced in weekly parts. From now on, too, all his novels (except the unfinished *Edwin Drood*) are divided into 'Books'.
2. John Butt and Kathleen Tillotson, *Dickens at Work*, p. 203.
3. An examination of the author's use of the Lancashire dialect is outside the scope of the present work, but about it Norman Page writes: 'One has the sense of Dickens somewhat anxiously steering a course that will provide adequate indications of dialect speech without running aground on the shoals of obscurity' (*Speech in the English Novel*, p. 63).
4. A. E. Dyson, '*Hard Times*: the Robber Fancy', *Dickensian* (May, 1969) p. 75.
5. This novel appeared in 20 monthly parts from December 1855 to June 1857. Dickens had actually started to get down to the writing of the book in May 1855, but the three numbers which he completed in the following seven months were the result of an intense, for him unprecedented, struggle with his material and with himself. This was the beginning of the most turbulent, dissatisfied, and hence uneasy, period in his life, reaching a head when, in 1858, he separated from his wife.
6. Edmund Wilson, 'Dickens: the Two Scrooges', in *The Wound and the Bow* (London, 1941; reprinted in Methuen's University Paperbacks, 1961) p. 51.
7. Richard Stang, '*Little Dorrit*: a World in Reverse', in *DtC*, pp. 143–4.
8. Of course, it is equally possible that Dickens simply found the unusual syntax amusing in itself, grafting it on to the speech idioms of certain suitable characters (all lower or lower-middle class). In the author's last (unfinished) book, that hilarious throwback to earlier times, Mrs Billickin, also indulges in the 'backward manner': 'The door-plate is used as a protection ... and go from it I will not' (*ED*, 252).
9. The attitude towards foreigners of his countrymen, in particular their

manner of adjusting their English to what they considered a more understandable level, was obviously a source of perennial amusement to Dickens, and he makes it clear here (302–3), as well as in various passages scattered throughout his writings (cf. Podsnap, *OMF*, 131–3). He once wrote from Italy about the way in which his Italian servants and those he had brought with him from England conversed with each other: 'To hear one or other of them [the Italians] talking away to our servants with the utmost violence and volubility in Genoese, and our servants answering with great fluency in English (very loud: as if the others were only deaf, not Italian), is one of the most ridiculous things possible.' (*The Letters of Charles Dickens*, vol. IV, *1844–1846*, p. 157.)

10. James Kincaid, *Dickens and the Rhetoric of Laughter*, p. 208.
11. N. M. Lary has drawn attention to the parallel between Mr Dorrit (plus, to a degree, Mr Micawber) and General Ivolgin in Dostoevsky's *The Idiot* (*Dostoevsky and Dickens*, London, 1973, pp. 93–104).
12. Sapsea's epitaph for his deceased wife (*ED*, 36), although it reflects the conceit and pomposity of a self-inflated character who stands at the other end from that part of the scale of feeling occupied by modest John, comes stylistically close to this. When considering the references in *DS* (552–3), *DC* (15) and *GE* (42) to the same, it becomes obvious that Dickens' undying fascination for all the language forms around him extended even to the gravestone inscriptions so beloved of the Victorian mind.
13. George Gissing, *Charles Dickens: a Critical Study*, p. 156.

CHAPTER 11: *GREAT EXPECTATIONS* TO *EDWIN DROOD*

1. *Great Expectations*, for which Dickens was once more forced to turn to weekly numbers, was brought out between December 1860 and August 1861.
2. Cf. Sylvère Monod, 'Some Stylistic Devices in *A Tale of Two Cities*', in *DtC*, pp. 165–86.
3. Graham Greene, 'The Young Dickens', in *DCr*, pp. 246–7.
4. Ibid. pp. 245–6.
5. There are, in fact, many examples in *A Tale of Two Cities*: 'it is always preparing' (170); 'It could not be otherwise' (318); etc.
6. This point has been very cogently made by Ruth Vande Kieft ('Patterns of Communication in *Great Expectations*', in *AGE*, pp. 170–80) in an answer to rather far-fetched theories put forward regarding Joe's (assumed) unintelligibility by, among others, Dorothy Van Ghent in her book *The English Novel*, pp. 125–38.
7. On page 196 of the OUP edition of *Great Expectations*, there is, incidently, a rather peculiar deviation, 'How am you?', which I can only assume to be a printer's error.
8. With *Our Mutual Friend*, Dickens returned once more to the monthly serial form, the novel appearing in 20 numbers between May 1864 and November 1865. During this time, he nearly lost one of the numbers in a disastrous train crash in Kent, the accident occurring on 9 June 1865, exactly five years previous to the day of his death.

9. John Lucas, *The Melancholy Man*, p. 344.
10. Norman Page, *Speech in the English Novel*, p. 140.
11. I certainly do *not* feel that the defects of the book arise 'because Dickens was losing his faculty for writing serious comedy' (Robert Barnard, 'The Choral Symphony: *Our Mutual Friend*', *REL*, II, 3 (July, 1961) p. 93). The novel, in fact, abounds with comedy, though now in a less wildly exotic, more subtle or ironic vein. One need only mention the comments on and language of 'Podsnappery' (cf. 128–43).
12. John Forster, *The Life of Charles Dickens*, p. 811.
13. Since writing these lines, I have had the opportunity to read Michael Slater's extremely comprehensive, illuminating and stimulating book *Dickens and Women* (London, 1983) in which he rejects the general tendency 'to see in Bella a portrait of Ellen' (p. 196). After clearly pointing out that she (Bella) 'is no more a "portrait" of any individual than any other of Dickens's major female chapters' (ibid.), Dr Slater submits the view that the author's favourite daughter 'Katey was, to some extent, [the] model for his wilful young heroine' (p. 197), concluding that 'As Bella Wilfer is ... the most fascinating and attractive young woman that Dickens ever created, so Katey is surely the most remarkable and attractive of all the women in his life who were privileged to know him intimately' (p. 200). So much for Ellen Ternan!
14. Robert Morse, '*Our Mutual Friend* (1949)', in *DMJ*, p. 266.
15. Jack Lindsay, *Charles Dickens* (London, 1950) p. 380.
16. Dickens had completed all but six of the *twelve* monthly numbers (a new turn) planned for *The Mystery of Edwin Drood* when he died suddenly on 9 June 1870.
17. Barbara Hardy, 'Dickens: the Later Novels', *WTW* (London, 1968) p. 39.
18. It was not until after he had started *The Mystery of Edwin Drood* that Dickens finished his last and most intense series of public readings, a series which, physically, had taken serious toll of him (cf. Philip Collins, *Charles Dickens: The Public Readings*, Oxford University Press, 1976).
19. I am assuming that in this unfinished novel Edwin Drood is actually murdered, and that Jasper is responsible for his nephew's murder.
20. George Gissing, *Charles Dickens: a Critical Study*, p. 160.
21. It is about this passage that A. O. J. Cockshut writes: 'A subtler, briefer, and more blistering comment even than is to be found in *Hard Times* upon the Manchester school, the commercial greatness of England, and the "immutable laws of supply and demand".' ('*Edwin Drood*: Early and Late Dickens Reconciled', in *DTC*, p. 234.)
22. G. L. Brook, *The Language of Dickens*, p. 115. After going on to analyse the construction and possible source of this non-standard pronunciation, Professor Brook underlines that 'no one can say exactly how much of the resultant word is due to phonetic changes and how much to blending' (ibid., p. 116).
23. With this in mind, it is clear that the book by no means deserves G. B. Shaw's contemptuous cry that it was 'only a gesture by a man three quarters dead' (cf. Edmund Wilson, 'Dickens: the Two Scrooges', p. 75).

Index

Ainsworth, Harrison, 74, 238
Allen, Benjamin (*PP*), 31
alliteration, 146
American Notes (*AN*), 11
anacoluthon, 239
anadiplosis, 51, 216
anaphoric mode, 10, 50, 106, 130, 149–50, 177, 178, 183, 185, 186, 188, 194, 216
aphasic speech, 127, 129, 131, 223
Arnold, Matthew, 73
Artful Dodger [Jack Dawkins] (*OT*), 38, 75, **85–7,** 105, 108, 109, 112, 122–3, 139, 219
'Astley's' (*SB*), 40, 94
Austen, Jane, 21, 232, 237

Bagnet, Matthew (*BH*), 20, 43
Bagstock, Major (*DS*), 18, 20, 31, 126, 127, 128, 131, **133–4,** 222–3, 240
Bailey Junior (*MC*), 108–9, 113
Bar (*LD*), 30
Barkis, Mr (*DC*), 135–6
Barnaby Rudge, 54, 65–6, 100–1, **102–7,** 124, 125, 221, 237, 238, 239
Barnacle, Clarence [Barnacle Junior] (*LD*), 27, 225, 227
Barnacle, Lord Decimus (*LD*), 50, 68, 225, 227
Barney (*OT*), 11, 84
Barsad (*TTC*): *see* Pross, Solomon
Bayham Badger, Mrs (*BH*), 31

Billickin, Mrs (*ED*), 40, 208, 211, 228
Bishop (*LD*), 31
Blackpool, Stephen (*HT*), 11, 159, 178
Blathers (*OT*): *see* Bow Street Runners
Bleak House, 40, 52, 54–7, 58, 59, 60, 61, 67, **145–56,** 157, 218, 224–5, 226
Blight, Young (*OMF*), 42–3
Blimber, Dr (*DS*), 66
Blimber, Miss (*DS*), 31
Bloom, Molly, 235
'Bloomsbury Christening, The' (*SB*), 76
Bloss, Mrs (*SB*), 39, 75
'Boarding-house, The' (*SB*), 75
Boffin, Mr (*OMF*), 29, **186–7,** 189, 191, 194, 195
Boffin, Mrs (*OMF*), 20, 29, 185, 189
Bounderby, Mr (*HT*), 40, 158, 159, 160
Bow Street Runners (*OT*), 38–9, 42
Brass, Sally (*OCS*), 94–5, 97, 100
Brass, Sampson (*OCS*), 30, 94–5, 97, 98, 100
Briggs (*DS*), 66
Brontë, Emily, 34
Browdie, John (*NN*), 11
Brown, Alice (*DS*), 129
Brown, Mrs (*DS*), 129
Browning, Robert, 73
Bucket, Inspector (*BH*), 28, 42, 55–7,

Bucket, Inspector – *cont.*
    149, 152, **154–6,** 224, 234, 239, 242
Budd, Rosa ['Rosebud'] (*ED*), 34, 70, 201, **202–4,** 206, 207
Bumble, Mr (*OT*), 39, 84–5, 87, 219
Bunsby, Jack (*DS*), 3, 42, 52–3, 132–3, 223
Burns, Robert, 34
Buzfuz, Serjeant (*PP*), 29
Byron, Lord, 73, 152

Carker, James (*DS*), 42, 127, 128–9, 131, 134
Carlyle, Thomas, 102, 176
Carroll, Lewis [C. L. Dodgson], 94, 138
Carton, Sydney (*TTC*), 30, 69
Casby, Mr (*LD*), 163, 168
Cavalletto, John Baptist (*LD*), 11, 163
Cervantes, Miguel de, 3
Chadband, Mrs (*BH*), 155
Chadband, Rev. Mr (*BH*), 32, 44, **148–50,** 152, 155, 224, 241–2
Chester, Sir John (*BR*), 27
Chick, Mrs (*DS*), 11
Chicken, The Game (*DS*), 43, 66
Childers, Mr E. W. B. (*HT*), 40–1
Chivery, John (*LD*), 9, 126, 162, **168,** 243
Chivery, Mrs (*LD*), 9, 162
Chopin, Frédéric, 235
Christmas Books, 235, 236
Christmas Stories, 62, 235, 236
Christopher, a headwaiter ['Somebody's Luggage'] (*CS*), 234
Chuckster, Mr (*OCS*), 42, 96, 99, 151
Chuzzlewit, Jonas (*MC*), 66, 108, 111, 114, 119, 133
Chuzzlewit, Martin, Jr (*MC*), 66, 121, 122
Chuzzlewit, Martin, Sn (*MC*), 121, 122, 123
Chuzzlewit, Mercy (*MC*): *see* Pecksniff, Mercy
circumlocution: *see under* speech
Cleaver, Fanny (*OMF*): *see* Wren, Jenny

Clennam, Arthur (*LD*), 41, 47, 164, 166, 167, 168, 225
Codlin, Tom (*OCS*), 18
Collins, Wilkie, 234
Copperfield, David (*DC*), 20, 41, 136–7, 139, 141, 144, 145, 226
Corney, Mrs (*OT*), 84
Coutts, Miss Angela Burdett, 109
Creakle, Mr (*DC*), 139
'Criminal Courts' (*SB*), 75
Crisparkle, Rev. Septimus (*ED*), 32, **204–6**
Cruikshank, George, 232
Crummles troupe (*NN*), 33, 40, 88, 94, 220
Cuttle, Captain (*DS*), 3, 18, 42, 52–3, 125, 126, **131–3,** 223

Darnay, Charles (*TTC*), 68
Datchery, Mr (*ED*), 211
David Copperfield, 3, 5, 8, 16, 17, 18, 54, 58–9, 67, **134–45,** 223–4, 236, 241
Dawkins, Jack: *see* Artful Dodger
Dedlock Cousin (*BH*), 27
Dedlock, Lady (*BH*), 37, 55, 57, 151, 154, 155, 241
Dedlock, Sir Leicester (*BH*), 27, 154, 155
Defarges (*TTC*), 11
Defoe, Daniel, 3
Dennis, Ned (*BR*), 18, 43, 65, 102–3, 133
Deputy ['Winks'] (*ED*), 200, **208–11,** 228
dialect, definition of, 1, 230
    American English, 11, 231
    English of foreigners, 11, 22
    English of Jews, 11
    regional dialects, 11, 34, 159, 231, 233, 242
dialogue: *see under* idiolects, interaction of
Dickens, Catherine (Mrs Charles), 242
Dickens, Charles, *passim*;
    authorial interpolation, 55, 87, 93, 135, 234
    authorial prose modalities, 7, **61–4,** 74–5, 77, 83, 102, 107, 108,

124, 125–6, 131, 134, 135, 145, 146–7, 161–2, 172, 185, 199–200, 213, 217
Bildungsroman, 59, 134, 223
childhood, spirit of, 134, 172
Cockney, attitude towards, 35, 74, 108, 220, 223
comic genius, 75, 77, 244
crime, 73, 74, 237–8
detective story, 146
determinism, philosophy of, 176
dissociation, 41, 200–2, 203, 227–8
Doppelgänger theme, 219
education, 30–1, 233
Ellen Ternan, 194, 244
English insularity, attitude towards, 193, 242–3
fairy tale elements in his fiction, 3, 26, 94, 134, 157, 172
fictional conventions of his time, use of, 74–5, 215, 235
'flat' characters, 116, 241
humour, cruelty of, 106, 122, 152
improvisation, 93, 100, 124, 213, 220, 228
industrial unrest, 157
inventive powers, 4, 16, 75, 84, 90, 146, 222, 224, 231
language, command of, 6, 7, 64, 65, 69, 107, 145, 171, 213
language, flexibility of, 42, 64, 162, 172–3, 184, 199, 200, 215, 217, 218, 225, 227, 241
law, 4–5, 29, 42–3, 96–7, 217
literary craftsman, 107
'Little Man', theme, 56, 148, 236, 241
Maria Winter, *née* Beadnell, 165, 231
mimicry: selection–concentration–exaggeration technique, 2, 4–5, 35, 36, 50, 81, 117, 123, 147–8, 185, 214, 215, 218, 227, 234
mirror metaphor, use of, 51, 185
natural gifts and early influences, 2–6, 17–21, 73–5, 231
Nonsense, world of, 53, 83, 94, 123–4, 188, 223
Parliament, 5–6, 33

pathetic fallacy, use of, 97, 108, 126, 146, 185, 234
poetic mode (authorial voice), 102, 107, 126, 145, 146, 162, 172, 225
Poor Law, 84, 185
professional recorder of speech, 5–6, 29, 33, 231
public readings, 50, 62, 115, 184, 199, 217, 235, 236, 244
psychological penetration, 161, 164, 176, 181, 183, 184, 199, 208, 212, 218, 225, 226
rapport with reading public, 53, 117, 235
rapport with his time through his art, 57–8, 74, 113, 116–17, 131, 145, 172, 180–1, 188, 191, 202
ridiculous, sense of the, 3, 231
realism, 38, 234
religion, 31–2, 102, 106, 148–9, 204–5, 242
Romantic movement, 73
self-centred aestheticism, theme of, 153–4, 191
serialization and demands thereof, 35, 74, 119, 125, 127, 134, 138, 142, 157, 178, 214, 238, 239, 240, 241, 242, 243, 244
sexuality in his fiction, 119, 120, 121, 133, 145, 240
society, parodic criticism of, 68, 140, 145–6, 148, 150, 160–1, 184–5, 188, 190, 192, 198–9, 200, 202, 206, 208, 209, 211–12, 216–17, 220, 223, 224–5, 226–7, 228
structure, growth in mastery of, 107–8, 124, 125–6, 134, 135
stylized theatrical storytelling world, 2, 6, 36, 38–9, 45, 51–3, 58, 61, 63–4, 69, 83–4, 85, 94, 125, 133, 146, 171, 179, 184, 185, 213, 215, 216, 217–18, 222, 228–9
symbolism, 37, 102, 184, 190, 192, 198, 202, 209
theatre, influence of, 4, 74, 79, 83–4, 87–8, 201, 214

Dickens, Charles – *cont.*
   vulgarity, nature of, 104, 113, 142
   women, attitude towards, 106
Dickens, Elizabeth (Mrs John), 3, 21, 93
Dickens, John, 3, 137
Dickens, Kate, 244
Dickens, Mamie, 5, 231
Disraeli, Benjamin, 235
Dodson, Mr (*PP*), 30
Dombey & Son, 3, 7, 16, 52, 54, 55, 58, 59, 66, 83, 124, **125–34,** 140, 214, 221, 222–3, 232, 236, 239, 240
Dombey, Edith (*DS*), 127, 128–9, 131, 133, 240
Dombey, Florence (*DS*), 128, 132, 240
Dombey, Mr (*DS*), 20, 126, 127, 128, 134
Dombey, Paul (*DS*), 125, 135
Dorrit, Amy (*LD*), 22, 68, 165, 166, 168, 170, 171, 194, 225, 232
Dorrit, Edward (*LD*), 22
Dorrit, Fanny (*LD*), 22, **170–1**
Dorrit, Frederick (*LD*), 22, 163–4
Dorrit, William (*LD*), 3, 22–3, 68, 162, **163–5,** 170, 171, 225, 233, 243
Dostoevsky, Feodor, 144, 241, 243
Dowler, Captain (*PP*), 20, 31
'Dr Marigold' (*CS*), 40
Drood, Edwin (*ED*), 70, **202–4,** 207, 227–8, 244
'Drunkard's Death, The' (*SB*), 45
Duff (*OT*): *see* Bow Street Runners
Durdles (*ED*), 43, 200, **208–11,** 227, 228

eccentric speech: *see under* speech
Egon, Pierce, 35, 74
Eliot, George, 34, 164, 240
Eliot, Thomas Stearns, 185
Emily, Little (*DC*), 135, 142, 143
Endell, Martha (*DC*): *see* Martha
epistolary mode: *see under* idiolects, typification, personal
epistrophe, 51, 103, 201, 216
epizeusis, 51
Estella (*GE*), 41, 173, 174, **175–7,** 194, 225–6

Fagin (*OT*), 39, 83–4, 85, 87, 232
Feenix, Cousin (*DS*), 27
Fielding, Henry, 3
Finching, Flora (*LD*), 9, 17, 21, 48, 52, 95, 133, 162, 163, **165–7,** 169, 222, 225–6
Flaubert, Gustave, 237
Fledgeby, Mr (*OMF*), 186, 187, 189, 190, 196
Flintwinch, Affery (*LD*), 47
Fogg, Mr (*PP*), 30
Forster, John, 17, 21, 192–3, 231, 232
free indirect speech: *see* speech

Gamp, Mrs (*MC*), 7, 8, 9, 10, 21, 35, 36, 37, 47, 48, 50, 52, 75, 104, 105, 107, 108, **109–17,** 119, 120, 122, 123, 124, 127, 131, 138, 214, 221–2, 233, 234, 235, 239, 240
Gargery, Joe (*GE*), **177–9,** 226, 243
Gargery, Mrs (*GE*), 177
Gashford, Mr (*BR*), 103
Gaskell, Mrs, 34
Gay, Walter (*DS*), 20, 42, 132
General, Mrs (*LD*), 170, 233
'George Silverman's Explanation' (*UT/RP*), 50, 51, 67
Gills, Sol (*DS*), 127
Gissing, George, 38, 234, 238, 242, 243
'Going into Society' (*CS*), 40
Golding, William, 240
Goldsmith, Oliver, 3
Gordon, Lord George (*BR*), 102
Gordon riots, 102, 103–4
Gowan, Henry (*LD*), 22, 27, 136, 225, 227
Gowan, Pet, *née* Meagles (*LD*), 22
Gradgrind, Louisa (*HT*), 159–60
Gradgrind, Mr (*HT*), 41, 60–1, 158, 160, 225
Gradgrind, Tom (*HT*), 159–60
Graham, Mary (*MC*), 119, 121
Granger, Mrs (*DS*): *see* Dombey, Edith
Great Expectations, 7, 47, 62, 67, **172–84,** 226, 227, 236, 243
Greene, Graham, 172, 235, 243
'Greenwich Fair' (*SB*), 40
Greenwood, James, 35

Gregsbury, Mr (*NN*), 32
Grewgious, Mr (*ED*), 30, 203, **206–8,** 227
Gridley, Mr (*BH*), 57, 156
Grummer, Daniel (*PP*), 42
Gummidge, Mrs (*DC*), 11
Guppy, William (*BH*), 30, 42, 43, 55, **150–2,** 224

Ham (*DC*), 11
Hard Times, 60–1, 62, **157–60,** 215, 225, 226, 227, 242, 244
Hardy, Thomas, 34
Haredale, Emma (*BR*), 25
Harmon, John (*OMF*), 186, 194
Harthouse, James (*HT*), 27, 136, 159–60, 225
'Haunted Man, The' (*CB*), 50
Havisham, Miss (*GE*), 67, **173–5,** 176, 177, 180, 183, 225, 226
Hawdon, Captain (*BH*), 55, 67, 211, 241
Hawke, Sir Mulberry (*NN*), 88, 93
Hawkyard, Brother (*GSE*), 32
Headstone, Bradley (*OMF*), 30–1, 33–4, 191, 197, 225
Heep, Uriah (*DC*), 42, 138, 139, 140, **143–5,** 224, 241
Hexam, Charlie (*OMF*), 197
Hexam, Gaffer (*OMF*), 63, 185, 190
Hexam, Lizzie (*OMF*), 26, 33, 63, 188, 192, 197–8, 234
Higden, Betty (*OMF*), 37, 185
Hogarth, William, 238
'Hollow Men' [T. S. Eliot], 185
Honeythunder, Mr (*ED*), 32, 205, 211
Hopkins, Gerald Manley, 73
'Horatio Sparkins' (*SB*), 75
Hortense, Mademoiselle (*BH*), 11, 28, 155
Household Narrative, 67
Household Words, 41, 231
Howler, Rev. Melchisedech (*DS*), 32, 148
Hugh (*BR*), 45, 102
Hunt, Leigh, 152

idiolects: *see also* speech
  analysis of (chronological), **77–212;**
    changes and fluctuations, 10, 123, 142–3, 174–7, 185–7, 201–3, 208, 218, 220, 221, 222, 227–8
  coda, 63, 86, 123, 139, 167
  collage (manufactured speech), 2, 8, 35, 36, 116, 137, 147, 187, 213–14, 215, 221–2, 227, 228, 234
  creative procedure, 38, 40, 214, 231
  critical approach to, 213
  development of (overview), 6–7, **213–29**
  idiolect pairs, 132–3, 139–40, 165–7, 187–92, 202–4, 208–11, 218–19, 221, 223, 225–6, 227
  increasing density of features, 7, 93, 214, 219, 221, 222, 228
  individual brilliance of, 213
  intelligibility of, 39, 243
  interaction of, 37, 52–3, 55–8, 70, 78, 94, 160, 163–4, 173, 175, 183, 187–92, 197–8, 203, 216, 223, 224, 227
  linguistic features: abrupt colloquialisms, 9, 100, 108, 120; blend words, 104, 110, 127, 203, 244; comparisons, irregular, 110; double negatives, 108; formulaic language, 192, 227; imagery of riches, 120–1; indefinites, use of, 169; lexical characterization, 110–11, 118–19, 128, 132, 144, 152–3, 179, 203; malapropisms, 3–4, 9, 35, 39, 78, 85, 104, 178, 186, 233; religious vocabulary, 36, 105, 106, 112–13, 114, 120–1, 149, 222; streams of plurals, 104–5, 106; syntactic waywardness, 110, 162–3, 166, 168; V/W confusion, 35, 85, 104, 115, 178, 233
  rhetorical features: advice, rhetoric of, 137, 141; accumulation technique, 89–90, 123; animal imagery, 89, 121, 128, 170, 241; apostrophizing incriminations, 133, 159, 222; baby talk, 89–90, 202; 'but', use of, 114,

idiolects – cont.
126–7; Cockney impudence, metaphoric and picturesque, 79, 82, 97, 105, 108, 113–14, 142–3; 186, 187, 196, 220; comparisons, exotic, 89, 113, 149, 169; comparisons, Weller-type, 9, 17, 18–19, 78–9, 82, 214, 232; distorted quotations, 9, 36, 131–2; doll metaphor, 197–8; 'earthy' folk wisdom, 209; echoes, 50, 122; emphasis, rhetoric of, 36, 79, 82, 108, 109, 118, 138, 141, 143, 167, 178, 180, 182, 186, 202, 204, 226; endearment, terms of, 89, 114, 132; epithetical excess, 9, 80, 82, 84, 92, 133–4, 189, 194, 196, 222; exaggeration, rhetoric of, 92, 105; first-person singular, use of, 105, 106, 153, 180; gravestone inscriptions, 168, 243; hypocrisy, rhetoric of, 114, 119, 128, 130, 133–4, 143–5, 222; interrogative mode, 183–4; irrelevant self-questioning and asides, 92, 129–30, 166, 220; names, variations on, 9, 141, 166; nicknames, 80, 97, 142–3, 170, 180; parenthetical rhetoric, 113, 120, 123, 139; punishment conceits, 196, 198; quoting others, 9, 36, 105, 111–12, 139, 222; reasoning, love of, 97, 98, 139; retrospective phraseology, 92; rhymes and scraps of verse, 36, 81, 86, 95, 97–8, 99, 100, 137, 144, 187, 197, 202, 209, 210, 216, 227; rhetorical questions and imperatives, 85, 95, 103, 105, 108, 129–30, 142, 149, 169, 170, 173–4, 175, 223; robot-like vituperation, 176; salutation urge, 9, 97, 118, 128, 149; speaking of oneself in the third person, 153, 209; speech tags, 9, 15–18, 36, 89, 103, 129, 131–2, 137, 139, 140, 151, 166, 170, 178, 196, 210, 214, 219; staccato-like phrases, 85, 138, 194; 'threeing', 50, 86–7, 123, 139, 167, 174, 216; 'unnecessary detail', 80, 82, 105, 111, 139

rhythmic patterns: *see* speech

sub-idiolects, 42, 95, 127, 129–31, 152, 154–6, 170–1, 181–3, 188–90, 218, 223, 224, 239

typifying registers (personal): affected, 22–3, 89, 128; 'backward', 9, 162–3, 168, 242; Chadbandian, 148–50, 224, 242; Christian, 179; colloquial, 202–3; contrast, 10, 95–6, 119–20, 127, 137, 220; county, 91; epistolary, 76, 137–8, 139, 223; 'exalted', 198; 'Heart–Nature–Soul', 128–9, 130; 'heroic', 26, 215, 232, 234; never-ending, 9, 17, 21, 91–2, 111, 166, 214, 220, 225–6, 235; prison, 165; Regency, 28, 89–90, 127–31, 220; sensual, 121; sentimental, 150–2, 166–7, 187–8; 'smooth', 143–5, 224; staccato, 9, 17, 19–20, 214, 219; variable, 203

working plan of idiolect features, 8–10, 231

Ikey (*SB*), 37, 75–6
Inspector, Mr (*OMF*), 42
Irish orator (*SB*), 32, 44

Jaggers, Mr (*GE*), 30, 173, 175, 178, 181, 182, **183–4**
James, Henry, 116, 164
Jasper, John (*ED*), 34, **200–2,** 203, 205, 206, 207, 208, 209, 210, 211, 225, 228, 244
Jenny (*BH*), 56–7, 234
Jingle, Alfred (*PP*), 9, 17, **19–20,** 41, 219
Jo (*BH*), 37–8, 45, 55–7, 67, 149, 150, 154, 156, 178, 211, 224, 234, 237, 241
Job (*PP*), 80
Jobling, Dr John (*MC*), 31

Jobling, Mr [alias Weevle] (*BH*), 42, 43, 151
Joyce, James, 235

Kafka, Franz, 156
Keats, John, 73, 150, 152
Kenge, Mr ['Conversation'] (*BH*), 30
Kenwigs, Mr (*NN*), 40, 88
key-word technique: *see* speech
Kidderminster, Mr ['Cupid'] (*HT*), 40–1
Knag, Miss (*NN*), 18
Krook, Mr (*BH*), 55

Lammle, Alfred (*OMF*), 185–6, **188–90,** 191, 198, 227
Lammle, Sophronia (*OMF*), 186, **188–90,** 191, 198, 227
Landless, Helena (*ED*), 70, 206, 211
Landless, Neville (*ED*), 70, 203, 205, 206, 211
Lear, Edward, 94
Lightwood, Mortimer (*OMF*), 20, 27, 30, 185, **190–2,** 227
Lirriper, Mrs ['Mrs Lirriper's Legacy'] (*CS*), 9, 17, 21, 48–50, 235
Littimer (*DC*), 60, 140
Little Dorrit, 21–4, 54, 61, 62, 68, 87, 146, **160–71,** 199, 215, 225–6, 242
Liz (*BH*), 56–7
Lord High Chancellor (*BH*), 55
Lowton, Mr (*PP*), 42
Lupin, Mrs (*MC*), 122
Lytton, Edward Bulwer [Lord Lytton], 74, 177, 235, 238

Macready, William, 33, 233
Madman, the (*NN*), 94
Magwitch, Abel (*GE*), 172, 175, 177, **179–81,** 183, 226
malapropisms: *see* idiolects
Manette, Dr (*TTC*), 50
Mantalini, Alfred (*NN*), 28, **88–90,** 220
Marchioness, The (*OCS*), 96, 100
Martha (*DC*), 135
Martin Chuzzlewit, 7, 45, 54, 66, 100–1, **107–24,** 214, 221–2, 239

Martin, Miss (*SB*), 65
Master Humphrey's Clock, 238, 239
Mathews, Charles, 17–21, 231, 232
Mayhew, Augustus, 35
Maylie, Rose (*OT*), 25, 45
Merdle, Mr (*LD*), 31, 32, 68, 161
Merdle, Mrs (*LD*), 161
Micawber, Wilkins (*DC*), 3, 10, 20, 67, 96, 119, 120, 127, 136, **137–8,** 139, 140, 144, 167, 222, 223, 233, 239, 243
Micawber, Emma (*DC*), 3, 67, 136, **139–40,** 167, 223, 233
Miggs, Miss (*BR*), 64–6, **103–7,** 120, 221, 239
Milliken, E. J., 35
Milvey, Rev. Frank (*OMF*), 205
Molly (*GE*), 175
Montague, Tigg (*MC*): *see* Tigg, Montague
Mould, Mr (*MC*), 111, 117
Mowcher, Miss (*DC*), 43, **142–3,** 197, 223, 241
Mr F's Aunt (*LD*), 133, 162, **167,** 225–6
Murdstone, Miss Jane (*DC*), 139
Murdstone, Edward (*DC*), 136, 139, 141
Mutanhed, Lord (*PP*), 27
Mystery of Edwin Drood, The, 47, 69–70, **199–212,** 217, 219, 227–8, 236, 242, 244

Nancy (*OT*), 45, 86
Nandy, John Edward (*LD*), 162, 164–5
Neckett, Mr ['Coavinses'] (*BH*), 58
Nell, Little (*OCS*): *see* Trent, Nell
'Newgate' novel, 102, 237, 238
Nicholas Nickleby, 33, **87–94,** 219–20, 238
Nickleby, Kate (*NN*), 88, 91, 92, 93
Nickleby, Mrs (*NN*), 3, 9, 17, 21, 48, 52, 88, **91–4,** 130, 220, 233
Nickleby, Nicholas (*NN*), 33, 45, 88, 91, 200
Nickleby, Ralph (*NN*), 88, 91, 200
Nipper, Susan (*DS*), 126–7

Nonsense, world of: *see* Dickens, Charles

O'Connell, Daniel, 6
Old Curiosity Shop, The, 46, **94–100,** 101, 220–1, 238, 239
Oliver Twist, 16, 38–9, 46, **83–7,** 219, 232, 234, 237, 238
'oral style': *see* speech
Our Mutual Friend, 50, 62–3, 69, 146, **184–99,** 200, 219, 226–7, 232, 236, 243, 244

Pancks, Mr (*LD*), 163, **168–9**
'Parlour Orator, The' (*SB*): *see* Rogers, Mr
'Passage in the Life of Mr Watkins Tottle, A' (*SB*), 75–6
Pecksniff, Charity [Cherry] (*MC*), 66, 119
Pecksniff, Mercy [Merry] (*MC*), 50, 66, 114
Pecksniff, Seth (*MC*), 7, 5, 66, 108, 111, **117–24,** 137, 138, 139, 144, 154, 214, 221–2, 233
Peggotty, Clara (*DC*), 20, 141
Peggotty, Daniel (*DC*), 11
Peggotty, Emily (*DC*): *see* Emily, Little
Peggotty, Ham (*DC*): *see* Ham
Pell, Solomon (*PP*), 30, 78
Perker, Mr (*PP*), 29
Phunky, Mr (*PP*), 30
Physician (*LD*), 31
Pickwick Papers, 32, 39, 45, 74, **77–83,** 94, 219, 232, 236, 238, 239
Pickwick, Samuel (*PP*), 19, 31, 79, 80, 82
Pinch, Ruth (*MC*), 66
Pinch, Tom (*MC*), 66
Pip (*GE*): *see* Pirrip, Philip
Pirrip, Philip ['Pip'] (*GE*), 41, 67, 172–84 *passim*, 225, 226, 232
Plornish, Mr (*LD*), 162
Plornish, Mrs (*LD*), 11, 68, 163
Pluck (*NN*), 93
Pocket, Herbert (*GE*), 182
Pocket, Matthew (*GE*), 183
Pocket, Mrs (*GE*), 233

Podsnap, Georgiana (*OMF*), 185, 189
Podsnap, John (*OMF*), **192–3,** 211, 227, 233, 243
Prig, Betsey (*MC*), 115
'Private Theatres' (*SB*), 40
Pross, Solomon [Barsad] (*TTC*), 68–9
Proust, Marcel, 172
Pumblechook, Mr ['Uncle'] (*GE*), 39, 40
Pyke (*NN*), 93

Quilp, Daniel (*OCS*), 94–5, 97–100 *passim*, 103, 121, 133, 220–1

Rachael (*HT*), 159
repetition: *see* speech
Reform Bill (1832), 5
rhetorical features: *see* idiolects
rhythmic patterns: *see* speech
Riah, Mr (*OMF*), 11, 187, 196, 198
Richardson, Samuel, 46
Riderhood, Pleasant (*OMF)*, 187–8
Riderhood, Rogue (*OMF*), 37, 185, 187
Rigaud [alias Blandois alias Lagnier] (*LD*), 11, 22
Rob the Grinder (*DS*), 42, 132, 143
Rogers, Mr [the 'Parlour Orator'] (*SB*), 32, 44, 76
Rokesmith, John (*OMF*): *see* Harmon, John
Rouncewell, George (*BH*), 155–6
Rudge, Barnaby (*BR*), 102
Russell, Lord John, 6

Sapsea, Thomas (*ED*), 209, 211, 233, 243
Sawyer, Bob (*PP*), 31
Scott, Sir Walter, 3, 34, 74, 102
'Seven Dials' (*SB*), 75
Shakespeare, William, 6, 83, 141, 145, 199
Shaw, George Bernard, 87, 244
Shelley, Percy Bysshe, 73, 152
Sikes, Bill (*OT*), 38, 83–4, 87, 103, 133, 234
Sketches by Boz, 16, 32, 33, 37, 40, 44, 45, 65, **74–6,** 77, 217, 238
Skewton, Hon Mrs ['Cleopatra'] (*DS*), 7, 88, 125, 126, **127–31,**

134, 159, 170, 188, 222–3, 233, 239, 240
Skimpin, Mr (*PP*), 30
Simpole, Harold (*BH*), 20, 58, **152–4**, 191, 224–5, 233
Sleary, Mr (*HT*), 40
Sluffen, Mr [the mastersweep] (*SB*), 37, 75
Smallweed, Mr (*BH*), 155
Smike (*NN*), 91, 93, 232
Smollett, Tobias, 3–4, 31, 46, 214
Smorltork, Count (*PP*), 11
Snagsby, Mr (*BH*), 55–7, **147–8**, 149, 156, 235, 241
Snagsby, Mrs (*BH*), 155
Snubbin, Mr (*PP*), 30
'Somebody's Luggage' (*CS*), 234
Sowerberry, Mrs (*OT*), 84
Sparkins, Horatio (*SB*), 75
Sparsit, Mrs (*HT*), 159, 233
speech: *see also* idiolects
  archaic usage, 36, 119, 175, 202
  'cataloguing' technique, 51, 63, 185, 201, 207, 216
  circumlocution (ornate gentility), 28–9, 118, 137–8, 148, 163, 223
  eccentric speech, 3, 15, 82, 87, 125, 132–3, 162–3, 208–11, 230, 231, 233
  'eye-dialect', 8–9, 35–6, 85
  free direct speech, 126, 237
  free indirect speech, 6, 50, 62, **64–70,** 104, 108, 125, 135, 153, 162, 164, 217–18, 225, 236–7, 239
  functional speech, 138, 169, 176–7, 181–3, 184, 188, 190, 192, 226
  individualization through speech, 6, **15–24,** 54, 56–7, 60, 78, 85, 87, 147, 166, 214, 219, 220, 221–2, 228
  irony, 103, 164–5, 174, 176, 200, 203, 209, 217, 228
  key-word technique, 47, **60–1,** 125, 143, 157–8, 160–1, 165, 217, 236
  'languages to suit the occasion', 28
  music and speech, 36, 49–50, 231, 235
  need for speech identifiers, **15–17,** 214, 232
  'oral style', 6, 7–8, **61–4,** 125, 156, 171, 172–3, 184, 185, 193, 199–200, 212, 217, 228
  repetition, 50–2, 69, 82, 90, 92–3, 105–6, 122, 125–6, 157–8, 162, 165, 174, 183, 185, 186, 188, 194, 197, 227
  rhythmic patterns, 6, 10, 35, 36, **46–53,** 69, 86–7, 89–90, 97, 98, 105–6, 114–16, 122–3, 130, 135, 138, 139, 141, 143, 149–50, 166–7, 174, 176–7, 180, 185, 194, 195, 197, 198, 201, 202, 214, 215, 216, 219, 221, 222, 223, 225, 228, 235, 240
  schizophrenic ('disjointed') speech, 200, 201–2, 203, 227–8
  structural significance (representational speech), 6, 7, 8, 37–8, 45, 47, **54–9,** 60, 66, 67, 69, 84, 87, 98–100, 106–7, 124, 125–6, 130–1, 134, 135–6, 138, 141–2, 145, 147–8, 150, 152, 153, 162, 163, 167, 168, 171, 173, 175, 177, 179, 180–1, 182–3, 184, 190–1, 193, 195, 197–8, 199, 200, 202, 204, 206, 207–8, 211–12, 213, 214, 216–17, 219, 221, 222–3, 224–5, 227, 228, 234, 235, 241
  typification, general, 6, 9–12, 16, **25–45,** 54, 56–7, 60, 77, 88, 147, 214–16, 219, 220, 222, 223, 228; cant, 10, **38–9,** 84, 85, 215, 234; genteel register, non-standard, 3, 10, **39–40,** 84, 88, 150–2, 186, 187–8, 211, 218; genteel register, standard, 10, **28–9,** 88, 91, 95, 96, 97, 98, 117–18, 120, 137–8, 139–40, 152, 163, 166, 170–1, 174, 176, 177, 192, 193, 200, 205, 211, 215, 218, 223, 225, 226, 227; melodramatic register, non-standard, 10, **44–5,** 113, 215, 219–20; melodramatic register,

speech – *cont.*
 standard, 10, 33–4, 83, 88, 96, 100, 137, 142, 200–1, 215, 219–20, 221, 225, 226; non-standard London register (Cockney), 10, 11, 16, **34–8,** 74, 75, 77, 78–80, 84, 85–7, 103, 104, 108, 109–11, 112, 115–16, 126, 131, 132, 142, 150–1, 177–8, 179–81, 186–8, 195, 208–11, 213, 214–15, 222, 224, 228, 231, 233, 239; occupational registers, non-standard: general, 10, 16, 40, 215; articulator, 43, 187–8; boxing, 43; coachman, 43, 77, 80–1, 83; hairdresser and manicurist, 43, 142; hangman, 43, 103; law, 4, 5, 42–3, 74, 150–2, 181; soldier, 43; nurse, 111, 113; policeman, 41–2, 154–6, 234; railway, 43; seafarer, 3, 42, 131–3; servant, 77; show world, 40–1; stonemason, 43, 209; teacher, 88; waiter, 41, 234; occupational registers, standard: general, 10, 16, 29, 215; architecture, 118; military, 31; business, 96–7; religion, 31–2, 117, 204–6; law, 29–30, 95, 96–7, 183–4, 206–8, 233; medicine, 31; teaching, 30–1; oratorical register, non-standard, 10, 16, **43–4,** 215; oratorical register, standard, 6, 10, 16, 32–3, 118, 148–50, 205, 215; situational typification, 45; standard speech in Dickens, 10, 11, **25–6,** 89, 91, 94, 95, 96, 140, 142, 152, 165–6, 170, 173, 176, 181, 200, 215–16, 221, 234; upper-class register, 10, **26–8,** 89, 159–60, 181, 215, 220, 225, 227
 zany speech, 18, 39, 75, 78, 83, 84, 97, 99, 109, 113, 116, 121–2, 123–4, 129, 132, 166, 206, 211, 222–3, 228
Spenlow, Dora (*DC*), 135–7, 141, 194, 204, 223

Squeers, Fanny (*NN*), 40, 76
Squeers, Wackford (*NN*), 88, 133
Stareleigh, Mr (*PP*), 30
Steerforth, James (*DC*), 27, 41, 60, 135–6, 142, 223, 227, 241
Steerforth, Mrs (*DC*), 135
Sterne, Lawrence, 46
Stiggins, Rev. Mr (*PP*), 32, 44, 148–9
Stone, Marcus, 197
Strong, Dr (*DC*), 144
structural representation: *see* speech
Stryver, Mr (*TTC*), 30, 69
Summerson, Esther (*BH*), 20, 25, 67, 150–1, 152, 224, 226, 241
'Sunday Under Three Heads' (*UT/RP*), 32
Surtees, Robert, 35, 74
Sweedlepipe, Mr (*MC*), 43
Swiveller, Dick (*OCS*), 10, 30, 33, 47, 94, **95–100,** 119, 151, 220, 239
symploce, 51, 216
syntactic eccentricity: *see* idiolects

Tale of Two Cities, A, 7, 62, 68–9, 103, 158, 172, 236, 237, 243
Tapley, Mark (*MC*), 18
Tappertit, Simon (*BR*), 103
Tartar, Lieutenant (*ED*), 31
Tennyson, Alfred, 73
Thackeray, William Makepeace, 35, 135, 233, 237
Thurber, James, 19, 236
Tigg, Montague (*MC*), 31, 66, 108
Tippens, Lady (*OMF*), 69, 159, 193
Todgers, Mrs (*MC*), 121
Toodle, Mr (*DS*), 43
Toodle, Rob (*DS*): *see* Rob the Grinder
Toots, Mr P. (*DS*), 18, 66, 126, 132, 134, 168
Tope, Mr (*ED*), 205
Tox, Lucretia (*DS*), 133
Traddles, Thomas (*DC*), 135–6, 223
Trent, Fred (*OCS*), 100
Trent, Nell (*OCS*), 94, 98, 99, 100, 116
Trotwood, Betsey (*DC*), 137, **140–2,** 144, 223–4, 231
Tuckle, Mr (*PP*), 80
Tuggs Family (*SB*), 39

Tulkinghorn, Mr (*BH*), 30, 55, 56, 146, 148, 155
Turveydrop, Mr (*BH*), 28, 89
Twemlow, Melvin (*OMF*), 27, 193
Twinkleton, Miss (*ED*), 31, 40, 70, 204, 211
Twist, Oliver (*OT*), 26, 38, 83–4, 86, 232, 234
typification: *see* idiolects *and* speech

Varden, Dolly (*BR*), 65, 103, 221
Varden, Gabriel (*BR*), 65, 103
Varden, Mrs (*BR*), 65, 103, 105, 106
Veneering, Anastasia (*OMF*), 69, 193
Veneering, Hamilton (*OMF*), 193
Venus, Mr (*OMF*), 43, **187–8,** 227
Verisopht, Lord (*NN*), 27
Vholes, Mr (*BH*), 30

Wagner, Richard, 23, 199
Wardle, Rachel (*PP*), 20, 106
'Waste Land, The' [T. S. Eliot], 185
Weevle, Mr (*BH*): *see* Jobling, Mr
Wegg, Silas (*OMF*), 20, 43, 186, **187–8,** 227
Weller, Mrs (*PP*), 80

Weller, Sam (*PP*), 9, 17, 18–19, 35, 36, 40, 74, **77–83,** 97, 105, 111, 138, 219, 220, 232, 233
Weller, Tony (*PP*), 9, 17, 18–19, 42, 43, 76, **77–83,** 105, 111, 138, 219
Wells, Herbert George, 235–6, 241
Wemmick, John (*GE*), 42, 43, **181–3,** 226
Westlock, John (*MC*), 66, 121
Wickfield, Agnes (*DC*), 25, 135, 144
Wickfield, Mr (*DC*), 144
Wield, Inspector (*UT/RP*), 234
Wilde, Oscar, 29, 153–4, 191, 227
Wilfer, Bella (*OMF*), **193–5,** 204, 227, 244
Wilfer, Mrs (*OMF*), 29, 233
Wititterly, Mrs (*NN*), 88, 233
Woodcourt, Allan (*BH*), 25, 148, 234
Wordsworth, William, 73
Wrayburn, Eugene (*OMF*), 27, 30, 136, 153–4, 159, 188, **190–2,** 197–8, 225, 227
Wren, Jenny [Fanny Cleaver] (*OMF*), 143, **195–9,** 227

zany speech: *see* speech